IRISH-ENGLISH RELATIONS

THE **BROADVIEW**
SOURCES SERIES

Irish-English Relations

A HISTORY IN DOCUMENTS

edited by KAREN SONNELITTER

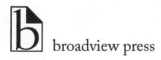 broadview press

BROADVIEW PRESS – www.broadviewpress.com
Peterborough, Ontario, Canada

Founded in 1985, Broadview Press remains a wholly independent publishing house. Broadview's focus is on academic publishing; our titles are accessible to university and college students as well as scholars and general readers. With over 800 titles in print, Broadview has become a leading international publisher in the humanities, with world-wide distribution. Broadview is committed to environmentally responsible publishing and fair business practices.

© 2023 Karen Sonnelitter

Library and Archives Canada Cataloguing in Publication

Title: Irish-English relations: a history in documents / edited by Karen Sonnelitter.
Names: Sonnelitter, Karen, editor.
Series: Broadview sources series.
Description: Series statement: The Broadview sources series | Includes bibliographical references.
Identifiers: Canadiana (print) 20220438633 | Canadiana (ebook) 20220438811 | ISBN 9781554815708 (softcover) | ISBN 9781770488731 (PDF) | ISBN 9781460408094 (EPUB)
Subjects: LCSH: Ireland—Relations—England—Sources. | LCSH: England—Relations—Ireland—Sources.
Classification: LCC DA964.A2 I75 2022 | DDC 327.415042—dc23

Broadview Press handles its own distribution in North America:
PO Box 1243, Peterborough, Ontario K9J 7H5, Canada
555 Riverwalk Parkway, Tonawanda, NY 14150, USA
Tel: (705) 743-8990; Fax: (705) 743-8353
email: customerservice@broadviewpress.com

For all territories outside of North America, distribution is handled by Eurospan Group.

Broadview Press acknowledges the financial support of the Government of Canada for our publishing activities.

Copy-edited by Juliet Sutcliffe
Book design by Em Dash Design

PRINTED IN CANADA

CONTENTS

Acknowledgements   ix
Introduction   1
Chronology   21
Questions to Consider   25

PART 1: MEDIEVAL IRELAND AND ENGLAND (700–1500)   27

1. From The Venerable Bede, *The Ecclesiastical History of the English People* (c. 731)   27

2. From *The Anglo-Saxon Chronicle* (9th–12th century)   31

3. From *Early Medieval Kings* (893 and c. 1103)   33

4. From William of Malmesbury, *Chronicle of the Kings of England* (c. 1125)   37

5. *Laudabiliter* (1155)   38

6. *The Treaty of Windsor* (1175)   40

7. From Gerald of Wales, *Topographia Hibernica* (c. 1188)   42

8. From Gerald of Wales, *Expugnatio Hibernica* (c. 1189)   45

9. From William of Newburgh, *The History of English Affairs* (c. 1190s)   47

10. From Sean Mac Ruaidhrí Mac Craith, *The Triumphs of Turlough* (mid-14th century)   50

11. From Statutes of Kilkenny (1367)   53

12. Poynings' Law (1495)   56

13. Irish Annals   57

PART 2: EARLY MODERN IRELAND AND ENGLAND (1500–1800)   65

14. The Crown of Ireland Act (1542)   65

15. Tadhg Dall Ó Huiginn, "To Conn O'Donnell" (late 16th century)   67

16. From Edmund Spenser, *A View of the Present State of Ireland* (1596)   72

17. From Tadhg Óg Ó Cianáin, *Departure of the Lords* (1608)   76

18. Lochlann Óg Ó Dalaigh, *Where Have the Gaels Gone?* (c. 1608)   79

19. From John Davies, *Discovery of the True Causes Why Ireland Was Never Entirely Subdued* (1612)   82

20. From Geoffrey Keating, *Foras Feasa as Éirinn* (1634)   86

21. The Confederation of Kilkenny, *The Oath of Association* (1642)   89

22. From John Temple, *The Irish Rebellion* (1646) 90

23. Oliver Cromwell, *Letters from Ireland* (1649) 93

24. Anthony O'Connor, *Ireland's Lamentation* (1659) 95

25. The Treaty of Limerick (1691) and the Penal Laws 97

26. From William Petty, *The Political Anatomy of Ireland* (1691) 102

27. From William Molyneux, *The Case of Ireland Being Bound by Acts of Parliament in England, Stated* (1698) 107

28. From *Bogg-Witticisms: or, Dear Joy's Common-Places* (1698) 110

29. From Jonathan Swift, *Drapier's Letters* (1724–25) 113

30. From Charles O'Conor, *The Case of the Roman-Catholics of Ireland* (1755) 117

31. From Arthur Young, *A Tour in Ireland* (1780) 120

32. Seághan Ó Coileáin, *Lament over the Ruins of the Abbey of Teach Molag* (late 18th century) 122

33. Henry Grattan, Speech in the Irish Parliament (16 April 1782) 125

34. From *The Utility of an Union between Great Britain and Ireland, Considered* (1787) 128

35. Theobald Wolfe Tone, et al., *Declaration and Resolutions of the Society of United Irishmen of Belfast* (1791) 130

36. From Patrick Sheehy, *Union a Plague* (1799) 132

PART 3: MODERN IRELAND AND ENGLAND BEFORE INDEPENDENCE (1800–1921) 135

37. From An Act for the Union of Great Britain and Ireland (1800) 135

38. From the Catholic Relief Act (1829) 138

39. British and Irish newspaper cartoons of Daniel O'Connell (1840s) 141

40. From Daniel O'Connell, Speeches on Catholic emancipation and the repeal of the Act of Union (1840s) 143

41. From Benjamin Disraeli, Speech in the House of Commons on the Irish Question (1844) 149

42. Thomas Davis, "A Nation Once Again" (1844) 151

43. From Charles Trevelyan, *The Irish Crisis* (1848) 153

44. James Mahony, "Condition of Ireland: Illustrations of the New Poor-Law," *Illustrated London News* (22 December 1849) 157

45. From John Mitchel, *The Last Conquest of Ireland, Perhaps* (1861) 165

46. From J.L. Porter, *The Life and Times of Henry Cooke* (1871) 168

47. *Punch* Cartoons on Ireland 171

48. Charles Stewart Parnell, *Speech at Cork* (1885) 174

49. From A.V. Dicey, *England's Case against Home Rule* (1887) 176

50. Douglas Hyde, *The Necessity of De-Anglicizing Ireland* (1892)   178

51. From George Bernard Shaw, *John Bull's Other Island* (1904)   184

52. The Solemn League and Covenant (1912)   187

53. Gaelic League Poster (1913)   188

54. John Redmond, Woodenbridge Speech (20 September 1914)   189

55. The Easter Rising Proclamation (1916)   191

56. W.B. Yeats, "Easter 1916" (1920)   193

57. From The Anglo-Irish Treaty (1921)   196

PART 4: IRELAND AND ENGLAND POST-INDEPENDENCE (1921–PRESENT)   201

58. From Coal-Cattle Pact Debates in the Dáil Éireann (13 June 1935)   201

59. From Bunreacht Na hÉireann (Constitution of Ireland) (1937)   204

60. Winston Churchill, Telegram to Éamon de Valera, 9 December 1941, and extract from Speech on V-E Day (1941 & 1945)   208

61. Éamon de Valera, Response to Churchill (1945)   211

62. The Republic of Ireland Act (1948)   215

63. From the Ireland Act (1949)   216

64. From *A Catholic Handbook for Irish Men & Women Going to England* (1953)   219

65. From Oliver Reilly, *A Worker in Birmingham* (1958)   221

66. From Sean Lemass, Statement to the European Economic Community (18 January 1962)   224

67. From Terence O'Neill, *Ulster Stands at the Crossroads* (1968)   227

68. From Bernadette Devlin, Maiden Speech in the House of Commons (1969)   229

69. From William Whitelaw, *The Future of Northern Ireland* (1972)   232

70. From Jack Lynch, Speech at the Dáil Éireann (21 March 1972)   235

71. From Radio Interview with British Prime Minister Margaret Thatcher (8 December 1980)   238

72. From *An Camchéacta/The Starry Plough*, "Why it is murder ..." (June 1981)   241

73. From The Good Friday Agreement (1998)   243

74. From Tony Blair, Address to the Dáil Éireann (26 November 1998)   248

75. Queen Elizabeth II, Speech at Dublin Castle (18 May 2011)   252

76. Michael D. Higgins, Shadow and Shelter Speech (8 April 2014)   255

Glossary of Key Figures and Terms   259

Select Bibliography   261

Permissions Acknowledgements   263

ACKNOWLEDGEMENTS

I would like to thank the anonymous reviewers of the proposal for this volume and of the completed volume. Their insightful commentary was essential to the shaping of this collection. I would also like to thank Stephen Latta from Broadview, who helped to develop the idea for this collection. Special thanks to my research assistant Brendan McDonnell, who sorted through many volumes of primary sources and made a number of important contributions to this work. Without his help I would likely still be compiling this collection. Thanks to the Siena College Center for Undergraduate Research and Creative Activity, which funded Brendan's work on this book. Finally, thanks to my family for their support of this project and to my dog Jack, who sat not-so-patiently at my side during the writing process waiting for me to put away my laptop and play fetch with him.

INTRODUCTION

On 22 December 1919 David Lloyd George, the prime minister of the United Kingdom of Great Britain and Ireland, rose to address the House of Commons on the topic of Ireland. By that point it had been almost a year since the 73 Sinn Féin representatives elected to parliament in 1918 had refused to take their seats in Westminster and declared themselves the Dáil Éireann. Violence had broken out not long after and in September 1919 the Lord Lieutenant of Ireland, Viscount French, had declared the Dáil illegal. Lloyd George characterized the ongoing conflict as "an old family quarrel, a quarrel which has degenerated many a time into a blood feud."[1] He would go on to describe the relationship between Ireland and England as one of mutual misunderstanding and miscommunication by saying, "There is a path of fatality which pursues the relations between the two countries, and makes them eternally at cross purposes. Sometimes Ireland demands too much; sometimes when Ireland is reasonable England offers too little; sometimes when Ireland is friendly England is sulky; sometimes when England has been friendly, Ireland had been angry; and sometimes when both Britain and Ireland seem to be approximating toward friendship, some untoward incident sweeps them apart, and the quarrel begins again."[2]

As prime minster, Lloyd George would oversee one of the more consequential periods in that long and often fraught relationship. The Easter Rising broke out months before he became prime minister in December 1916, his attempts to extend conscription to Ireland in 1918 played a role in Sinn Féin's landslide victory in the elections that year, the Government of Ireland Act of 1920 partitioned Ireland into north and south, and, finally, towards the end of his tenure as prime minister the Anglo-Irish Treaty was signed in December 1921. It's not surprising that in 1919 Ireland and England would seem to be "eternally at cross purposes." In 2014 during a very different stage in the relationship between Ireland and England the Irish President Michael D. Higgins argued that, "Ireland and Britain live in both the shadow and in the shelter of one another, and so it has been since the dawn of history. Through conquest and resistance, we have cast shadows on each other, but we have also gained strength from one another as neighbours and, most especially, from the contribution of those who have travelled between our islands in recent decades" (Document 76). Over the years politicians on both sides of the Irish Sea have used many metaphors to explain the relationship between Ireland and England.

---

1   House of Commons, 22 December 1919, vol. 123, cc 1168–1233.
2   Ibid.

In many ways the modern relationship between England and Ireland fits neatly into the dynamics that often exist between larger nations and their smaller neighbors. In 2020 the United Kingdom of Great Britain and Northern Ireland had a population of 67 million people, 56.5 million of them in England, and a gross domestic product (GDP) of 2.8 trillion US dollars.[3] The Republic of Ireland, as of 2021, has only 5.01 million people and a GDP of 418 billion US dollars.[4] Northern Ireland adds an additional 1.9 million people to the population of the island of Ireland.[5] England is vastly larger in terms of population, economy, and even land mass; it is about 18,000 square miles larger than the island of Ireland.[6] While the size of their respective populations and economies have varied considerably over time England has always been the larger of the two geographically and demographically. There are numerous examples of this dynamic around the world as physically, demographically, or economically larger nations are able to overshadow their smaller neighbors. The smaller nation and its residents are often acutely aware of almost everything that happens within the larger nation, while the larger nation and its residents have the privilege of ignorance about the smaller one. For Ireland and England this dynamic is complicated by a long and tumultuous shared history, either a "family quarrel" or a "path of fatality," in the words of Lloyd George, that provide extra layers of meaning to even the most seemingly innocuous interaction.

This book is an attempt to provide context to help explain those extra layers of meaning. The documents presented here come from a variety of sources, both English and Irish, to help illuminate a greater understanding of the course of the relationship between England and Ireland. The documents will focus on the evolution of the cultural and political relationship between both nations. They will also explore how that relationship has been shaped by their views of each other. As with all primary sources they must be read critically with attention paid to the medium, the author, and the intent of the document. These documents are meant to provide insight into the political, cultural, and economic relationship between these two nations over the long history of their direct connection with each other. To aid in this analysis this volume begins with a brief introduction, a chronology of events, and a list of questions to consider.

---

3 "Population Estimates," Office for National Statistics UK, 25 June 2021. "Gross Domestic Product," ONS UK, 30 September 2021.

4 "Population and Migration Estimates, April 2021," Central Statistics Office Ireland, 31 August 2021. "GDP Ireland," World Bank, 25 October 2021.

5 "Northern Ireland population," ONS UK, 25 June 2021.

6 "Land area—United Kingdom," World Bank.

The paths of English and Irish history diverged centuries before the first arrival of Norman knights in Ireland in 1169. Beginning in 43 CE the Roman Empire invaded and settled within most of what is now England; following the collapse of the Roman Empire, the island of Britain was invaded once again in the fifth century by Germanic tribes such as the Angles, Saxons, Jutes, and Frisians. The Celtic Britons gradually merged with the Germanic settlers, although Celtic languages survived in a few pockets of what is now England, as well as in Wales and Scotland.

Ireland meanwhile remained separate from these events. Celtic groups remained dominant until the Normans. Irish tribes traded with the Roman Empire and the rest of Europe, and regularly sent raiding parties to the island of Britain to capture slaves. Most famously, St. Patrick, the patron saint of Ireland, was such a captive, the son of a Roman official from near the Scottish border. In his "Confessio" Patrick recounts spending six years as a shepherd in western Ireland before escaping and returning home.[7] Once home he received visions which told him to return to Ireland and convert the people there. While in reality Patrick was not the only Christian missionary sent to Ireland he is certainly the most iconic.

In the centuries that followed St. Patrick, Irish Christianity developed along a decentralized model that favored the power of abbots and monasteries more so than bishops. The Germanic arrival in England delayed the widespread adoption of Christianity there. In 597 St. Augustine arrived to establish a mission in Canterbury. In England Augustine established a church that ran along continental models that centered the power of bishops and dioceses. Irish monks, particularly those based out of the monastery at Iona, continued to be very influential in spreading Christianity in England. The differences between these traditions was solidified and symbolically settled in the Synod of Whitby in 664, when the King of Northumbria determined to calculate the date of Easter according to Roman models and not Ionan ones.[8]

Despite these religious differences early Medieval England and Ireland had many similarities. Both consisted of a number of separate kingdoms who were constantly fighting each other for land, wealth, and power. Both also had similar experiences of the Viking era. Beginning with the attack at the monastery of Lindisfarne in 793, both islands dealt with a consistent pattern of Viking raids, which eventually evolved into permanent Viking

---

7 St. Patrick, "Confessio," translated by Pádraig McCarthy, www.confessio.ie.

8 Henry Mayr-Harting, *The Coming of Christianity to Anglo-Saxon England* (University Park: Pennsylvania State UP, 1991), 104–19.

settlements. Viking kingdoms became important players in the politics of both countries.[9]

The Norman Invasion of England marks another significant point of departure between England and Ireland. It transformed the politics and society of the island of Britain. Shortly after establishing their rule in England, the Normans began to intervene in Wales and in Scotland. It is not immediately apparent whether William I or his direct heirs had plans for Ireland as well. Wales proved very difficult to conquer and the succession crisis brought on by the death of Henry I in 1135 likely delayed any such ambitions. Between 1135 and 1154 Henry I's sole surviving legitimate child Matilda fought a series of civil wars against her cousin Stephen, who had usurped the throne, in a period known as 'the anarchy.' That conflict ended in 1153 when King Stephen agreed to recognize Matilda's son Henry as his heir. The new king Henry II had substantial properties to consolidate his rule over; through his father he was count of Anjou and Maine, through his grandfather he was Duke of Normandy, and through his wife Eleanor of Aquitaine he became the Duke of Aquitaine.[10]

The exact origins of the Norman invasion of Ireland are up for debate. The immediate cause of the invasion was Diarmait Mac Murchada, the king of Leinster, fleeing Ireland and seeking assistance from Henry II in 1165. But it is likely a possible invasion of Ireland had been broached with Henry II years before. The Archbishop of Canterbury Theobald of Bec claimed jurisdiction over the Irish church, but the Archbishop of Armagh had a competing claim. In 1155 during a royal council at Winchester Henry II is said to have enthusiastically discussed invading Ireland and making his brother William its king. The plan was apparently abandoned due to the disapproval of their mother the Empress Matilda, who did not think Ireland worth invading. Meanwhile 1155 is also widely accepted as the year that Pope Adrian IV issued the papal bull the *Laudabiliter* (Document 5), which commissioned Henry II to intervene in Ireland to reform the Irish church. Despite this, Henry II made no plans to actually intervene in Ireland.[11]

When Mac Murchada sought assistance in 1165 Henry II also declined to directly intervene in Ireland. At that point he was in the midst of his long quarrel with his new Archbishop of Canterbury Thomas Becket, which would end in Becket's murder by Henry's knights in 1170. The king did allow Mac Murchada to recruit military assistance from his vassals. Mac Murchada was able to recruit most famously Richard Fitzgilbert de Clare, the Earl of

---

9   Jeremy Black, *A History of the British Isles*, 4th ed. (London: Palgrave Macmillan, 2017), 11–35.

10 Ibid., 36–93. Thomas Bartlett, *Ireland: A History* (Cambridge: Cambridge UP, 2010), 34–35.

11 F.X. Martin, "Diarmait Mac Murchada and the Coming of the Anglo-Normans," in *A New History of Ireland, Volume II: Medieval Ireland 1169–1534* (Oxford: Oxford UP, 2008), 55–60.

Pembroke, commonly known as Strongbow. Strongbow granted assistance in exchange for a marriage to Mac Murchada's daughter Aoife and the promise that he would succeed Mac Murchada as king of Leinster. Other Norman Welsh nobles also joined the campaign in exchange for promises of land. Most were from families who were not in favor with Henry II and so had little hope of advancement in the rest of his empire.[12]

The Normans arrived in 1169 and met with quick success. They captured the cities of Wexford, Waterford, and Dublin. In August of 1170 the promised marriage between Strongbow and Aoife Mac Murchada took place. The next year when Diarmait Mac Murchada died Strongbow became king of Leinster. Henry II had been prepared to allow his vassals to claim territory in Ireland, but he was not prepared for one of his vassals to become a king there and so he prepared his own expedition to Ireland. Henry II landed in 1171 near Waterford with a sizable army. He stayed in Ireland for six months receiving the homage of both the Norman nobles who had invaded Ireland, and a number of Irish kings. Strongbow was demoted from King to Lord of Leinster. Notably Rory O'Connor (or Ruadhrí Ó Conchobair) of Connacht, the most powerful of the Irish kings, did not pay homage to Henry. In 1175 Henry and O'Connor agreed to the Treaty of Windsor (Document 6) which was meant to settle the territorial disputes in Ireland but did not last long. In 1185 Henry II's son Prince John was sent to Ireland; he seems to have planned to declare him king of a separate kingdom of Ireland. Those plans did not come to fruition and John was only ever Lord of Ireland.[13]

Ireland at the time of the Norman invasion consisted of a number of separate kingdoms, all of varying size, and each almost constantly at war with each other. This disunity benefited the invaders: some Irish kings found it beneficial to fight alongside English invaders because of longstanding local conflicts. The arrival and settlement of English and Welsh settlers in large portions of Ireland set into motion a number of patterns that repeat over the centuries. In 1183 and 1185 Gerald of Wales would travel in Ireland to visit relatives who had settled there and to accompany Prince John on his travels. The subsequent works that he produced on Ireland, most famously the *Topographia Hibernica* (Document 7) played an important role in how Ireland was viewed. Gerald of Wales describes Ireland as a beautiful place and the Irish as a primitive and barbaric people. He would also establish another idea: the tense negotiation of identities for those who settled in Ireland. In his *Expugnatio Hibernica* he records Maurice Fitzgerald declaring, "Is it succour from our own country that we expect? Nay, such is our lot that

---

12 Bartlett, 35–37.
13 Black, 53–54.

what the Irish are to the English, we too, being now considered as Irish, are the same" (Document 8).

Earlier in that speech Fitzgerald lamented the state of the colonization of Ireland. "For awhile we were in the ascendant, but now the wheel is turned, and we are in a low estate."[14] That low estate continued as the colony of Ireland slowly declined over the next few hundred years. Royal neglect was certainly a factor. King John visited in 1210, and after him the next English king to come to Ireland was Richard II in 1394. Traditionally the late thirteenth century is seen as the high point of the Norman colony of Ireland, while the rest of the fourteenth century marked a slow decline.[15] The invasion of Edward Bruce, brother of Robert Bruce, the king of Scotland, in 1315, contributed to this decline. Over the fourteenth century the English lordship in Ireland experienced loss of revenue and loss of territory. The Bruce campaign had been devastating in Ireland, it coincided with a European wide famine, and the looting of the army only exacerbated those conditions. The *Annals of Loch Cé* refer to Edward Bruce as "the destroyer of all Erinn."[16] The Black Death further weakened the lordship, with depopulation in both England and Ireland making it impossible to recruit new settlers from England to go to Ireland. In Ireland the disease, which spread more in towns, is thought to have disproportionately affected English colonists.[17]

In 1361 Edward III sent his third son Lionel, Duke of Clarence to Ireland to restore order in the colony. The most significant result of this campaign was the Statutes of Kilkenny in 1366 (Document 11). The statutes placed blame for the decline of the lordship in Ireland squarely on colonists who were insufficiently English. The statutes essentially attempted to forbid contact between the two communities; they forbade marriage, fosterage, or even acting as godparents. In practical terms the Statutes of Kilkenny changed little about the status of Ireland or the strength of the lordship. But they are significant in stating an avowed condemnation of integration or accommodation between the English and Irish communities.[18]

The Statutes of Kilkenny did little to stabilize or expand the English lordship of Ireland, and in 1394 King Richard II arrived with an army of 8–10,000 men to punish rebellious Gaelic lords and "establish good government."[19] The plan failed and after Richard's return to England the next year the English lordship diminished to the area surrounding Dublin known as the Pale. After

---

14 Giraldus Cambrensis, *The Conquest of Ireland*, translated by Thomas Forester (Ontario: In Parentheses Publications, 2000), 31.

15 Robin Frame, *Ireland and Britain: 1170–1450* (London: Bloomsbury, 1998), 191.

16 *Annals of Loch Cé*, translated by William Hennessy, https://celt.ucc.ie.

17 J.A. Watt, "The Anglo-Irish Colony under Strain, 1327–99," *A New History of Ireland, vol. II*, 352–96.

18 Bartlett, 58–60.

19 Qtd. in Nigel Saul, *Richard II* (New Haven: Yale UP, 1999), 277.

Richard II's excursion in 1394 Ireland took a backseat for English monarchs who were distracted by the Hundred Years' War and dynastic struggles such as the Wars of the Roses. The first Tudor monarch, Henry VII, was inclined to ignore Ireland except for the tendency of significant Anglo-Irish lords to support pretenders to his throne. Henry VII's reign did see the appointment of Sir Edward Poynings as Lord Deputy of Ireland and the passage of Poynings' Law in 1495 (Document 12). That law would be used for centuries to justify Ireland's political subjugation to England.

EARLY MODERN HISTORY

The Tudor era brought a number of changes to Ireland. In 1542 the Parliament of Ireland, first created in 1297, passed the Crown of Ireland Act, which created the title King of Ireland and gave it to Henry VIII (Document 14). Several years earlier Henry VIII also introduced the Protestant Reformation to Ireland; in 1536 the Irish parliament passed the Act of Supremacy, which declared Henry VIII to be head of the Church of Ireland, as he was head of the Church of England. Making himself king of Ireland was one part of the broader Tudor conquest of Ireland, a plan which began following the failure of the Kildare Rebellion in 1534.[20] Unable to rely on the Earls of Kildare to govern Ireland as Lord Deputies, Henry VIII and his advisors sought to expand the crown's control across Ireland. The Reformation was one part of this campaign but Henry also sought to expand his political authority using a policy known as 'surrender and regrant.' Irish lords were asked to surrender their lands to the king and in exchange they would be granted them back by royal charter. Irish lords were granted English titles and admitted into the Irish Parliament for the first time. Henry termed the policy one of "amiable persuasions."[21]

Crown policy did not always remain amiable, and the Tudor Conquest also brought about new rebellions (the **Desmond Rebellions**, the **Nine Years' War**, the **1641 Rebellion**) and the plantation scheme. Under the plantation policy Irish land was confiscated by the crown and then colonized with settlers from England and later Scotland. The goal was to both civilize Ireland but also to spread the political control of the English crown. The earliest plantation scheme began in 1556, in the reign of the Catholic English monarch Mary I, in what are now counties Offaly and Laois, but which were then called King's County and Queen's County. Under Elizabeth I

Desmond Rebellions: 1569–73 and 1579–83, successive rebellions in Munster led by the Earl of Desmond against the extension of English government over the region.

Nine Years' War: 1593–1603 war against the extension of English rule led by Hugh O'Neill, Earl of Tyrone and Hugh Roe O'Donnell, Earl of Tyrconnell.

1641 Rebellion: Rebellion led by Irish Catholics against the plantation system, Catholic discrimination, and the expansion of English rule.

---

20 G.A. Hayes-McCoy, "The Royal Supremacy and Ecclesiastical Revolution, 1534–47," in *A New History of Ireland*, vol. III, 39–48.

21 Ibid., 48–52. Hugh Kearney, *The British Isles: A History of Four Nations* (Cambridge: Cambridge UP, 2012), 159.

the plantations were extended to Munster as punishment against the Earls of Desmond for rebelling.[22]

By far the most ambitious and ultimately the most significant of the plantation schemes was the one for Ulster. Plans for that plantation began after the end of the Nine Years' War, which had been led by Hugh O'Neill, the Earl of Tyrone. The plantation scheme was partially enabled by the Flight of the Earls in 1607, when Hugh O'Neill and other Irish lords who had rebelled in the Nine Years' War fled Ireland to seek assistance from Spain for a new rebellion and never returned. Arthur Chichester, the lord deputy of Ireland took advantage of the opportunity created by the fleeing of the Irish leadership to plan a large-scale plantation of the entire province. By this point the crown of England had passed to King James VI of Scotland (James I of England) and the decision was made to recruit settlers from Scotland as well as England.[23]

The plantation transformed the landscape and the population of Ulster. Thousands of settlers were imported from England and Scotland to take possession of most of the land in the province. The native Irish population remained, but few had land grants; about 300 Irish families who had sided with the English in the Nine Years' War received grants. The rest of the native Irish population remained as tenants in the same areas where they had lived before. The plantation was not well received by the native population and Chichester described them in 1610 as "generally discontented."[24] Violence did exist in the early years of the plantation: a group called the **wood-kern** would attack settlements. By the 1630s it seemed that the situation had settled down and a degree of religious tolerance existed within the plantation. However, the events of 1641 cast that into question. In response to rising tensions on the island of Britain, between King Charles I and the English parliament and between King Charles and his Scottish Presbyterian subjects, in October a group of Ulster Catholics led by Phelim O'Neill and Rory O'More, planned a rebellion. In the aftermath of this attempted coup d'état the native Irish population turned on the colonists and killed or expelled thousands. The massacres of 1641 helped to create a persistent siege mentality in the Ulster Protestant population that persists in some segments to the present day.[25]

Wood-kern: Kern were Irish soldiers, basically light infantrymen. Wood-kern were displaced soldiers who operated as bandits.

---

22 G.A. Hayes-McCoy, "The Completion of the Tudor Conquest and the Advance of the Counter-Reformation, 1571–1603," in *A New History of Ireland*, vol. III, 113–15.

23 Aidan Clarke and R. Dudley Edwards, "Pacification, Plantation, and the Catholic Question, 1603–23," in *A New History of Ireland*, vol. III, 187–96.

24 Oliver Rafferty, *Catholicism in Ulster, 1603–1983: An Interpretive History* (Columbia: U of South Carolina P, 1994), 12.

25 A.T.Q. Stewart, *The Narrow Ground: The Roots of Conflict in Ulster* (London, 1989), 52

Meanwhile, the aborted coup attempt of O'Neill and O'More spread south and gained followers as other Catholic landowners both native Irish and Anglo-Irish joined in the rebellion. The outbreak of civil war in England prevented an effective armed response from England and so the Catholic nobility of Ireland set up an alternative government known as the Confederacy. The Confederacy would effectively rule Ireland until 1649, when Oliver Cromwell invaded Ireland with the New Model Army and put an end to the rebellion. The Cromwellian conquest of Ireland had vast consequences in both the short and the long term. In the short term the Confederate government of Ireland was overthrown and tens of thousands of people died in a famine that resulted from the army's destruction of food supplies. William Petty estimated by 1652 616,000 people had died from this famine, or about forty percent of the island's population (Document 26). In the long term, the Cromwellian land settlement changed landholding structures as almost all Catholic-owned land was confiscated and given to British settlers.

When the monarchy was restored in 1660, King Charles II allowed the land settlement to largely stand although he did make some efforts to compensate Irish Catholics. Religious divisions persisted in Ireland and reappeared again in 1688 with the Glorious Revolution. The Catholic monarch James II fled England in 1688 in response to the invasion carried out by his daughter and son-in-law, William and Mary. James fled to France to gain the support of King Louis XIV and in 1689 he traveled to Ireland with French troops. James's son-in-law William of Orange, William III, led an army into Ireland and eventually defeated James II and his Irish supporters at the Battle of the Boyne in 1690, after which James fled for France. Irish forces fought for another year until finally they were defeated at the Battle of Aughrim in 1691.[26]

The Treaty of Limerick of 1691 put an end to Jacobite wars in Ireland, and the defeat of the Jacobite cause halted the political aspirations of Irish Catholics for decades. The eighteenth century broadly speaking saw the establishment of English domination of the British Isles. In 1707 the English relationship with Scotland was formalized through the Act of Union. There was some discussion of a similar act for Ireland in the beginning of the eighteenth century but it gained little traction. Instead eighteenth-century Ireland was dominated by an Anglo-Irish elite commonly referred to as the Protestant Ascendancy. At times throughout the century this class came to resent their legal subordination to the parliament of Great Britain. This resentment culminated in the political career of Henry Grattan. In 1782

---

26 Black, 149–50.

Grattan, with the help of the Irish Volunteer movement, was able to secure legislative independence for the Irish parliament.[27]

This independence did not last long. The United Irishmen was founded in Belfast in 1791; inspired by the French Revolution, they advocated for civil and religious equality in Ireland (Document 35). In 1798 they led a rebellion in Ireland with the goal of establishing a fully independent and republican form of government in Ireland. That rebellion and its failure eventually contributed to the passage in 1800 of an Act for the Union of Great Britain and Ireland (Document 37). This act would dissolve the Irish parliament in Dublin and create the United Kingdom of Great Britain and Ireland.[28]

MODERN HISTORY BEFORE INDEPENDENCE

The Act of Union effectively introduced a new stage of the Anglo-Irish relationship by clarifying the political relationship. Ireland was now one part of a larger United Kingdom. The independent Irish parliament was dissolved and Ireland was now governed directly from Westminster. The Act of Union brought about a new stage in Irish political action, which began in particular with the political career of Daniel O'Connell (Document 40). O'Connell focused his career first on the goal of Catholic Emancipation, which was achieved through the Catholic Relief Act of 1829. He next turned his energy to the repeal of the Act of Union, the major political issue which would energize and divide Irish politics throughout the nineteenth and early twentieth century.[29]

Several decades into the union other events would emerge to cast a pall over English–Irish relations. Beginning in 1845 an oomycete, *phytophthora infestans,* then unidentified and simply called the blight, destroyed potato crops around the world. Ireland, which for a variety of reasons had a large population of people largely dependent on the potato for food, was particularly badly hit. Over the next several years the Great Famine would reduce the Irish population significantly leading to a number of deaths from disease and starvation as well as widespread emigration. The response to the famine by the government of the United Kingdom further damaged the relationship between Ireland and England, leading the Irish nationalist leader John Mitchel to famously declare in 1861 "the Almighty, indeed, sent the potato blight, but the English created the famine" (Document 45).[30]

---

27   Ibid., 150–52.

28   Ibid., 185.

29   Bartlett, 262–64.

30   Karen Sonnelitter, *The Great Irish Famine: A History in Documents* (Peterborough: Broadview Press, 2018), 1–20.

The Irish Question plagued the politics of the United Kingdom throughout the nineteenth century. Benjamin Disraeli defined the Irish Question in 1844 as:

> Let them consider Ireland as they would any other country similarly situated, in their closets. Then they would see a teeming population, which with reference to the cultivated soil, was denser to the square mile than that of China; created solely by agriculture, with none of those sources of wealth which are developed with civilization; and sustained consequently upon the lowest conceivable diet, so that in case of failure they had no other means of subsistence upon which they could fall back. That dense population in extreme distress inhabited an island where there was an established church which was not their church; and a territorial aristocracy, the richest of whom lived in distant capitals. Thus they had a starving population, an absentee aristocracy, and an alien Church, and, in addition, the weakest executive in the world. That was the Irish question. (Document 41)

The years that followed the famine saw a UK government that was more willing to make concessions to Irish concerns. The Liberal prime minister William Gladstone agreed to disestablish the Church of Ireland in 1869, passed several different land-reform acts which sought to address the issues of the Irish Land League, and in 1886 introduced a bill for Irish Home Rule. Meanwhile Conservative party administrations sought to "kill Home Rule by kindness." They pursued policies known as constructive unionism, which included public works and economic subsidies.[31]

One of the major complications in the Irish Question was the opposition to Home Rule from a significant portion of the population of Ulster. Hundreds of years after the plantation, Ulster differed from the rest of Ireland economically and there were significant religious differences as well; a slight majority of the population of Ulster was protestant, mainly Presbyterian. For many in Ulster the Act of Union was seen as an uncomplicated good. The unionist leader Henry Cooke once noted, "Look at the town of Belfast. When I was a youth it was almost a village. But what a glorious sight does it now present! The masted grove within our harbor— our mighty warehouses teeming with the wealth of every clime—our giant manufactures lifting themselves on every side, and all this we owe to the UNION" (Document 46). For Unionist leaders like Cooke membership

---

31 Hilary Larkin, *A History of Ireland, 1800–1922: Theatres of Disorder?* (Cambridge: Cambridge UP, 2014), chaps. 13, 15.

in the United Kingdom was the biggest factor in the thriving industrial economy of Belfast.

However, economic concerns were not the only factor energizing unionist opposition to Home Rule. The slogan "Home Rule equals Rome Rule" was coined by the radical Quaker MP John Bright during the first Home Rule crisis in 1886.[32] The phrase resonated with Irish Unionists and continued to be used in the twentieth century to express opposition to Irish Home Rule, Irish independence, or a united Ireland. The concern was that an independent Ireland with its overwhelmingly Catholic population of Ireland would allow domination by the Catholic Church and that Protestants would face discrimination and repression.

Strong feelings both for and against Home Rule continued throughout the late nineteenth and early twentieth century. When the third Home Rule Bill was introduced in 1912 it sparked a crisis in Ireland. Nearly half a million Ulster Protestants signed what they termed "Ulster's Solemn League and Covenant" (Document 52) expressing their opposition to the bill. Many went a step further and organized a militia, the Ulster Volunteers, which armed and drilled in preparation for violent conflict to prevent Home Rule in Ireland. Irish nationalists responded by forming their own militia, the Irish Volunteers, with the intent of fighting to secure Home Rule should it become necessary. With Ireland on the verge of civil war the idea of partitioning Ireland began to be discussed in parliament. An amending bill was proposed that would have temporarily excluded Ulster counties from Home Rule.[33]

The outbreak of World War I on 4 August 1914 put a stop to these debates. The Home Rule Bill was passed without amendments and given royal assent on 18 September. It was also immediately suspended by the Suspensory Act, meaning that Home Rule would be postponed until the end of the war. Meanwhile both Nationalist and Unionist leaders in Ireland worked to secure support for the war effort. The Unionist MP Sir Edward Carson encouraged members of the Ulster Volunteers to enlist in the army, while John Redmond the leader of the Irish Home Rule movement encouraged Irish Volunteers to enlist as well (Document 54).[34]

The outbreak of the war also provoked a crisis in the Irish Volunteer movement. The majority supported the war effort and joined Irish regiments in the British Army. Many others, however, opposed joining a British war effort and felt that Ireland should remain neutral. Many of these volunteers were members of the Irish Republican Brotherhood, a secret organization

---

32 G.R. Searle, *A New England? Peace and War 1886–1918* (Oxford: Clarendon Press, 2005), 142.

33 Bartlett, 367–68.

34 Bartlett, 374–76.

dedicated to securing not merely Home Rule but complete independence for Ireland as a democratic republic. The duration of the war and the continued suspension of the Home Rule Bill provided an opportunity for the Brotherhood. Almost as soon as World War I began the Supreme Council of the IRB began planning an insurrection against British rule in Ireland. The Easter Rising was eventually launched on 24 April 1916. It was the largest uprising in Ireland since the 1798 rebellion. The Irish Republican Brotherhood together with the Irish Citizen Army, Cumann na mBan, and some Irish Volunteers seized control of several sites around Dublin and declared an Irish Republic (Document 55). The rebels managed to hold out against British army forces in the city until 29 April, when they surrendered unconditionally.[35]

In the aftermath of the Easter Rising the leaders of the rebellion were quickly tried by court martial and executed. The executions more so than the Rising itself seemed to inspire more people in Ireland to support the goal of an independent Irish republic. Prior to 1916 most Irish voters outside of Ulster supported the moderate Home Rule Party, the Irish parliamentary party led by John Redmond. A combination of World War I, the Easter Rising, and the 1918 Representation of the People Act, which expanded the electorate across the United Kingdom, contributed to the results of the 1918 general parliamentary election. It was the first election in which all men over the age of 21 and women over the age of 30 could vote. In Ireland the result was a massive victory for the republican Sinn Féin party.[36] Sinn Féin had been founded in 1905 by Arthur Griffith with the goal of establishing a dual monarchy between Ireland and Great Britain.[37] In the aftermath of the Easter Rising the party came to be dominated by Irish republicans and the platform shifted to the goal of establishing an Irish Republic. In 1918 Sinn Féin candidates won 73 of the 105 seats available. In January of 1919 the newly elected MPs assembled in Dublin and proclaimed themselves the Dáil Éireann. They promptly issued a declaration of independence and proclaimed themselves the parliament of the Irish Republic. The British administration refused to recognize the new government and the Irish War of Independence began.[38]

The war was primarily a guerrilla war fought between the Irish Republican Army and the British forces, which consisted of the Royal Irish Constabulary and auxiliary forces. The constabulary forces were bolstered with reinforcements from Britain, most famously the Black and Tans, the majority of which were former soldiers just out of World War I. The Black and Tans and other

---

35 Bartlett, 379–96.
36 Black, 269.
37 Bartlett, 352.
38 Bartlett, 400–01.

auxiliary units became famous for extrajudicial killings, reprisal attacks on civilians, and property destruction. The Irish Republican Army meanwhile was descended from the Irish Volunteers. They organized into small mobile units called flying columns to carry out attacks against British forces.[39]

The cost of the British occupation of Ireland was rapidly increasing and in the immediate aftermath of World War I there was little support for more expenditure. There was also increasing criticism of British policy in Ireland both within Great Britain but also internationally. It is within this context that David Lloyd George gave his speech in the House of Commons describing the two nations as on "a path of fatality." Each of these factors contributed to the British government being willing to first make a truce with Irish forces on 11 July 1921. The Irish government sent representatives led by Arthur Griffith and Michael Collins to negotiate a treaty. The result was the Anglo-Irish Treaty of 1921 (Document 57). The treaty did not grant Ireland complete independence. Instead the southern 26 counties were granted dominion status as the Irish Free State. The six counties of Ulster were permitted to opt out of the Irish Free State, and Northern Ireland was created and granted its own parliament. The compromises of the treaty split the Dáil Éireann, which only narrowly approved the treaty. A number of representatives walked out and several months later the Irish Civil War broke out between pro- and anti-treaty forces. By May of 1923 pro-treaty forces with the military support of the United Kingdom had defeated anti-treaty forces and a ceasefire was agreed to.[40]

POST-INDEPENDENCE

Self-governance and partition created new issues that came to define the relationship between England and Ireland. The Irish Free State would go on to pass a new constitution in 1937 (Document 59), which among other things removed any constitutional role for the British monarchy. In 1948 it would go on to formally declare itself a republic (Document 62) and withdrew from the British Commonwealth of Nations. In the intervening years Ireland would attempt to assert its independence from the United Kingdom through economic policies such as during the Anglo-Irish Economic War, eventually settled by the Coal-Cattle Pact of 1936 (Document 58). The Irish government, led by Éamonn de Valera, ceased reimbursing Great Britain for land annuities as required of them in the Anglo-Irish Treaty. The result was a series of retaliatory tariffs issues by both sides. These tariffs were far

---

39 Ibid., 401–04.
40 Ibid., 406–19.

more damaging to Ireland, which had a smaller more agricultural economy, and which relied far more on trade with Great Britain than Great Britain did on trade with Ireland.[41]

The Irish government also chose to remain neutral during the Second World War, a decision which caused tension in its relationship with Great Britain. In December of 1941 Winston Churchill, the prime minister of the United Kingdom, sent a telegram to de Valera that seemed to indicate he would be willing to support Irish unification if Ireland formally allied with the United Kingdom (Document 60). De Valera, for his part, regarded neutrality as practical, since joining a conflict on the side of Britain would have been deeply unpopular and very expensive, but also as an opportunity to assert Ireland's sovereignty.[42]

In the second half of the twentieth century the relationship between Britain and Ireland was affected by a variety of factors, particularly their membership in the European Economic Community (now called the European Union) and the conflict in Northern Ireland known as the Troubles. For Ireland, membership in the EEC was desirable as a way to secure economic growth and to reduce their reliance on trade with Great Britain. **Taoiseach** Sean Lemass first applied for membership in 1961, the same year that Great Britain first applied as well. Ireland and Great Britain's applications were viewed as inextricably linked because of their close ties. When French President Charles de Gaulle decided to block British membership in 1962 this meant that Ireland was de facto rejected as well. In 1969 de Gaulle relinquished the French presidency and there was no longer a vocal or powerful opponent to British membership in the EEC. Great Britain applied again, as did Ireland. Negotiations began and Ireland as well as Great Britain and Denmark were formally admitted into the EEC in 1972.[43]

Their mutual membership into the EEC came at a fraught time for relations between Great Britain and Ireland as longstanding community tensions in Northern Ireland had boiled over into violence. In 1967 civil rights organizers in Northern Ireland formed the Northern Ireland Civil Rights Association (NICRA), with the goal of protesting discrimination against Irish Catholics in Northern Ireland. Inspired by the American Civil Rights movement, NICRA planned to use nonviolent methods such as marching, petitioning, and letter-writing campaigns.[44] Since its foundation in 1921, Northern Ireland had been dominated by a Protestant elite. The Ulster

Taoiseach: Literally chieftain in Irish, this is the title given to the head of the Irish government, similar to a prime minister.

---

41 Kevin O'Rourke, "Burn Everything British but Their Coal: The Anglo-Irish Economic War of the 1930s," *Journal of Economic History*, vol. 51, no. 2 (1991): 357–66.

42 Bartlett, 452.

43 Garret FitzGerald, "Ireland and the European Union," *Radharc*, vol. 3 (2002): 66, 124–25.

44 Bob Purdie, *Politics in the Streets: The Origins of the Civil Rights Movement in Northern Ireland* (Newtonards: Blackstaff Press, 1990), 132–33.

Unionist party held a monopoly on political power, and policies such as gerrymandering meant that the Irish Catholic population had little to no political representation.[45]

At the same time that NICRA was beginning to gain prominence, a Presbyterian minister named Ian Paisley began to organize a concerted opposition to the cause of Catholic civil rights. Paisley was virulently anti-Catholic and regularly referred to the pope as the "antichrist." Paisley believed that NICRA was a front for the Irish Republican Army (IRA). He and his followers founded the Ulster Constitution Defence Committee to oppose Catholic civil rights. They also founded loyalist paramilitary groups such as the Ulster Protestant Volunteers. Beginning in 1968, loyalist paramilitaries began organizing counter-protests to NICRA civil rights marches. During a march in Derry in 1968 the Royal Ulster Constabulary (RUC) attempted to stop a NICRA march and officers began attacking protestors. In response to the rising tension and increasingly violent clashes, Terence O'Neill, the prime minister of Northern Ireland, gave a speech declaring that Ulster was at a crossroads (Document 67).[46]

O'Neill urged peace and reconciliation between both Catholic Nationalists and Protestant Loyalists. However, many Loyalists were convinced that legal equality with Catholics would mean oppression for them. Catholic communities meanwhile viewed the RUC with distrust, and communities were radicalized by attacks by loyalist paramilitaries. The Provisional Irish Republican Army, known as the Provos, was started in 1969. The Provos denounced the official IRA for failing to adequately defend Catholic areas in Northern Ireland. By the early 1970s the Provos had become the dominant faction of the IRA. Meanwhile, the British Army was first deployed in Northern Ireland in 1969 in response to rioting that had broken out in Derry. In 1972 the parliament of Northern Ireland was suspended and direct rule from London was introduced.[47]

Over the course of the next thirty years the Troubles, as the conflict in Northern Ireland was known, would kill or injure approximately 50,000 people.[48] The Troubles also served as a consistent source of tension between Great Britain and the Republic of Ireland. The government of the Republic of Ireland claimed sovereignty over the entire island in their constitution, and every major political party in the Republic supported an end to the partition of Ireland. Great Britain meanwhile remained committed to

---

45 James Lydon, *The Making of Ireland: A History* (London: Routledge, 1998), 393–94.

46 Paul Arthur and Keith Jeffrey, *Northern Ireland Since 1968* (Oxford: Blackwell Publishers, 1996).

47 David McKittrick and David McVea, *Making Sense of the Troubles: The Story of the Conflict in Northern Ireland* (Chicago: New Amsterdam Books, 2002), 53–75.

48 "Table NI-SEC-05: Persons injured (number) due to the security situation in Northern Ireland, 1969 to 2003," *Cain Archive*, https://cain.ulster.ac.uk/ni/security.htm#05.

the maintenance of the United Kingdom and its commitment to loyalists in Northern Ireland who were violently opposed to Irish reunification. Nationalists in Northern Ireland were just as violently opposed to partition and to the presence of what they saw as a British occupying force. The violence also spread beyond Northern Ireland: there were loyalist bombs planted in the Republic of Ireland and the Provos regularly took to planting bombs in England. Attempts to broker a peace between all sides were made multiple times over the years but both the Sunningdale Agreement (1973) and the Anglo-Irish Agreement (1985) broke down.[49] In 1994 a ceasefire agreement was reached between both nationalist and loyalist paramilitaries as well as political leaders for both communities. Paramilitaries did break the ceasefire at several points in 1996, 1997, and 1998. However, negotiations continued and the result was the Good Friday Agreement of 1998 (Document 73). The Agreement restored self-government to Northern Ireland and created a power-sharing arrangement between the then four major political parties in Northern Ireland. This included Ian Paisley's Democratic Unionist Party and Sinn Féin which had close ties to the Provos.[50]

The Good Friday Agreement marked the beginning of a new era in Northern Ireland and a new era of relations between the Republic of Ireland and Great Britain. The agreement noted the close ties between the two countries, who "wish[ed] to develop still further the unique relationship between their peoples and the close co-operation between their countries as friendly neighbours and as partners in the European Union" (Document 73). In the aftermath of the agreement both countries made attempts to follow through on that wish. The British prime minister Tony Blair formally addressed the Dáil Éireann in 1998 (Document 74) and Queen Elizabeth II made a formal state visit in 2011 (Document 75). In 2014 the Irish president Michael D. Higgins made a formal state visit to England (Document 76). Each of these leaders stressed the close ties both culturally and geographically that exist between the countries and expressed hope that the success of the Northern Ireland Peace Process would bring about a new era of closeness and cooperation between the two countries but on very different terms than earlier in their mutual history.

Up until 2016 their common membership in the European Union was one of the ties that existed between both countries. Their economic ties were so close that Ireland was only admitted alongside Great Britain. The years since admission have brought about great changes to Ireland, which has seen tremendous economic growth and social change. The tone of hopeful cooperation and a bright future, in the words of Queen Elizabeth II "close

---

49 Bartlett, 514–23.
50 Ibid, 562–68.

as good neighbours should always be" (Document 75), seemed to define Anglo–Irish relations in the years following the Good Friday Agreement. The 2016 vote by Great Britain to leave the European Union has created new complications and challenges for the Anglo–Irish relationship.[51] In particular, the partition of Ireland has become a renewed issue.[52] The present solution to this is the Northern Ireland protocol, which has been designed to avoid a hard border on the island of Ireland. This solution has been upsetting to many in the Unionist community in Northern Ireland, who dislike the existence of a customs border between Northern Ireland and Great Britain. It remains to be seen how the challenges presented by Brexit will fully play out, or how they will continue to change the Anglo–Irish relationship.

HISTORIOGRAPHY

The relationship between Ireland and England is the subject of a number of monographs and articles, and the topic appears in virtually everything that has ever been written on Irish history. Traditionally many works of English history have found it easier to leave out the relationship with Ireland. However, recent historiographical turns have worked to reintegrate Irish, Scottish, and Welsh history into the study of England. This Three Kingdoms approach to English history has provided valuable new insights into a number of debates in English history.

The history of Anglo–Irish relations is rife with mutual misunderstanding and distrust. Historical study of this relationship has frequently reflected or even at times perpetuated the central conflict. Beginning in the nineteenth century, Irish nationalist historians sought to write a history of the Irish nation that served their goal of political independence and so focused on the relationship with England as one defined by colonial oppression. Following Irish independence a new school of revisionist historians in Ireland sought to move beyond this focus, finding it dogmatic and fearing in part that it served to perpetuate violent conflict during the Troubles in Northern Ireland. Subsequently, revisionist historians generally sought to write Irish history in a way that did not center on the relationship with England. From the 1990s onward Irish historians have embraced a post-revisionist ideology. Post-revisionists have rejected the revisionist emphasis on writing "value-free" history, noting that such an approach is not actually possible. While many post-revisionist historians continue to attempt to write a less Anglo-centric version of Irish history, in many cases they have proven more

---

51 Tony Connelly, *Brexit & Ireland* (London: Penguin Random House UK, 2018).
52 Feargal Cochrane, *Breaking Peace: Brexit and Northern Ireland* (Manchester: Manchester UP, 2020).

willing to acknowledge the colonial nature of the relationship and to write critically of English policy towards Ireland.

This book aims to take a balanced approach to the history of this relationship and to present a range of primary source documents that introduce the complex realities of the relationship between Ireland and England. The documents that follow fall into four sections: first, those that address the medieval relationship between Ireland and England beginning centuries before the Norman arrival in Ireland and ending in the fifteenth century. Next, documents that focus on the shifting relationship in the early modern period beginning with the The Crown of Ireland Act of 1542 (Document 14) and ending with the debate over the Act of Union of 1800 (Document 37). Third, documents that cover the relationship in the modern era before Irish Independence, starting with the Act of Union of 1800 and ending with the Anglo-Irish Treaty of 1921. Finally, documents that focus on the relationship following Irish independence through to the present day. This collection attempts to balance sources that focus on the political conflicts with those that illuminate cultural interactions and connections. Editorial interventions have been kept to a minimum in most cases, but most documents have been edited for length, and medieval and early modern documents have been edited for spelling. This is a classroom edition and the intention has been to make the texts accessible and to include as broad a range of sources as possible.

CHRONOLOGY

431 St. Patrick, born in Roman Britain, is said to have come to Ireland to spread Christianity.

1166 Diarmait Mac Murchada, King of Leinster, is banished from Ireland and flees to Bristol.

1170 Richard de Clare, also known as Strongbow, arrives in Ireland capturing Wexford and marries Mac Murchada's daughter Aoife.

1171 Henry II arrives in Ireland and receives submission from the kings of Leinster and Dublin.

1175 Henry II and King Rory O'Connor sign the Treaty of Windsor.

1177 Henry II's ten-year-old son John is named "Lord of Ireland."

1366 The Statutes of Kilkenny are introduced; they attempt to ban Anglo-Norman lords in Ireland from adopting Irish language and customs.

1494 Poynings' Law is introduced by Sir Edward Poynings

1537 Silken Thomas Rebellion.

1542 Henry VIII is proclaimed King of Ireland by the Irish parliament.

1555 Pope Paul IV declares that Ireland is a kingdom under the Catholic Queen Mary I.

1568 Desmond Rebellions begin.

1593 The Nine Years' War or Tyrone's Rebellion breaks out.

1603 Hugh O'Neill, the Earl of Tyrone, surrenders at Mellifont ending the Nine Years' War.

1607 Flight of the Earls.

1610 Settlers from England and Scotland begin to arrive for the Plantation of Ulster.

1641 A rebellion breaks out in Ulster.

1642 A Catholic confederacy known as the Confederation of Kilkenny is created.

1649	Oliver Cromwell arrives in Ireland and takes command of parliamentary forces.
1652	Following Cromwell's victory, land is confiscated from Irish landowners and given as payment to Cromwellian soldiers.
1690	Irish Catholic forces under the command of King James II are defeated at the Battle of the Boyne.
1691	King William III wins final victory over Jacobite forces at the Battle of Aughrim.
1718	George I declares the right of the British parliament to legislate for Ireland.
1741	Severe famine in Ireland.
1782	Henry Grattan achieves legislative independence for the Irish parliament.
1798	United Irishmen rebellion.
1801	The Union of Great Britain and Ireland takes effect on January 1.
1803	Robert Emmet's rising takes place in Dublin.
1829	The Relief Act is passed allowing Catholics to enter parliament and hold state offices.
1845	The potato blight is first reported in Ireland.
1847	The worst year of the famine.
1879	The Irish National Land League is founded.
1886	William Gladstone introduces a bill for Irish Home Rule but it is defeated.
1893	The Gaelic League is founded.
1905	Sinn Féin is founded.
1914	The Third Home Rule Bill for Ireland is approved in the United Kingdom but implementation is delayed due to the outbreak of World War I.

1916 Easter Rising.

1918 Sinn Féin wins 73 seats in the United Kingdom general election.

1919 Sinn Féin representatives form the first Dáil Éireann; the Irish War of Independence begins.

1921 The Anglo-Irish Treaty is signed in London, southern Ireland becomes a free state, Northern Ireland is partitioned from southern Ireland.

1922 A civil war breaks out in Ireland between those who opposed and those who supported the Anglo-Irish Treaty.

1932 Éamon de Valera withholds payments of land annuities to the British government. This begins an economic war.

1937 A new constitution is approved for Ireland; it has no mention of the British crown.

1939 World War II breaks out; Ireland remains neutral.

1949 The Republic of Ireland Act abolishes the British monarchy in Ireland.

1969 British troops are deployed in Northern Ireland; the Troubles begin.

1973 Ireland and the United Kingdom are both admitted to the European Economic Community.

1980 First hunger strike by Republican prisoners in Northern Ireland over the loss of special category (political) status.

1981 Second hunger strike by Republican prisoners in Northern Ireland results in the death of 10 prisoners by starvation. The leader of the strike, Bobby Sands, is elected to parliament prior to his death from starvation in May of that year.

1998 The Good Friday agreement is signed; the Troubles end.

1999 Ireland yields its official currency, the Irish pound, and adopts the Euro.

2011 Queen Elizabeth II makes a state visit to Ireland.

2016 In a popular referendum the United Kingdom votes to withdraw from the European Union.

QUESTIONS TO CONSIDER

1. How does the portrayal of Ireland by Gerald of Wales (Documents 7 and 8) influence later writers on Ireland?

2. How have English portrayals of Ireland and the Irish shaped the Anglo–Irish relationship over time?

3. How have English portrayals of Ireland and the Irish changed over time? Why?

4. What is the impact of settler colonialism on Ireland and Irish history?

5. Early modern Irish writers described some Anglo-Norman settler families as "more Irish than the Irish themselves." Is this an accurate description of English settlers in Ireland?

6. How does the nature of Irish resistance to English rule change over time? In what ways do the central conflicts change and in what ways do they stay the same?

7. What role does religion play in shaping the relationship between Ireland and England over time?

8. Why are eighteenth-century Anglo-Irish writers like Molyneux, Swift, and Grattan (Documents 27, 29, and 33) so critical of the relationship with England?

9. Why was the Act of Union (Document 37) so controversial? How did it go on to shape Anglo–Irish relations?

10. In Document 41 Benjamin Disraeli gives his definition of the Irish Question. Do you agree with his interpretation? How would you define the Irish Question in English politics?

11. Why is Douglas Hyde (Document 50) so concerned about "Anglicization" in Ireland?

12. Compare and contrast the Irish nationalist views in Documents 40, 42, 45, 48, 50, 53, 54, and 55. What values and goals do they share? In what way do their views of Irish nationalism differ?

13. How does the relationship between Ireland and England change after the Anglo-Irish Treaty (Document 57)?

14. How do Margaret Thatcher (Document 71) and the writers of *The Starry Plough* (Document 72) see the issue of special category status and the hunger strike differently? Why?

15. How do English and Irish political leaders in the late twentieth and early twenty-first century (Documents 72, 75, and 76) sum up the relationship between England and Ireland? What are the common themes in these speeches? How does the context of the period inform their speeches?

16. In Document 75 Queen Elizabeth II begins her speech with some words in Irish. Why was this gesture and the speech overall so widely praised in Ireland? How does the history between Ireland and England inform reactions to the speech?

17. In 2014 Irish President Michael D. Higgins (Document 76) described Ireland and England as being in both the "shadow" and the "shelter" of each other. In what ways are Ireland and England each other's shadow and in what ways are they each other's shelter?

PART 1

Medieval Ireland and England (700–1500)

DOCUMENT I:

From The Venerable Bede, *The Ecclesiastical History of the English People* (c. 731)[1]

St. Bede, or the Venerable Bede (673–735), was a Benedictine monk in Northumbria, then an independent Old English kingdom. He completed his *Ecclesiastical History of the English People* in 731. The book includes an account of the history of England and the history of Christianity. There is a particular focus on the theological controversy between Celtic and Roman Christianity. In these passages Bede reflects on the Irish influence on the development of Christianity in England and the controversy that developed over such issues as the date of the celebration of Easter at the Synod of Whitby in 664.

∾

Ireland, both in its average breadth and in healthfulness, as well as in the serenity of its air, is much superior to Britain, so that snow there rarely remains longer than three days. No one for winter use either cuts hay in the summer or builds sheds for beasts of burden; no reptile is wont to be seen, no serpent is able to live there; for often serpents brought thither from Britain, on the ship approaching the shore, die, as if overcome with the scent of the air. Nay, more; almost all things brought from that island are efficacious against poison. In short, leaves of books brought from Ireland have been scraped, and the scrapings, when put in water and given to drink to persons bitten by a serpent, have been known to absorb and allay immediately the whole force of the venom working in such persons, and all the swelling of the body. The island abounds in milk and honey, nor is it destitute of vines, fishes, and birds; it is moreover noted for the hunting of stags and goats....

But whatsoever [**Columba**] was himself, we hold this as certain concerning him, that he left successors remarkable for their great continence, and divine love, and regular discipline: as to the time indeed of the chief

Columba: St. Columba (521–97) was an Irish monk and missionary primarily in what is now Scotland; he helped to introduce Christianity to the Picts of Scotland, and founded the monastery of Iona.

---

1   *Bede's Ecclesiastical History of the English Nation*, translated by L. Gidley (Oxford: James Parker and Co., 1870).

festival they followed doubtful cycles, since, as they were situated far beyond the world, no one had brought them the synodal decrees for the observance of Easter, only they diligently practised those works of piety and chastity which they were able to learn in the prophetical, evangelical, and apostolic writings. Moreover, this manner of keeping Easter continued among them for no short time, that is, for 150 years, until the year of the Lord's incarnation 715....

Aidan: St. Aidan (590–651) was an Irish monk and missionary who converted the people of Northumbria to Christianity, and founded the monastery of Lindisfarne.

From this island, then, and from the college of these monks, **Aidan** was sent to instruct the province of the Angles in Christ, having received the degree of bishop.... Whence, among other examples of living, he left a most salutary example of abstinence as well as continence to the clergy; and his doctrine was most chiefly commended to all by the circumstance that he himself taught not otherwise than he and his followers lived. For he cared not to seek anything or to love anything of this world. All things which were given him by kings or rich men of the world, he delighted presently to dispense to the poor whom he met with. He was wont to go about through all places, both in town and in country, on foot, and not on horseback, unless any urgent necessity compelled him; in order that wheresoever he beheld in his walks any, whether rich or poor, he might immediately turn aside to them, and either invite them to the sacrament of receiving the faith, if they were infidels; or, if they were believers, strengthen them in the same faith, and excite them, both by his words and deeds, to alms and the performance of good works....

Oswald: King Oswald of Northumbria, reigned 634–42.

Moreover, they relate that when King **Oswald** asked for a prelate from the province of the Scots, to minister to himself and his people the word of faith, there was at first another man sent of more austere disposition, who, when after preaching for some time to the nation of the Angles, he made no progress, and was not listened to willingly by the people, returned to his country, and related in the assembly of the elders, that he had not been able to effect anything in teaching the nation to which he had been sent, on account of their being intractable men, and of a harsh and barbarous disposition. Then they, as is reported, began to hold a great debate in council as to what was to be done, being desirous to afford to the nation those means of salvation which they were asked to confer, but grieving because the preacher whom they had sent had not been received. Then said Aidan, for he also was present in the council, to that priest concerning whom the meeting was held, "It seems to me, brother, that you have been too hard with your unlearned hearers, and have not afforded them, according to the apostolic teaching, first the milk of easier doctrine, until being nourished by degrees by the Word of God, they should be capable of receiving the more perfect, and of performing the sublimer precepts of God." Which being heard, the faces and eyes of all who sat there were turned towards him, and they earnestly discussed what he had said, and decreed that he himself was worthy of the episcopate, and ought to be sent to teach the unbelieving and unlearned, since above all things he was proved to be endued with the grace of discretion, which is the mother of virtues; and accordingly they ordained him, and sent him to preach. And he, in course of time, as he had before appeared to be adorned with the guidance of discretion, so afterwards exhibited the other virtues also....

However, on the death of **Finan**, who came after him, when **Colman** succeeded to the episcopate, being himself also sent by the Scots, a greater controversy arose concerning the keeping of Easter, and also concerning other rules of ecclesiastical life; whereupon this question moved the feelings and hearts of many, who feared lest perchance after they had received the name of Christians, they were running or had run in vain. It came even to the ears of the rulers—to wit, King **Oswy**, and his son Alchfrid; which Oswy, forsooth, having been instructed and baptized by the Scots, and also being well skilled in their language, thought that nothing was better than what they had taught him. Further, Alchfrid, having for his instructor in Christian erudition **Wilfrid**, a most learned man (for he had gone to Rome previously for the sake of ecclesiastical learning, and had spent much time with Dalfinus, archbishop of Lyons in Gaul, from whom also he had received the crown of the ecclesiastical tonsure), knew that his doctrine was justly to be preferred to all the traditions of the Scots.

And first King Oswy having said by way of preface, that it behoved those who together served one God to hold one rule of living, and those who all expected one kingdom in the heavens, not to differ in the celebration of the heavenly sacraments; but that they should enquire rather what was the truest tradition, and that this should be followed by all in common; commanded his bishop, Colman, first to declare what that custom was which he followed, and whence it derived its origin. Then said Colman, "This **paschal** feast which I am accustomed to keep, I received from my elders, who sent me hither as bishop, which all our fathers, men beloved by God, are known to have celebrated in the same manner. And this may not appear to any to be condemned or rejected, since it is the very feast which the blessed evangelist St. John, the disciple specially beloved by the Lord, together with all the Churches over which he presided, is recorded to have celebrated." And when he had said these and such like things, the king commanded **Agilberct** also to proclaim openly the custom of his observance, whence it had its beginning, or by what authority he followed it. Agilberct replied, "Let my disciple Wilfrid the presbyter speak, I entreat you, in my place, because we both think the same thing, together with the rest of the observers of ecclesiastical tradition, who are sitting here, by us; and he can explain in the tongue of the Angles what we think, better and more clearly

Finan: An Irish monk and Bishop of Lindisfarne from 651 to 661.

Colman: An Irish monk and Bishop of Lindisfarne from 661 to 664. Here he represents the viewpoint of Celtic Christianity in the debate over how to calculate Easter. After losing this debate Colman resigned as bishop and traveled to Scotland.

Oswy: King of Northumbria, reigned 642–70.

Wilfrid: A Northumbrian nobleman, he was appointed Bishop of York in 664 following his speech here.

Paschal: Easter.

Agilberct: Originally a Frank, at this time he was bishop of the West Saxons.

than I can by an interpreter." Then Wilfrid, the king commanding that he should speak, began thus: "The paschal feast which we observe," said he, "we have seen celebrated by all at Rome, where the blessed apostles Peter and Paul lived, taught, suffered, and were buried; this feast in Italy, and in Gaul, which countries we passed through for the sake of learning or of praying, we saw kept by all. We found Africa, Asia, Egypt, Greece, and all the world, wherever the Church of Christ is spread abroad, through divers nations and tongues, keeping this feast in one, and not a different, order of time, except these only, and their accomplices in obstinacy, I mean the Picts and the Britons, together with whom, from two most remote islands of ocean, nor yet from the whole of these, they contend with foolish labour against the whole world." To whom, saying these things, Colman replied: "It is marvellous that you will call our labour foolish, in which we follow the example of so great an apostle, who was worthy to lie upon the Lord's bosom, when all the world knows that he lived most wisely."

DOCUMENT 2:

From *The Anglo-Saxon Chronicle* (9th–12th century)[2]

The Anglo-Saxon Chronicles is a collection of annals written in Old English. Originally composed during the reign of Alfred the Great (r. 871–99) they were continuously updated until approximately 1154. The entry below is for the year 1087 and commemorates the death of William I, also known as William the Conqueror (r. 1066–87), who conquered England in 1066. The writer speculates that had he lived he would have conquered Ireland as well.

ℰ

A.D. 1087 ... In the same year also, before the Assumption of St. Mary, King William went from Normandy into France with an army, and made war upon his own lord **Philip, the king**, and slew many of his men, and burned the town of Mante, and all the holy minsters that were in the town; and two holy men that served God, leading the life of **anachorets**, were burned therein. This being thus done, King William returned to Normandy. Rueful was the thing he did; but a more rueful him befel. How more rueful? He fell sick, and it dreadfully ailed him. What shall I say? Sharp death, that passes by neither rich men nor poor, seized him also. He died in Normandy, on the next day after the Nativity of St. Mary, and he was buried at Caen in St. Stephen's minster, which he had formerly reared, and afterwards endowed with manifold gifts. Alas! how false and how uncertain is this world's weal! He that was before a rich king, and lord of many lands, had not then of all his land more than a space of seven feet! and he that was whilom enshrouded in gold and gems, lay there covered with mould! He left behind him three sons; the eldest, called **Robert**, who was earl in Normandy after him; the second, called **William**, who wore the crown after him in England; and the third, called **Henry**, to whom his father bequeathed immense treasure. If any person wishes to know what kind of man he was, or what honour he had, or of how many lands he was lord, then will we write about him as well as we understand him: we who often looked upon him, and lived sometime in his court. This King William then that we speak about was a very wise man, and very rich; more splendid and powerful than any of his predecessors were. He was mild to the good men that loved God, and beyond all measure severe to the men that gainsayed his will.... But amongst other things is not to be forgotten that good peace that he made in this land; so that a man of any account might go over his kingdom unhurt with his bosom full of gold. No man durst slay another, had he never so much evil done to the other;

Philip, the king: Philip I, King of France 1060–1108.

Anachoret: Also spelled anchorite, someone who withdraws from society usually for religious reasons.

Robert: Eldest son of William the Conqueror, Robert was Duke of Normandy from 1087 until 1106. He was estranged from his father at the time of his death and his younger brother claimed the throne of England.

William: William II, second son of William the Conqueror and King of England from 1087 until 1100.

Henry: Henry I, fourth son of William the Conqueror and King of England from 1100 until 1135.

---

2 *The Anglo-Saxon Chronicle*, https://avalon.law.yale.edu/medieval/ang09.asp.

and if any **churl** lay with a woman against her will, he soon lost the limb that he played with. He truly reigned over England; and by his capacity so thoroughly surveyed it, that there was not a hide of land in England that he **wist** not who had it, or what it was worth, and afterwards set it down in his book. The land of the Britons was in his power; and he wrought castles therein; and ruled **Anglesey** withal. So also he subdued Scotland by his great strength. As to Normandy, that was his native land; but he reigned also over the earldom called **Maine**; and if he might have yet lived two years more, he would have won Ireland by his valour, and without any weapons. Assuredly in his time had men much distress, and very many sorrows.

DOCUMENT 3:

From Early Medieval Kings: Extracts from *Asser's Life of King Alfred* (893)[3] and *Cogad Gáedel re Gallaib* (c. 1103)[4]

In the early Middle Ages both England and Ireland consisted of a number of smaller, constantly warring kingdoms. The experience of Viking invasions beginning in the eighth century encouraged the emergence of kings who attempted to centralize multiple kingdoms under their rule: in England Alfred the Great of Wessex (849–99) and in Ireland Brian Boru of Munster (941–1014). Asser, a Welsh monk and later Bishop of Sherborne, first wrote his *Life of King Alfred* in 893. The *Cogad Gáedel re Gallaib* was likely composed between 1103 and 1111 to promote the interest of the O'Briens, who were struggling to remain high kings of Ireland.

Asser's Life of King Alfred

In the year of our Lord's incarnation 876, being the twenty-eighth year of King Alfred's life, the oft-mentioned army of the **heathen**, leaving Cambridge by night, entered a fortress called Wareham, where there is a monastery of nuns between the two rivers Froom (and Tarrant), in the district which is called in Welsh Durngueir, but in Saxon Thornsæta, placed in a most secure location, except on the western side, where there was a territory adjacent. With this army Alfred made a solemn treaty to the effect that they should depart from him, and they made no hesitation to give him as many picked hostages as he named; also they swore an oath on all the relics in which King Alfred trusted next to God, and on which they had never before sworn to any people, that they would speedily depart from his kingdom. But they again practiced their usual treachery, and caring nothing for either hostages or oath, they broke the treaty, and, sallying forth by night, slew all the horsemen that they had, and, turning off, started without warning for another place called in Saxon Exanceastre, and in Welsh Cairwisc, which means in Latin The City (of Exe), situated on the eastern bank of the river Wisc, near the southern sea which divides Britain from Gaul, and there passed the winter....

What shall I say of his repeated expeditions against the heathen, his wars, and the incessant occupations of government? ... [O]f the nations which dwell on the Tyrrhene Sea to the farthest end of Ireland? For we have seen

Heathen: A reference to the Viking invaders of England.

---

3   *Asser's Life of King Alfred*, translated by Albert S. Cook (Boston: Ginn & Co, 1906).

4   *The War of the Gaedhil with the Gaill*, translated by James Henthorn Todd (London: Longmans, Green, Reader, and Dyer, 1867).

and read letters, accompanied with presents, which were sent to him from Jerusalem by the patriarch Elias. What shall I say of his restoration of cities and towns, and of others which he built where none had been before? Of golden and silver buildings, built in incomparable style under his direction? Of the royal halls and chambers, wonderfully erected of stone and wood at his command? Of the royal **vills** constructed of stones removed from their old site, and finely rebuilt by the king's command in more fitting places?

Not to speak of the disease above mentioned, he was disturbed by the quarrels of his subjects, who would of their own choice endure little or no toil for the common need of the kingdom. He alone, sustained by the divine aid, once he had assumed the helm of government, strove in every way, like a skillful pilot, to steer his ship, laden with much wealth, into the safe and longed-for harbour of his country, though almost all his crew were weary, suffering them not to faint or hesitate, even amid the waves and manifold whirlpools of this present life. Thus his bishops, earls, nobles, favorite thanes, and prefects, who, next to God and the king, had the whole government of the kingdom, as was fitting, continually received from him instruction, compliment, exhortation, and command; nay, at last, if they were disobedient, and his long patience was exhausted, he would reprove them severely, and censure in every way their vulgar folly and obstinacy; and thus he wisely gained and bound them to his own wishes and the common interests of the whole kingdom. But if, owing to the sluggishness of the people, these admonitions of the king were either not fulfilled, or were begun late at the moment of necessity, and so, because they were not carried through, did not redound to the advantage of those who put them in execution—take as an example the fortresses which he ordered, but which are not yet begun or, begun late, have not yet been completely finished—when hostile forces have made invasions by sea, or land, or both, then those who had set themselves against the imperial orders have been put to shame and overwhelmed with vain repentance. I speak of vain repentance on the authority of Scripture, whereby numberless persons have had cause for sorrow when they have been smitten by great harm through the perpetration of deceit. But though by this means, sad to say, they may be bitterly afflicted, and roused to grief by the loss of fathers, wives, children, thanes, man servants, maid servants, products, and all their household stuff, what is the use of hateful repentance when their kinsmen are dead, and they cannot aid them, or redeem from dire captivity those who are captive? For they cannot even help themselves when they have escaped, since they have not wherewithal to sustain their own lives. Sorely exhausted by a tardy repentance, they grieve over their carelessness in despising the king's commands; they unite in praising his wisdom, promising to fulfil with all their might what before they had declined to do, namely, in the construction of fortresses, and other things useful to the whole kingdom.

Vills: The smallest rural land unit in England.

Cogad Gáedel re Gallaib

Now, when these [Brian and his brother Mathgamhain] saw the bondage, and the oppression, and the misrule, that was inflicted on **Mumhain**, and on the men of Erinn in general, the advice they acted on was to avoid it, and not submit to it at all. They therefore carried off their people, and all their chattels, over the **Sinann** westwards; and they dispersed themselves among the forests and woods of the three tribes that were there. They began to plunder and kill the foreigners immediately after that. Neither had they any **termonn** or protection from the foreigners; but it was woe to either party to meet the other, or come together, owing to the plunders, and conflicts, and battles, and skirmishes, and trespasses, and combats, that were interchanged between them during a long period. When at length, each party of them became tired of the other, they made peace and truce between them for some time, viz, Mathgamhain, son of Cennedigh, king of the Dal Cais, and the chieftains of the **foreigners** of Mumhain in general....

So Brian returned from his great royal visitation around all Erinn made in this manner; and the peace of Erinn was proclaimed by him, both of churches and people; so that peace throughout all Erinn was made in his time. He fined and imprisoned the perpetrators of murders, trespass, and robbery, and war. He hanged, and killed, and destroyed the robbers and thieves, and plunderers of Erinn. He extirpated, dispersed, banished, caused to fly, stripped, maimed, ruined, and destroyed the foreigners in every district and in every territory throughout the breadth of all Erinn. He killed also their kings, and their chieftains, their heroes, and brave soldiers, their men of renown and valour. He enslaved and reduced to bondage their stewards and their collectors, and their swordsmen, their mercenaries, and their comely, large, cleanly youths; and their smooth youthful girls....

By him were erected also noble churches in Erinn and their sanctuaries. He sent professors and masters to teach wisdom and knowledge; and to buy books beyond the sea, and the great ocean; because their writings and their books in every church and in every sanctuary where they were, were burned and thrown into water by the plunderers, from the beginning to the end; and Brian, himself, gave the price of learning and the price of books to every one separately who went on this service ... He continued in this way prosperously, peaceful, giving banquets, hospitable, just-judging, wealthily, venerated, chastely, and with devotion, and with law and with rules among the clergy; with prowess and with valour; with honour and with renown among the laity; and fruitful, powerful, firm, secure; for fifteen years in the chief sovereignty of Erinn ...

There was not done in Erinn, since Christianity, excepting the beheading of **Cormac Mac Cuilennain**, any greater deed than this. In fact he was one

Mumhain: Munster.

Sinann: The Shannon River.

Termonn: An Irish word for a sanctuary or boundary.

Foreigners: A reference to the Vikings.

Cormac Mac Cuilennain: An Irish bishop and King of Munster 902–08.

of the three best that ever were born in Erinn; and one of the three men who most caused Erinn to prosper, namely, **Lugh Lamha-fada**, and **Finn Mac Cumhaill**, and **Brian Mac Ceinneidigh**. For it was he that released the men of Erinn, and its women, from the bondage and iniquity of the foreigners, and the pirates. It was he that gained five-and-twenty battles over the foreigners, and who killed and banished them as we have already said. He was the beautiful, ever-victorious **Octavin**, for the prosperity and freedom of his country and his race. He was the strong, irresistible, second **Alexander**, for energy, and for dignity, and for attacks, and for battles, and for triumphs. And he was the happy, wealthy, peaceable **Solomon** of the Gaedhil. He was the faithful, fervent, honourable, gallant **David** of Erinn, for truthfulness, and for worthiness, and for the maintenance of sovereignty. He was the magnificent, brilliant Moses, for chastity, and unostentatious devotion.

Lugh Lamha-fada: Lugh of the Long-hand, a warrior king in Irish mythology

Finn Mac Cumhaill: Finn McCool, a hunter and warrior in Irish mythology.

Brian Mac Ceinneidigh: Brian Boru; mac Cennétig means "son of Cennetig."

Octavin: Octavian or Augustus Caesar, emperor of Rome (27 BCE–14 CE).

Alexander: Alexander the Great, king of Macedon (335–323 BCE).

Solomon: King of Israel in the Bible, noted for his wealth and wisdom.

David: King of Israel in the Bible, noted for killing the giant Goliath.

DOCUMENT 4:

From William of Malmesbury, *Chronicle of the Kings of England* (c. 1125)[5]

William of Malmesbury (c. 1095–c. 1143) was an English historian and monk. As a historian William modeled himself after the Venerable Bede and consciously patterned his work after *The Ecclessiastical History of the English People*. His work spanned the period from 449 to 1120. In this section he reflects on the relationship between Henry I and an Irish king.

ev

[A.D. 1119.]   MURCARD, KING OF IRELAND.

Murcard, king of Ireland, and his successors, whose names have not reached our notice, were so devotedly attached to our Henry that they wrote no letters but what tended to soothe him, and did nothing but what he commanded; although it may be observed that Murcard, from some unknown cause, acted, for a short time, rather superciliously towards the English; but soon after on the suspension of navigation and of foreign trade, his insolence subsided. For of what value could Ireland be if deprived of the merchandize of England? From poverty, or rather from the ignorance of the cultivators, the soil, unproductive of every good, engenders, without the cities, a rustic, filthy swarm of natives; but the English and French inhabit the cities in a greater degree of civilization through their mercantile traffic. Paul, earl of Orkney, though subject by hereditary right to the king of Norway, was so anxious to obtain the king's friendship, that he was perpetually sending him presents; for he was extremely fond of the wonders of distant countries, begging with great delight, as I have observed, from foreign kings, lions, leopards, lynxes, or camels,—animals which England does not produce. He had a park called Woodstock, in which he used to foster his favourites of this kind. He had placed there also a creature called a porcupine, sent to him by William of Montpelier; of which animal, Pliny the Elder, in the eighth book of his Natural History, and Isodorus, on Etymologies, relate that there is such a creature in Africa, which the inhabitants call of the urchin kind, covered with bristly hairs, which it naturally darts against the dogs when pursuing it: moreover, these are, as I have seen, more than a span long, sharp at each extremity, like the quills of a goose where the feather ceases, but rather thicker, and speckled, as it were, with black and white.

Murcard: or Muirchertach O'Brien (c. 1050–c. 1119), was the great-grandson of Brian Boru. He was king of Munster and self-declared high king of Ireland.

---

5   *William of Malmesbury's Chronicle of the Kings of England,* edited by J.A. Giles (London: Henry G. Bohn, 1847).

DOCUMENT 5:

Laudabiliter (1155)[6]

Laudabiliter refers to a papal bull issued in 1155 by Pope Adrian IV. Adrian IV was pope from 1154 to 1159; he was the only Englishman to ever hold that office. The bull granted to King Henry II of England the right to invade and govern Ireland in order to enforce the Gregorian Reforms on the church there. Henry II did nothing at the time, but later leaders of the Norman Invasion of Ireland claimed the authority to do so from the *Laudabiliter*.

❧

Adrian, bishop, servant of the servants of God, to his most dearly beloved son in Christ, the illustrious king of the English, greeting and apostolical blessing.

Laudably and profitably doth your Majesty consider how you may extend the glory of your name on earth and lay up for yourself an eternal reward in heaven, when, as becomes a Catholic prince, you labour to extend the borders of the Church, to teach the truths of the Christian faith to a rude and unlettered people, and to root out the weeds of vice from the field of the Lord; and to accomplish your design more effectually you crave the advice and assistance of the Apostolic See, and in so doing we are persuaded that the higher are your aims, and the more discreet your proceedings, the greater, under God, will be your success; because, whatever has its origin in ardent faith and in love of religion, always has a prosperous end and issue. Certainly it is beyond a doubt, as your Highness acknowledged, that Ireland and all the other islands, on which the Gospel of Christ hath dawned and which have received the knowledge of the Christian faith, belong of right to St Peter and the holy Roman church. Wherefore we are the more desirous to sow in them the acceptable seed of God's word, because we know that it will be strictly required of us hereafter. You have signified to us, our well-beloved son in Christ, that you propose to enter the island of Ireland in order to subdue the people and make them obedient to laws, and to root out from among them the weeds of sin; and that you are willing to yield and pay yearly from every house the pension of one penny to St Peter, and to keep and preserve the rights of the churches in that land whole and inviolate.

We, therefore, regarding your pious and laudable design with due favour, and graciously assenting to your petition, do hereby declare our will and pleasure, that, for the purpose of enlarging the borders of the Church, setting bounds to the progress and wickedness, reforming evil manners,

---

6 *Laudabiliter*, in *A History of Ireland and Her People*, by Eleanor Hull (Oxford: G.G. Harrap, 1926).

planting virtue, and increasing the Christian religion, you do enter and take possession of that island, and execute therein whatsoever shall be for God's honour and the welfare of the same.

And, further, we do also strictly charge and require that the people of that land shall accept you with all honour, and dutifully obey you, as their liege lord, saving only the rights of the churches, which we will have inviolably preserved; and reserving to St Peter and the holy Roman Church the yearly pension of one penny from each house. If, therefore, you bring your purpose to good effect, let it be your study to improve the habits of that people, and take such orders by yourself, or by others whom you shall think fitting, for their lives, manners, and conversation, that the Church there may be adorned by them, the Christian faith be planted and increased, and all that concerns the honour of God and the salvation of souls be ordered by you in like manner; so that you may receive at God's hands the blessed reward of everlasting life, and may obtain on earth a glorious name in ages to come.

DOCUMENT 6:

The Treaty of Windsor (1175)[7]

Signed in 1175 between King Henry II of England and the High King of Ireland Rory O'Connor, the treaty was a territorial agreement made following the Norman invasion of Ireland. The agreement did not last long, as both men interpreted the terms differently. Henry II saw Rory O'Connor as his feudal subordinate, while Rory O'Connor saw himself as the independent high king of Ireland subject to a small annual tribute to the king of England.

ϑ

Michaelmas: The Feast of St Michael and all the angels at that time held on October 6th.

This is the agreement which was made at Windsor in the octaves of **Michaelmas** in the year of Our Lord 1175, between Henry, king of England, and Roderic [Rory], king of Connaught, by Catholicus, archbishop of Tuam, Cantordis, abbot of Clonfert, and Master Laurence, chancellor of the king of Connaught, namely: The king of England has granted to Roderic, his liegeman, king of Connacht, as long as he shall faithfully serve him, that he shall be king under him, ready to his service, as his man. And he shall hold his land as fully and as peacefully as he held it before the lord king entered Ireland, rendering him tribute. And that he shall have all the rest of the land and its inhabitants under him and shall bring them to account [**justiciet eos**], so that they shall pay their full tribute to the king of England through

Justiciet eos: "Do justice to."

him, and so that they shall maintain their rights. And those who are now in possession of their lands and rights shall hold them in peace as long as they remain in the fealty of the king of England, and continue to pay him faithfully and fully his tribute and the other rights which they owe to him, by the hand of the king of Connaught, saving in all things the right and honour of the king of England and of Roderic. And if any of them shall be rebels to the king of England and to Roderic and shall refuse to pay the tribute and other rights of the king of England by his hand, and shall withdraw from the fealty of the king of England, he, Roderic, shall judge them and remove them. And if he cannot answer for them by himself, the constable of the king of England in that land [Ireland] shall, when called upon by him, aid him to do what is necessary. And for this agreement the said king of Connaught shall render to the king of England tribute every year, namely, out of every ten animals slaughtered, one hide, acceptable to the merchants both in his land as in the rest; save that he shall not meddle with those lands which the lord king has retained in his lordship and in the lordship of his batons; that is to say, Dublin with all its **appurtenances**;

Appurtenances: A legal term referring to a minor property right belonging to another more important right.

---

7 "The Treaty of Windsor (1175)." The original treaty can be seen on Wikipedia.

Meath with all its appurtenances, even as **Murchat Ua Mailethlachlin** [Murchadh O' Melaghlin] held it fully and freely [**melius et plenius**] or as others held it of him; Wexford with all its appurtenances, that is to say, the whole of Leinster; and Waterford with its whole territory from Waterford to Dungarvan, including Dungarvan with all its appurtenances. And if the Irish who have fled wish to return to the land of the barons of the king of England they may do so in peace, paying the said tribute as others pay it, or doing to the English the services which they were wont to do for their lands, which shall be decided by the judgment and will of their lords. And if any of them are unwilling to return and their lords have called upon the king of Connaught, he shall compel them to return to their land, so that they shall dwell there in peace. And the king of Connaught shall accept hostages from all whom the lord king of England has committed to him, and he shall himself give hostages at the will of the king. The witnesses are Robert, bishop of Winchester; Geoffrey, bishop of Ely; Laurence, archbishop of Dublin; Geoffrey Nicolas and Roger, the king's chaplains; William, Earl of Essex; Richard de Luci; Geoffrey de Portico, and Reginald de Courtenea.

Murchat Ua Mailethlachlin: King of Meath.

Melius et plenius: Latin for "better and fuller."

DOCUMENT 7:

From Gerald of Wales, *Topographia Hibernica* (c. 1188)[8]

Topographia Hibernica or *The Topography of Ireland* was written around 1188 by Gerald of Wales, a Welsh-Norman clergyman. In 1184 he became a royal clerk and chaplain to King Henry II and was chosen in 1185 to accompany Prince John, recently declared Lord of Ireland, on a trip to Ireland. Gerald had previously traveled to Ireland in 1183 to visit members of his family who had helped lead the Norman Invasion in 1169. It is likely that Gerald did not travel extensively around Ireland in either of his visits. He would later write an account of the invasion *Expugnatio Hibernica*. Taken together these two works play an important role in shaping English attitudes towards Ireland for centuries afterwards.

ം

Of the prodigies of our times, and first of a wolf which conversed with a priest

Earl John: Henry II's youngest son John was named Lord of Ireland in 1177; he first visited Ireland in 1185 with Gerald of Wales. John would eventually become King of England from 1199 until 1216.

About three years before the arrival of **earl John** in Ireland, it chanced that a priest, who was journeying from Ulster towards Meath, was benighted in a certain wood on the borders of Meath. While in company with only a young lad, he was watching by a fire which he had kindled under the branches of a spreading tree, lo! A wolf came up to them, and immediately addressed them to this effect: "Rest secure, and be not afraid, for there is no reason you should fear, where no fear is." The travellers being struck with astonishment and alarm, the wolf added some orthodox words referring to God. The priest then implored him, and adjured him by Almighty God and faith in the Trinity, not to hurt them, but to inform them what creature it was that in the shape of a beast uttered human words. The wolf, after giving catholic replies to all questions, added at last: "There are two of us, a man and a woman, natives of Ossory, who, through the curse of one **Natalis**, saint and abbot, are compelled every seven years to put off the human form, and depart from the dwellings of men. Quitting entirely the human form, we assume that of wolves. At the end of the seven years, if they chance to survive, two others being substituted in their places, they return to their country and their former shape. And now, she who is my partner in this visitation lies dangerously sick not far from hence, and, as she is at

Natalis: St. Natalis of Ulster was a sixth-century Irish monk; he was abbot of a monastery in Donegal.

---

8   Giraldus Cambrensis, *The Topography of Ireland,* translated by Thomas Forester (Ontario: In parentheses Publications, 2000).

the point of death, I beseech you, inspired by divine charity, to give her the consolations of your priestly office."

At this word the priest followed the wolf trembling, as he led the way to a tree at no great distance, in the hollow of which he beheld a she-wolf, who under that shape was pouring forth human sighs and groans. On seeing the priest, having saluted him with human courtesy, she gave thanks to God, who in this extremity had vouchsafed to visit her with such consolation....

There rites having been duly, rather than rightly performed, the he-wolf gave them his company for during the whole night at their little fire, behaving more like a man than a beast.... At the close of their conversation, the priest inquired of the wolf whether the hostile race which had now landed in the island would continue there for the time to come, and be long established in it. To which the wolf replied:— "For the sins of our nation, and their enormous vices, the anger of the Lord, falling on an evil generation, hath given them into the hands of their enemies. Therefore, as long as this foreign race shall keep the commandments of the Lord, and walk in his ways, it will be secure and invincible; but if, as the downward path of illicit pleasures is easy, and nature is prone to follow vicious examples, this people shall chance, from living among us, to adopt our depraved habits, doubtless they will provoke the divine vengeance on themselves also." ...

Of the character, customs, and habits of this people

I have considered it not superfluous to give a short account of the condition of this nation, both bodily and mentally; I mean their state of cultivation, both interior and exterior. This people are not tenderly nursed from their birth, as others are; for besides the rude fare they receive from their parents, which is only just sufficient for their sustenance, as to the rest, almost all is left to nature. They are not placed in cradles, or swathed, nor are their tender limbs either fomented by constant bathing, or adjusted with art. For the midwives make no use of warm water, nor raise their noses, nor depress the face, nor stretch the legs; but nature alone, with very slight aids from art, disposes and adjusts the limbs to which she has given birth, just as she pleases. As if to prove that what she is able to form she does not cease to shape also, she gives growth and proportions to these people, until they arrive at perfect vigour, tall and handsome in person, and with agreeable and ruddy countenances. But although they are richly endowed with the gifts of nature, their want of civilization, shown in both their dress and mental culture, makes them a barbarous people. For they wear but little woollen, and nearly all they use is black, that being the colour of the sheep in this country. Their clothes are also made after a barbarous fashion....

The Irish are a rude people, subsisting on the produce of their cattle only, and living themselves like beasts—a people that has not yet departed from the primitive habits of pastoral life. In the common course of things, mankind progresses from the forest to the field, from the field to the town, and to the social condition of citizens; but this nation, holding agricultural labour in contempt, and little coveting the wealth of towns, as well as being exceedingly averse to civil institutions—lead the same life their fathers did in the woods and open pastures, neither willing to abandon their old habits or learn anything new. They, therefore, only make patches of tillage; their pastures are short of herbage; cultivation is very rare, and there is scarcely any land sown. This want of tilled fields arises from the neglect of those who should cultivate them; for there are large tracts which are naturally fertile and productive. The whole habits of the people are contrary to agricultural pursuits, so that the rich glebe is barren for want of husbandmen, the fields demanding labour which is not forthcoming …

This people, then, is truly barbarous in their dress, but suffering their hair and beards to grow enormously in an uncouth manner, just like the modern fashion recently introduced; indeed all their habits are barbarisms. But habits are formed by mutual intercourse; and as this people inhabit a country so remote from the rest of the world, and lying at its furthest extremity, forming, as it were, another world, and are thus secluded from civilized nations, they learn nothing, and practice nothing but the barbarism in which they are born and bred, and which sticks to them like a second nature. Whatever natural gifts they possess are excellent, in whatever requires industry they are worthless …

How the Irish are very ignorant of the rudiments of the faith

The faith having been planted in the island from the time of St. Patrick, so many ages ago, and propagated almost ever since, it is wonderful that this nation should remain to this day so very ignorant of the rudiments of Christianity. It is indeed a most filthy race, a race sunk in vice, a race more ignorant than all other nations of the first principles of the faith. Hitherto they neither pay tithes nor first fruits; they do not contract marriages, nor shun incestuous connections; they frequent not the church of God with proper reverence. Nay, what is most detestable, and not only contrary to the Gospel, but to everything that is right, in many parts of Ireland brothers (I will not say marry) seduce and debauch the wives of their brothers deceased, and have incestuous intercourse with them; adhering in this to the letter, and not to the spirit, of the **Old Testament**; and following the example of men of old in their vices more willingly than in their virtues.

Old Testament: Deuteronomy 25:5 says that brothers have a duty to marry their widowed sisters-in-law.

DOCUMENT 8:

From Gerald of Wales, *Expugnatio Hibernica* (c. 1189)[9]

> *Expugnatio Hibernica* or *The Conquest of Ireland* was written around 1189
> by Gerald of Wales. It was written after the *Topographia Hibernica* or *The
> Topography of Ireland* as a companion piece focusing on the Norman conquest.
> Gerald traveled to Ireland first in 1183 and again in 1185 on an expedition with
> Henry II's son John. Robert FitzStephen and Raymond FitzGerald, two of
> the leaders of the Norman invasion of Ireland were his uncles.

Speech of Hervey

Besides, we have already more enemies than guards in our camp; we are
surrounded with perils on every side; is it not enough that we are exposed
to them from without, and must we also have them within? Outside our
trenches the enemy's host is innumerable, within there are numbers who
plot our destruction.... We must so employ our victory that the death of
these men may strike terror into others, and that, taking warning from their
example, a wild and rebellious people may beware of encountering us again.
Of two things, we must make a choice of one: we subjugate this rebellious
nation by the strong hand and the power of our arms, or yielding to indulging
in deeds of mercy, as Raymond proposes, set sail homewards, and leave both
the country and patrimony to this miserable people....

Hervey: Hervey de Montmorency (c. 1130–85), uncle of Strongbow; he led one of the first contingents of Anglo-Normans to Ireland in 1169.

Speech of Maurice Fitzgerald

We get no supplies by sea, which is commanded by the enemy's fleet. **Fitz-Stephen**, likewise, whose valour and noble enterprise opened to us the way
into this island, is shut up in a sorry fortress, which is strictly watched by
a hostile people. What then do we look for? Is it succour from our own
country that we expect? Nay, such is our lot, that what the Irish are to
the English, we too, being now considered as Irish, are the same. The one
island does not hold us in greater detestation than the other. Away then
with hesitation and cowardice, and let us boldly attack the enemy, while our
short stock of provisions yet supplies us with sufficient strength. Fortune
helps the brave, and a well-armed though scanty force, inured to war, and
animated by the recollection of former triumphs, may yet crush this rude
and disorderly rabble....

Fitz-Stephen: Robert FitzStephen (d. 1183), a Welsh Norman soldier and leader of the Norman Conquest of Ireland; afterwards he was granted extensive lands in Ireland.

---

9 Giraldus Cambrensis, *The Conquest of Ireland.*

The Arrival of Henry II

Roderic: Rory O'Connor, who by this point claimed the title of high king of Ireland.

Vassal: Someone who holds land under a feudal lord to whom he owes homage and fealty. Rory O'Connor did not regard himself as Henry II's vassal: he did not submit to Henry II at this time but he did sign the Treaty of Windsor in 1175.

Thus did all the princes of Ireland, except those of Ulster, severally make their submission for themselves, and thing along, in the person of **Roderic**, prince of Connaught, and the titular head of the Irish and monarch of the whole island, they, all became **vassals** to the king of England. Indeed, there was scarcely any one of name or rank in the island, who did not, either in person or otherwise, pay to the king's majesty the homage due from a liege-man to his lord....

Happy indeed would it have been if, the first conquerors being men of worth and valour, their merits had been duly weighed, and the government and administration of affairs had been placed in their hands. For the Irish people, who were so astounded and thrown into such consternation at the arrival of the first adventurers, by the novelty of the thing, and so terrified by flights of arrows shot by the English archers, and the might of the men-at-arms, soon took heart, through delays, which are always dangerous, the slow and feeble progress of the work of conquest, and the ignorance and cowardice of the governors and others in command. And becoming gradually expert in the use of arrows and other weapons, as well as being practiced in stratagems and ambuscades by their frequent conflicts with our troops, and taught by their successes, although they might at first have been easily subjugated, they became in process of time able to make a stout resistance.

Read the Book of Kings, read the Prophets, examine the whole series of the Old Testament, and even consider familiar examples furnished by our own times and our own country, and you will find that no nation was ever conquered which did not bring down punishment on themselves for their sins and wickedness. But although the Irish people did well deserve, for their grievous offences and filthy lives, to be brought into trouble by the incursions of strangers, they had not so utterly offended God that it was his will they should be entirely subjugated; nor were the deserts of the English such as to entitle them to the full sovereignty over, and the peaceable obedience of, the people they had partly conquered and reduced to submission. Therefore, perhaps, it was the will of God that both nations should be long engaged in mutual conflicts, neither of them having merited or altogether forfeited his favour, so that the one did not gain the prize of triumphant success, nor was the other so vanquished as to submit their necks generally to the yoke of servitude.

From William of Newburgh, *The History of English Affairs* (c. 1190s)[10]

William of Newburgh (1136–98) was an English historian and clergyman. His *History of English Affairs* covers the period from 1066 until his death in 1198. In this section he recounts the Norman Invasion of Ireland which began in 1169.

ϲℓ

Chap. XXVL—Of The Subjugation Of The Irish By The English

About the same period, the English, under pretext of military service, secretly stole into the island of Ireland, intending to invade and possess a considerable portion of it hereafter, on gaining accession to their strength. Ireland (as we have heard) ranks next in magnitude to Britain among the islands; but (as the venerable Bede observes) far excels it in serenity and salubrity of atmosphere—it abounds wonderfully in pasturage and fish, and possesses a soil sufficiently fruitful, when aided by the industry of a skilful cultivator; but its natives are uncivilized, and barbarous in their manners, almost totally ignorant of laws and order; slothful in agriculture, and, consequently, subsisting more on milk than corn. Again, it obtains by nature this singular prerogative and gift, in preference to all other nations, that it produces no venomous animal, no noxious reptile; and should such be carried thither from other countries, sure and speedy death ensues with the first breath which they draw of Irish air. Whatever is brought thence has been ascertained to be a remedy against poison: and, again, this is a singular fact, with regard to this island, namely, that while Great—equally an island in the ocean, and not far remote—has experienced so many chances in war, so frequently fallen a prey to distant nations, so often been subjected to foreign sway—being subdued and possessed first, by the Romans, next, by the Germans, then, by the Danes, and lastly, by the Normans—Ireland (though the Romans had dominion even over the Orkney Isles), being difficult of access, and seldom and only slightly assailed by any nation in war, was never attacked and subdued, never subject to foreign control, until the year one thousand one hundred and seventy-one from the delivery of the Virgin, which was the eighteenth of the reign of Henry the second, king of England. For what the Britons assert as to this island having been under the subjugation of their **Arthur,** is merely fabulous, as well as other anecdotes of him, fabricated from pure lust of lying; but by what means the Irish, by

Arthur: The mythical King Arthur conquered Ireland according to Geoffrey of Monmouth's *History of the Kings of Britain* (c. 1136), a major source for King Arthur legends.

---

10 "The History of William of Newburgh," in *The Church Historians of England*, translated by Joseph Stevenson (London: Seeleys, 1856).

falling under the dominion of the king of England, put a period to their long, and, as it were, never-disturbed and inbred liberty, is easy to explain, as the occurrence is so recent.

The reason of this change is as follows. Ireland, after the ancient custom of Britain, dividing itself into several kingdoms, and accustomed to have numerous kings, was perpetually rent asunder by their quarrels; and, in proportion to her freedom from foreign warfare, had, at times, her vitals pitiably torn by her children rushing to mutual slaughter. It happened that **a certain king** in that country was assailed by the bordering princes, and, from being hard pressed and deficient in power, was nearly experiencing the rage of his enemies; whereupon, taking counsel, he hastily despatched his son into England, who summoned to his assistance military men, and a hardy band of youths, who were allured by the hope of great reward. Supported by their aid, he began first to take breath, then to gain strength, and, ultimately, to triumph over his enemies. Nor did he suffer his assistants to quit the country, but so nobly remunerated them, that, forgetful of their nation and their father's house, they took up their residence there. But when the fiercest of the people throughout Ireland began to rage and storm against this prince, for having introduced the English nation into the island, they, fearful on account of the scantiness of their numbers, sent to England for such persons as were struggling with poverty or greedy of gain, and by these means gradually augmented their power. Being as yet without a commander, they were like sheep without a shepherd; and, therefore, they invited **earl Richard**, a powerful nobleman from England, to become their leader. Being of high spirit, and extravagant beyond his fortune, for he had wasted his ample revenues and nearly exhausted his patrimony, and being harassed by the claims of his creditors, and, consequently, ripe for ambitious projects, he readily assented. Collecting a numerous and hardy band of young adventurers, he prepared within his territories a fleet to convey him to Ireland; but when he was just ready to depart, he was prohibited from sailing by persons acting on behalf of the king. He, however, would not delay out of regard for any property he seemed to possess in England, but sailed over, and gladdened his impatient associates with his wished-for presence. Having united their forces, he deemed it expedient to risk and attempt some enterprise, to impress the barbarians with terror for the future: with daring impetuosity, then, he rushed against Dublin, a maritime city, the metropolis of Ireland, and, from its far-famed harbour, the rival of our London in commerce and importation. Having with bravery and despatch assailed and carried the city, he compelled persons at a distance, through apprehension, to enter into affiance with him. By building fortresses in convenient places, and extending his dominion by degrees, he pressed with perseverance on the bordering districts, which endeavoured to maintain their ancient liberty.

A Certain King: Diarmait Mac Murchada, King of Leinster (1110–71).

Earl Richard: Richard de Clare, Earl of Pembroke, popularly known as Strongbow (1130–76).

Moreover, affecting some little regard for this barbarous nation by a connexion with it, he took the daughter of the confederate king to wife, and received a considerable portion of the kingdom under the title of dowry.

When these prosperous successes became known to the king of England, he was indignant at the earl for having achieved so great an enterprise, not only without consulting him, but even in defiance of him, and because he attributed to himself the glory of so noble an acquisition, which ought to have been ascribed to the king, as his superior. Hereupon he confiscated all the earl's property within his dominions; and lest any assistance should be derived to Ireland from England, he forbad all intercourse by sea. Threatening still severer measures, he obliged him, now nearly a king, quickly to recover his good graces. In consequence, he extorted from him the most famous city of Dublin, and all the best of his acquisitions; and leaving him the residue, and restoring to him the whole of his English property, bade him to be satisfied. After these things, this same earl, who shortly before, from the prodigal waste of his substance, had scarcely anything but his bare title of nobility, now was celebrated for his wealth in Ireland and England, and lived in great prosperity. Some years afterwards, a premature death, however, closed his career. By this event was evidently manifested the uncertainty of fortune, which in this man's case so quickly disappeared, as well as its fallacy, which, when possessed, so suddenly eluded his enjoyment. From his Irish spoils, for which he had so diligently laboured, and been so anxiously employed at the peril of his safety, he carried nothing with him on his departure; but, bequeathing his hard-earned, perilous acquisitions to his ungrateful heirs, left at the same time, by his fall, a wholesome lesson to numbers. The King of England, shortly afterwards, went over into Ireland with a numerous army, and subjugated, by the terror of his name, without bloodshed, those kings of the island who, until that time, had been in a state of resistance; and, disposing matters according to his wishes, returned into England, with safety and with gladness.

DOCUMENT 10:

From Sean Mac Ruaidhrí Mac Craith, *The Triumphs of Turlough* (mid-14th century)[11]

Sean Mac Ruaidhrí Mac Craith was an Irish historian in the fourteenth century, his family had long been attached as historians to the O'Brien kings of Munster. *The Triumphs of Turlough* is an account of the wars between the O'Briens and the Anglo-Norman de Clare family for control of the Thomond region, now County Clare and Limerick. The account includes both historical and mythological elements. The first volume, excerpted here, tells of the invasion of Ireland and the struggle of Irish dynasties to remain independent.

ev

Milesius: In Irish mythology Milesius, a soldier from what is now Spain, is the ancestor of the first settlers of Ireland.

Donough Cairbreach Mac Donall More O'Brien: Donnchadh O'Brien, king of Thomond 1198–1242.

Cuchullin: Cú Chulainn, a demigod figure from Irish mythology.

The government of Ireland being now in the year 1172 come into foreigners' hands, and regal dignity divorced from all and singular the clans of **Milesius** the Spaniard's blood, **Donough Cairbreach Mac Donall More O'Brien** (whose spears were tough and his battalions numerous) became chief in his father's stead and assumed the power, renowned of old, to maintain and govern Thomond's fair and pleasant countries; the entirety of which dominion was this: from **Cuchullin's** far-famed Leap to the Boromean Tribute's ford; from the borders of Birra to Knockany in Cliu máil, and from the Eoghanacht of Cashel to the northernmost part of Burren, land of white stones.

On the north bank of the Fergus, abreast of Inishalee (at this day called Clonroad), in the very heart of his own near dependants and of his domain, he built a circular hold and residence in which then he sat down to spend, consonantly with the rules of reason and of wisdom, his riches and great substance: dispensing righteous judgments, and serving both God and man by erection of many churches and monasteries, as well as by plentiful other benefactions covering the whole period of his vigorous rule.

He the first, when he dropped the royal style and title that before him ever had been his forefathers' use and wont, was inaugurated O'BRIEN; and so, after he had been chief for the long period of a score and eighteen years, he died in the year of Christ's Age 1242.

Donough Cairbreach therefore (after victory of unction and penance) being entered into angels' bliss, all heads of kindreds, captains of peoples, and all district assemblies, gathered at Moyare about **Conor O'Brien** to ordain him chief in his good father's room. Sheeda Mac Conmara it was that

Conor O'Brien: Son of Donough, he succeeded him as king of Thomond; he died in battle in 1268.

---

11 Sean Mac Ruaidhrí Mac Craith, *Caithréim Thoirdhealbhaigh*, translated by Standish Hayes O'Grady, https://celt.ucc.ie.

proclaimed him to begin with, after which the other chiefs acknowledged him [and the thing was done].

Propitious indeed was this chief's fortune, great his prosperity: in his time amity and peace and quiet prevailed; throughout the divisions of his stern jurisdiction were spacious and jovial winefeasts, largesse bountiful and constant, princely merriment. While he held sway every chieftain enjoyed his rightful heritage, every **hospitaller** his ancestral place, so that on all sides people were filled with divine blessing and temporal felicity. Verily and indeed had all Ireland's Gael but held their patrimonies against the English as did this chief his, such ground for glorification this island of ours never had furnished to the foreign adventurers that at this time, through excess of rapacity that grew and seethed in them, sought to exercise upon the Gael injustice and tyranny and violence and oppression, taking from them (wheresoever they could compass it) their blood and their land.

Hospitaller: In a religious house, someone whose office it was to receive and attend upon visitors.

[A.D. 1258] The Gael then, perceiving this, desired by election of one supreme king (to whom they all should submit) to be freed from this iniquity of the English and, as was their right, to vindicate Ireland for themselves. All together therefore they took counsel, and were resolved to appoint on the banks of island-studded Erne a place of meeting to which Ireland's chiefs and nobles in general should repair.

Then, with well nigh all the gentlemen of the Southern Half and of Connacht, Conor mac Donough cairbreach O'Brien's good son **Teigue** (afterwards surnamed "of Narrow-water") sets out to keep that tryst; under O'Neill, all Ulster's gentlemen come to meet them.

Teigue: Tadhg O'Brien c. 1230–59, eldest son of Conor O'Brien.

Now in time of old it was the custom that whoso, being ruler whether of a **cantred** or of a province, accepted another chief's gift or wage [for in this matter they are synonyms] did actually by such acceptance submit to the giver as to his chief paramount, and in virtue of the same take on himself to do him suit and service, to pay him rent and tribute. Therefore, and or ever they took their seats in order to this conference, northwards across the river O'Brien sent to O'Neill a hundred horses by way of stipend.

Cantred: A subdivision of a county during the Anglo-Norman Lordship of Ireland.

O'Neill, when he saw this, in violent anger commanded his people to send back over said river two hundred horses wearing gold-adorned white-edged bridles, which (with an eye to this congress) he had himself provided for bestowal on the men of Erin: so great he deemed both his right to have and his might to hold Ireland, before ever another of the Gael; also because that, previously to this occasion, [not his own country of Tirowen only but] the whole of Ulster already was agreed to have him.

But at sight of these horses with their bridles Teigue returned them, along with their due complement of armed men that whether by fair means or by forcible should compel acceptance of the stipend; whereat O'Neill, marking

O'Brien's pride and haughty temper, in dudgeon returned homeward. From which dissension it resulted that the men of Erin broke up without concert of measures to keep Ireland against the English, saving this alone: that after a while they would a second time assemble anent the same question. The major part of them however had been of one accord: that, in virtue of the gifts and favours which with such bounty the Holy Spirit had conferred on him, the noble Teigue ought to have taken the high lordship over them; for he was endowed with a presence comely and heroic, with great strength of body, a brave and gallant spirit, and in him moreover were the knowledge and all other special lineaments of a great chief; so that in fame and name he distanced the young heirs of Ireland at large. Him therefore they hoped for and continually expected, as being the latent spark that soon should be their flame, and their shelter in whom they trusted.

A good choice too was this that they would have made, seeing that from the date when first he was of strength to handle warlike arms, he never was day nor hour but he pondered and kept unremitting watch how he might cast off oppression from the Gael; for under heaven was nor animal nor other created thing that he hated and loathed more than he did an Englishman's progeny; neither throughout length and breadth of the country of his sway did he ever suffer one of the breed to occupy so much as a nutshell of a pauper's **bothie**. Proof of which be furnished by his deeds at Limerick, where [in 1257] he inflicted on them sore loss of knights and captains, besides all other affairs in which he had to do with them.

[A.D. 1259] Howbeit, for the vaingloriousness of the chiefs of the Gael, their Almighty King's will it was that their fair-foliaged thicket of refuge and lovely vine must be cut down before maturity of thickly promised fruit; as may be understood from these verses of a **duan** which after the chief's death the **Dalcassians'** chief poet made, and of which here I set down so much as (indistinctness of the ancient book notwithstanding) I might contrive to read:—

"Teigue being gone Ireland too is departed, woful her continued lamentation's sound; had the hero lived whole to old age, Ireland had not been given up to mourning. Donough's grandson, for whom we had a right to hope, alas that all beneath fine mould he's laid; surely his death is not the perishing of one man alone, but an outcry-raising loss multiplied many times. Since Teigue's exit, not a day but has borne miraculous crop of grief and desolation; before attaining to ripeness he dropped off, and never again has [seasonable] heat touched the clustered fruits. Since through the people's misdeeds 'tis, that he of whom they cherished so great expectation now is fallen; condign punishment of their sins being exacted thus, wondrous it is that the Creator's wrath must still endure."

Bothie: A small hut or cottage.

Duan: An epic poem.

Dalcassians: An Irish tribe in the region.

DOCUMENT 11:

From Statutes of Kilkenny (1367)[12]

In 1361 Edward III sent his son Lionel of Antwerp, the Duke of Clarence, to Ireland to serve as viceroy and recover territories in Ulster that had been lost over the years to Irish leaders. In 1366 he held a parliament at Kilkenny which passed the Statutes of Kilkenny. These were a series of laws aimed at stopping the decline of the Lordship in Ireland. The Hiberno-Norman lords were by this time regarded as "more Irish than the Irish themselves."

Whereas at the conquest of the land of Ireland, and for a long time after, the English of the said land used the English language, mode of riding and apparel, and were governed and ruled, both they and their subjects called **Betaghes**, according to the English law, in which time God and holy Church, and their franchises according to their condition were maintained and themselves lived in due subjection; but now many English of the said land, forsaking the English language, manners, mode of riding, laws and usages, live and govern themselves according to the manners, fashion, and language of the Irish enemies; and also have made divers marriages and alliances between themselves and the Irish enemies aforesaid; whereby the said land, and the liege people thereof, the English language, the allegiance due to our lord the king, and the English laws there, are put in subjection and decayed, and the Irish enemies exalted and raised up, contrary to reason; our lord the king considering the mischiefs aforesaid, in the consequence of the grievous complaints of the commons of his said land, called to his parliament held at Kilkenny, the Thursday next after the day of Cinders Ash Wednesday in the fortieth year of his reign, before his well-beloved son, Lionel Duke of Clarence, his lieutenant in his parts of Ireland, to the honour of God and His glorious Mother, and of holy Church, and for the good government of the said land, and quiet of the people, and for the better observation of the laws, and punishment of evils doers there, are ordained and established by our said lord the king, and his said lieutenant, and our lord the king's counsel there, which the assent of the archbishops, bishops, abbots and priors (as to what appertains to them to assent to), the earls, barons, and others the commons of the said land, at the said parliament

Betaghes: An Irish term for a tenant who provides food for a household.

---

12 James Hardiman, *A Statute of the Fortieth Year of King Edward III., enacted in a parliament held in Kilkenny, A.D. 1367, before Lionel Duke of Clarence, Lord Lieutenant of Ireland, Tracts relating to Ireland 2* (Dublin: Irish Archaeological Society, 1843). https://celt.ucc.ie.

there being and assembled, the ordinances and articles under written, to be held and kept perpetually upon the pains contained therein....

II. Also, it is ordained and established, that no alliance by marriage, **gossipred**, fostering of children, concubinage or by amour, nor in any other manner, be henceforth made between the English and Irish of one part, or of the other part; and that no Englishman, nor other person, being at peace, do give or sell to any Irishman, in time of peace or war, horses or armour, nor any manner of sustenance in time of war; and if any shall do to the contrary, and thereof be **attainted**, he shall have judgment of life and member, as a traitor to our lord the king.

III. Also, it is ordained and established, that every Englishman do use the English language, and be named by an English name, leaving off entirely the manner of naming used by the Irish; and that every Englishman use the English custom, fashion, mode of riding and apparel, according to his estate; and if any English, or Irish living amongst the English, use the Irish language amongst themselves, contrary to the ordinance, and therof be **attainted,** his lands and tenements, if he have any, shall be seized into the hands of his immediate lord, until he shall come to one of the places of our lord the king, and find sufficient surety to adopt and use the English language, and then he shall have restitution of his said lands or tenements, his body shall be taken by any of the officers of our lord the king, and commited to the next **gaol**, there to remain until he, or some other in his name, shall find sufficient surety in the manner aforesaid: And that no Englishman who shall have the value of one hundred pounds of land or of rent by the year, shall ride otherwise than on a saddle in the English fashion; and he that shall do to the contrary, and shall be thereof attainted, his horse shall be forfeited to our lord the king, and his body shall be committed to prison, until he pay a fine according to the king's pleasure for the contempt aforesaid; and also, that beneficed persons of holy Church, living amongst the English, shall have the issues of their benefices until they use the English language in the manner aforesaid; and they shall have respite in order to learn the English language, and to provide saddles, between this and the feast of Saint Michael next coming.

IV. Also, whereas diversity of government and different laws in the same land cause difference in allegiance, and disputes among the people; it is agreed and established, that no Englishman, having disputes with any other Englishman, shall henceforth make caption, or take pledge, distress or vengeance against any other, whereby the people may be troubled, but that they shall sue each other at the common law; and that no Englishman be governed in the termination of their disputes by March law nor **Brehon** law, which reasonably ought not to be called law, being a bad custom; but they shall be governed, as right is, by the common law of the land, as liege subjects of our lord the king; and if any do to the contrary, and thereof be attainted, he shall be taken and imprisoned and adjudged as a traitor; and that no difference of allegiance shall henceforth be made between the English born in Ireland, and the English born in England, by calling them English **hobbe**, or Irish dog, but that all be called by one, name, the English lieges of our Lord the king; and he who shall be found doing to the contrary, shall be punished by imprisonment for a year, and afterwards fined, at the king's pleasure; and by this ordinance it is not the intention of our Lord the king but that it shall be lawful for any one that he may take distress for service and rents due to them, and for **damage feasant** as the common law requires....

VI. Also, whereas a land, which is at war, requires that every person do render himself able to defend himself, it is ordained, and established, that the commons of the said land of Ireland, who are in the different marches at war, do not, henceforth, use the plays which men call **horlings**, with great sticks and a ball upon the ground, from which great evils and maims have arisen, to the weakening, of the defence of the said land, and other plays which men call **coiting**; but that they do apply and accustom themselves to use and draw bows, and throw lances, and other gentlemanlike games, whereby the Irish enemies may be the better checked by the liege people and commons of these parts; and if any do or practise the contrary, and of this be attainted, they shall be taken and imprisoned, and fined at the will of our lord the king....

XV. Also, whereas the Irish agents who come amongst the English, spy out the secrets, plans, and policies of the English, whereby great evils have often resulted; it is agreed and forbidden, that any Irish agents, that is to say, pipers, story-tellers, bablers, **rimers**, **mowers**, nor any other Irish agent shall come amongst the English, and that no English shall receive or make gift to such; and that shall do so, and be attainted, shall be taken, and imprisoned, as well the Irish agents as the English who receive or give them any thing, and after that they shall **make fine** at the king's will; and the instruments of their agency shall forfeit to our lord the king....

Brehon: The traditional Irish law.

Hobbe: At this time a generic term for a rustic or a clown.

Damage feasant: phrase that refers to the damage done by a tresspassing animal.

Horlings: The traditional Irish sport of hurling, which is still played today.

Coiting: Likely quoits, a ring tossing game.

Rimer: A rhymer or a poet.
Mower: A jester.

Make fine: Exemption from punishment by paying a sum of money.

DOCUMENT 12:

Poynings' Law (1495)

Named for Sir Edward Poynings, the Lord Deputy of Ireland under King Henry VII, the law was passed in the parliament of Ireland in 1495. It gave laws passed in the parliament of England the force of law in Ireland as well.

An Act confirming all the Statutes made in England.

Forasmuch as there been many and diverse good and profitable statutes late made within England by great labour, study, and policy, as well in the time of our sovereign lord the King, as in the time of his full noble and royal progenitors, late Kings of England, by the advise of his and their discrete council, whereby the said realm is ordered and brought to great wealth and prosperity, and by all likelihood so would this land, if the said statutes were used and executed in the same:

Wherefore all statutes, late made within England, concerning or belonging to the common and publique **weal** of the same, from henceforth be deemed good and effectuall in the law, and over that be accepted, used, and executed within Ireland in all points at all times requisite according to the tenor and effect of the same; and over that they and every of them be authorized, proved, and confirmed in Ireland. And if any statute or statutes have been made within this said land, hereafter to the contrary, they and every of them be annulled, revoked, void, and of none effect in the law.

Weal: Well-being.

DOCUMENT 13:

Irish Annals

Annals were concise historical records arranged chronologically, similar to a chronicle, traditionally kept by monks. Most Irish annals were kept until the seventeenth century. *The Annals of Ulster* were mostly compiled in the late fifteenth century. *The Annals of the Four Masters* were compiled from earlier annals in the 1600s. *The Annals of Tigernach* largely survives in fragments in a fourteenth-century manuscript. *The Annals of Inisfallen* was compiled by a single scribe around 1092 and then updated regularly after that until 1450. *The Annals of Loch Cé* were commissioned by King Brian MacDermot in the sixteenth century. *Mac Carthaigh's Book* was compiled from earlier annals by Fínghin Mac Carthaigh Mór (c. 1560–1640). Each of the excerpts below cover the years of the Norman Invasion and immediately after, roughly 1169 through 1176.

Annals of Ulster[13]

1169: The fleet of **Robert FitzStephen** came to Ireland in aid of **Mac Murchadha**.

1170: **Ath-cliath** was destroyed by Diarmait Mac Murchadha and by the transmarine men he brought with him from the east to destroy Ireland, in revenge for his expulsion over sea out of his own land and of the killing of his son. How be it, they inflicted slaughter upon the **Foreigners** of Ath-cliath and **Port-lairgi** and, on the other hand, many slaughters were inflicted upon themselves. Moreover, Leinster and the country of Meath, both churches and territories, were destroyed by them and they took Ath-cliath and Port-lairgi.

1171: Diarmait Mac Murchadha, king of the Fifth of Leinster, after destroying many churches and territories, died in Ferna without Unction, without Body of Christ, without penance, without a will, in reparation to Colum-cille and Finnian and to the saints besides, whose churches he destroyed....

There came into Ireland **Henry** (son of the Empress), most **puissant** king of England and also Duke of Normandy and Aquitaine and Count of Anjou and Lord of many other lands, with 240 ships. (So that that was the

Robert FitzStephen: A Welsh Norman solider, one of the leaders of the invasion. He died in 1183.

Mac Murchadha: Diarmait Mac Murchada, the exiled king of Leinster, deposed in 1167. He sought the assistance of Henry II to regain his kingdom.

Ath-cliath: The Irish term for the city of Dublin.

Foreigners: Vikings who had settled there in the tenth century.

Port-lairgi: The Irish term for the city of Waterford.

Henry: Henry II; his mother was Empress Matilda; she was called this because she had previously been married to the Holy Roman Emperor.

Puissant: Powerful.

---

13 *Annals of Ulster,* translated by W.M. Hennessy and B. Mac Carthy, https://celt.ucc.ie.

first advent of the Saxons into Ireland.) And he came to land at Port-lairgi and received the pledges of Munster. He came after that to Ath-cliath and received the pledges of Leinster and of the Men of Meath and of the Uí-Briuin and Airgialla and Ulidia.

Uí Briuin: The O'Brien family.

1172: The king of the Saxons (namely, Henry, son of the Empress) went from Ireland on Easter Sunday, after celebration of Mass.

Tigernan Ua Ruairc, king of Breifni and Conmaicni, a man of great power for a long time, was killed by the same Saxons and by Domnall, son of Annadh [Ua Ruairc] of his own clan along with them. He was beheaded also by them and his head and his body were carried ignominiously to Ath-cliath. The head was raised over the door of the fortress,—a sore, miserable sight for the Gaidhil. The body was hung in another place, with its feet upwards.

Saxon Earl: Richard Fitzgilbert de Clare, aka Strongbow, the Earl of Pembroke.

1176: The **Saxon Earl** died in Ath-cliath of an ulcer he got on his foot, through the miracles of Brigit and Colum-cille and the saints besides, whose churches he destroyed.

Annals of Tigernach[14]

Ruaidhrí Ó Conchobhair: Rory O'Connor, the High King of Ireland.

1169: A hosting by **Ruaidhrí Ó Conchobhair**, king of Ireland, into Uí Cennselaigh, and he brought away Mac Murchadha's son as a hostage.

A large body of knights came oversea to Mac Murchadha....

Ossory was ravaged, both church and district, by Mac Murchadha with Foreigners.

Erin's evil: A reference to the invasion of Ireland. Erin or Éirinn is an Irish term for Ireland.

Mailcoats: Norman knights wore chain mail armor, not then common in Ireland.

Earl Richard: Strongbow.

1170: The beginning of **Erin's evil** i.e. Robert Fitz Stephen came into Ireland with sixty **mailcoats**, and there was **Earl Richard** son of Gilbert, and they had two battalions, both knights and archers, come to help Mac Murchadha. And they entered Waterford by force and left some of their people there, and they invaded Wexford by force, and captured Mac Giolla Muire, the officer of the fort, and Ó Faeláin, king of the Déise, and his son, and slaughtered the garrison of the fort, so that seven hundred of them fell.

Mac Murchadha musters with the Foreigners thereafter to overcome Dublin. Then the king of Ireland, Ruaidhrí Ó Conchobhair, gathered his troops to the Green of Dublin, and remained there, awaiting battle, for three days and

---

14 *Annals of Tigernach*, translated by Gearóid Mac Niocaill, https://celt.ucc.ie.

three nights, until lightning struck Dublin and demolished it. Thereafter the Foreigners assented to the burning of the town, since they perceived that to be with Mac Murchadha was to revolt against the king of Ireland. Then the king of Ireland returned, with his army unhurt, after Mac Murchadha and the Foreigners had refused to give him battle. Then Mac Murchadha goes with the Foreigners and overcomes Dublin by force, and makes captives of all that were therein.

1171: Diarmaid Mac Murchadha, king of Leinstermen and Foreigners, the disturber of Banba and destroyer of Erin, after (bringing over) foreigners and constantly harming Gaels, after plundering and destroying churches and boundaries, after the end of a year of insufferable illness, died through the miracles of Finnén and Columcille and the other saints whom he had plundered.

Robert Fitz Stephan was captured by the Foreigners of Wexford, after a slaughter of his people, and he was afterwards set free by king Henry the son of the Empress Matilda.

The Earl went into England to meet Henry, king of England, and Henry arrived in Ireland at Waterford a week before Samhain, and Diarmaid Mac Carthaigh, king of Desmond, submitted to him. Thence he went to Dublin and received the kingship of Leinster and of the men of Meath, Breifne, Oriel and Ulster.

1172: Some of the troops of the son of the Empress went with Hugo de Lacy from Dublin to Fore, and for a fortnight consumed its food and they burned the town. Thence they fared to Cell Achaid, where they plundered the church and killed some of its people, and burned it afterwards.

Annals of Inisfallen[15]

1170: A great slaughter of the foreigners of Port Láirge by the oversea fleet.

Port Láirge was plundered by the oversea men, and they seized lands there. The Desmumu and Cormac's son assembled and inflicted a slaughter upon them. Cathal Ua Donnchada {i.e. son of Amlaíb Mór} by him was first fortified Ailén Maíl Anfaid, for he held the kingship of Uí Echach, and there were given to him before he was killed, the lands of Domnall his brother, and of Muiredach Ua Muirchertaig, viz. the two Eóganacht. For it

---

15 *Annals of Inisfallen*, translated by Seán Mac Airt, https://celt.ucc.ie.

was the grandson of Cormac himself who fostered him, after he had been banished, and thus they came to him [and] his fosterfather gave his lands to him and Ragnall Ua Rígbardáin, and the son of Ímar Ua Cathail were slain there by the oversea men.

Mac Murchada and the same foreigners plundered Áth Cliath…, both church and lay property, was also plundered and burned by the oversea men.

1171: Diarmait Mac Murchada, king of Laigin, died.

The son of the Empress came to Ireland and landed at Port Láirge. The son of Cormac and the son of Tairdelbach submitted to him there, and he proceeded thence to Áth Cliath and remained there during the winter.

1173: Les Mór was plundered by the grey foreigners.

Cathal Ua Domnaill and Torgar's son were also slain by the same foreigners.

Annals of the Four Masters[16]

Flemings: The Flemish are a Germanic ethnic group in modern-day Belgium; they were not involved in the Norman invasion of Ireland.

1169: The fleet of the **Flemings** came from England in the army of Mac Murchadha, i.e. Diarmaid, to contest the kingdom of Leinster for him: they were seventy heroes, dressed in coats of mail.

The King of Ireland, Ruaidhri Ua Conchobhair, afterwards proceeded into Leinster; and Tighearnan Ua Ruairc, lord of Breifne, and Diarmaid Ua Maeleachlain, King of Teamhair, and the foreigners of Ath-cliath, went to meet the men of Munster, Leinster, and Osraigh; and they set nothing by the Flemings; and Diarmaid Mac Murchadha gave his son, as a hostage, to Ruaidhri Ua Conchobhair.

1170: Robert Fitz Stephen and Richard, son of Gilbert, i.e. Earl Strongbow, came from England into Ireland with a numerous force, and many knights and archers, in the army of Mac Murchadha, to contest Leinster for him, and to disturb the Irish of Ireland in general; and Mac Murchadha gave his daughter to the Earl Strongbow for coming into his army. They took Loch Garman, and entered Port-Lairge by force; and they took Gillemaire, the officer of the fortress, and Ua Faelain, lord of the Deisi, and his son, and they killed seven hundred persons there.…

---

16 *Annals of the Four Masters*, translated by Charles O'Conor, https://celt.ucc.ie.

An army was led by Ruaidhri Ua Conchobhair, King of Ireland; Tighearnan Ua Ruairc, lord of Breifne; Murchadh Ua Cearbhaill, lord of Oirghialla, against Leinster and the Galls aforesaid; and there was a challenge of battle between them for the space of three days, until lightning burned Ath-cliath; for the foreigners Danes of the fortress deserted from the Connaughtmen and the people of Leath-Chuinn in general. A miracle was wrought against the foreigners Danes of Ath-cliath on this occasion, for Mac Murchadha and the Saxons acted treacherously towards them, and made a slaughter of them in the middle of their own fortress, and carried off their cattle and their goods, in consequence of their violation of their word to the men of Ireland. Asgall, son of Raghnall, son of Turcall, chief king of the foreigners Danes of Ath-cliath, made his escape from them.

1171: Diarmaid Mac Murchadha, King of Leinster, by whom a trembling sod was made of all Ireland,—after having brought over the Saxons, after having done extensive injuries to the Irish, after plundering and burning many churches … died before the end of a year after this plundering, of an insufferable and unknown disease; for he became putrid while living, through the miracle of God, Colum-Cille, and Finnen, and the other saints of Ireland, whose churches he had profaned and burned some time before; and he died at Fearnamor, without making a will, without penance, without the body of Christ, without unction, as his evil deeds deserved.

The King of England, the second Henry, Duke of Normandy and Aquitaine, Earl of Andegavia, and lord of many other countries, came to Ireland this year. Two hundred and forty was the number of his ships, and he put in at Port-Lairge.

1172: Tiernan O'Rourke, Lord of Breifny and Conmaicne, a man of great power for a long time, was treacherously slain at Tlachtgha by Hugo de Lacy and Donnell, the son of Annadh O'Rourke, one of his own tribe, who was along with them. He was beheaded by them, and they conveyed his head and body ignominiously to Dublin. The head was placed over the gate of the fortress, as a spectacle of intense pity to the Irish, and the body was gibbeted, with the feet upwards, at the northern side of Dublin.

Annals of Loch Cé[17]

1170: Ath-cliath was spoiled by Diarmaid Mac Murchadha, and by pirates whom he brought with him from the east, to spoil Erinn, in retaliation for

---

17 *Annals of Loch Cé*, translated by William Hennessy, https://celt.ucc.ie.

his expulsion beyond the sea from his own territory, and for his son having been slain.

They inflicted a slaughter, moreover, on the Foreigners of Ath-cliath and Port-Lairge, and a countless slaughter was, however, inflicted on them.

Earl Strongbow came into Erinn with Diarmaid Mac Murchadha, to avenge his expulsion by Ruaidhri, son of Toirdhealbhach O'Conchobhair; and Diarmaid gave him his own daughter, and a part of his patrimony; and Saxon Foreigners have been in Erinn since then.

1171: Diarmaid Mac Murchadha, king of the province of Laighen, after spoiling numerous churches and territories, died at Ferna—without the body of Christ, without penitence, without making a will—through the merits of Colum-Cille, and Finnen, and the other saints whose churches he had spoiled.

Saxon Earl: Strongbow, died of an infection in his leg or foot.

1176: The **Saxon Earl** died in Ath-cliath of an ulcer which attacked his foot, through the miracles of Brighid and Colum-Cille, and the other saints whose churches he had spoiled.

Miscellaneous Irish Annals (Mac Carthaigh's Book)[18]

Richard, Earl of Striguil: Strongbow, Earl of Striguil was one of his Welsh titles.

Áine: Most sources agree that Mac Murchada's daughter was named Aoife; she was given to Strongbow in marriage.

1169: **Richard, Earl of Striguil**, came to Ireland with two hundred knights and a thousand archers to the assistance of Mac Murchadha on St. Bartholomew's Day. Mac Murchadha came with his knights to meet them, and gave his married daughter, **Áine**, to the Earl, in consideration of his assisting him to conquer Ireland. On the following day they proceeded to Waterford and took it.

Mac Murchadha and the Earl went with their knights to Dublin, and they drove out all the Norse, the merchants, and the inhabitants who were there, killed or drowned many women and men and youths, and carried off much gold and silver and apparel. The English Earl left the care of these, as well as of the town, in the hands of Diarmaid Mac Murchadha, to avenge the wicked slaying of his father by the people of Dublin before that, when a dead dog was buried with his body in the ground as a mark of hatred and contempt.

---

18   *Mac Carthaigh's Book*, translated by Séamus Ó hInnse, https://celt.ucc.ie.

1172: Henry son of the Empress, King of England, Duke of Normandy, Aquitaine, and Anjou, came to Ireland with five hundred knights and numerous cavalry and infantry, and entered Waterford harbour on the feast of St. Luke the Apostle.

1173: The King of England departed from Ireland, leaving **Hugo de Lacy** as constable in his place with great power.

Numerous churches were destroyed by the English after the King had left.

Hugo de Lacy: Hugh de Lacy (1135–86), an Anglo-Norman lord named first viceroy of Ireland by Henry II.

PART 2

Early Modern Ireland and England (1500–1800)

DOCUMENT 14:
The Crown of Ireland Act (1542)

> This act, passed by the parliament of Ireland in June of 1542 and which took effect the next year, created the title of King of Ireland for Henry VIII of England and his successors, who up until then had ruled Ireland as Lord of Ireland. The act was passed in the midst of the Protestant Reformation and following the Kildare Rebellion of 1534–35.

I

The King's highness, his heirs and successors, Kings of England, be always Kings of Ireland, and that his Majesty, his heirs and successors, have the name, stile, title, and honour of King of Ireland, with all manner honours, preheminences, prerogatives, dignities, and other things whatsoever they be to the estate and majesty of a King imperial appertaining or belonging; and that his majesty, his heirs and successors, be from henceforth named, called, accepted, reputed, and taken to be Kings of Ireland, to have, hold and enjoy the said style, title, majesty, and honours of King of Ireland, with all manner preheminences, prerogatives, dignities, and all other the premisses unto the King's highness, his heirs and successors for ever, as united and knit to the imperial crown of England.

II

High treason by writing, deed, print, or act to occasion disturbance to his crown of Ireland, in name, style, &c. The forfeiture. Saving the rights of others.

And if any person or persons, of what estate, dignity, or condition soever they or he be, subject, or resident within Ireland, by writing or imprinting, or by any exterior act or deed, maliciously procure or doe, or cause to be procured or done, any thing or things to the peril of the King's majesty's most royal person, or maliciously give occasion by writing, deede, print, or act, whereby the King's majestie, his heirs or successors, or any of them might be disturbed or interrupted of the crown of Ireland, or of the name, stile, or title thereof, or by writing, deed, print, or act, procure or do, or cause to be procured or done, any thing or things, to the prejudice, slander, disturbance, or derogation of the King's majestie, his heirs or successors, in, of or for the crown of Ireland, or in, of or for the name, title, or stile thereof, whereby his Majesty, his heirs or successors, or any of them might be disturbed or interrupted in body, name, stile, or title of inheritance, of, in, or to the crown of Ireland, or of the name, style, title, or dignity of the same, that then every such person and persons, of what estate, degree or condition they be, subject or residents within Ireland, and their aiders, counselors, maintainers, and abbetors therein, and every of them, for every such offence, shall be adjudged high traitors, and every such offence shall be adjudged and deemed high treason, and the offenders, their aiders, counselors, maintainers, and abbetours therein, and every of them being lawfully convicted of any such offence, by presentment, verdict, confession, or proofes, according to the customs and laws of Ireland, [be liable to imprisonment for life], as in cases of high treason; and also shall lose and forfeit unto the King's highness, and to his heyres, Kings of Ireland, all such his mannors, landes, tenements, rents, reversions, annuities, and **hereditaments**, which they had in possession

Hereditaments: Any item of property that can be inherited.

as owner, and were sole seized in their own right, of, by, or in any title or means, or in any other person or persons, had to their use of any estate of inheritance, at the day of any such treason and offences by them committed and done. And that also every such offender shall lose and forfeit to the King's highness, and to his said heyres, as well all manner such estates of freehold, and interest for years of lands and rents, as all the goods, cattles and debts, which they or any of them had, at the time of their conviction or attainder of, or for any such offence, saving alway to every person and persons, and bodies politique, their heirs, successours, and assignees, and to every of them, other then such persons as shall be so convicted or attainted, their heirs and successors, and all other claiming to their use, all such right, title, use, interest, possession, condition, rents, fees, offices, annuities, commons and profits, which they or any of them shall happen to have, in, to or upon any such manors, lands, tenements, rents, reversions, services, annuities, and hereditaments, which so shall happen to be lost and forfeited, by reason and occasion of any of the treasons or offences above rehearsed, any time before the said treasons or offences committed or done.

Tadhg Dall Ó Huiginn, "To Conn O'Donnell" (late 16th century)[1]

Tadhg Dall Ó Huiginn (1550–91) was an Irish poet from a well-known Bardic family. The Dall in his name indicates that he was blind. He was a celebrated poet in his own life and addressed poems to many of the most powerful lords in Ireland, including this address to **Conn O'Donnell** (d. 1583). Ó Huiginn was murdered in 1591 by the Ó hEadhra after he composed a satirical poem about them.

᧫

Raise the veil from Ireland; long hath she sought a spouse, finding no mate for her couch after the happiness of the men of *Fál* was blasted.

It is long since the **Isle of Bregia** could discover herself to any; a luckless widow is the wife of *Flann*—land of splendid stone dwellings.

She could not but lose her beauty, it is thus with uncared for-women Ireland, land of sparkling, melodious streams, hath the complexion of loneliness.

Ushnagh's castle, darling of kings, hath been brought to such a state that it is a sorrowful omen to watch over the fair, modest contours of her bright countenance.

Ireland's capitals have been defiled, one after another; a garment of weeds invests each keep, the white rampart of every castle is become a trench.

Her round hills have been stripped, her boundaries plowed over, so that *Té*'s **Rampart**, with its firm dwellings of white masonry, is not recognized by the guides.

Nought remains of them save their traces, they have exchanged comeliness for uncomeliness; the brightly-tapestried castles of Niall's *Banbha*—a cause of sorrow are they.

Howbeit, we think the more lightly of this mournful gloom which hangs over Ireland, since *Té*'s Rampart, which was named of **Art**, succour hath been.

Conn O'Donnell: (d. 1583) member of the O'Donnell dynasty of Donegal; he was known to ally himself with either the English or with other Irish lords depending on what he thought to his personal advantage.

Fál: Name of a ceremonial stone at the Hill of Tara, often called the Stone of Destiny, associated with the High Kingship of Ireland.

Isle of Bregia: Breagh, a petty Irish kingdom that contained parts of Dublin, Louth, and Meath.

Flann: Flann Sinna (847?–916), a member of the powerful O'Neill Dynasty who claimed the high kingship of Ireland.

Ushnagh's castle: The Hill of Uisneach is an ancient ceremonial site in the center of Ireland.

Té's Rampart: A reference to the Hill of Tara, an ancient ceremonial site associated with Irish high kings.

Banbha: In Irish mythology, Banbha is one of the patron goddesses of Ireland along with her sisters Fódla and Ériu.

Art: Art Mac Cuinn, son of Conn of the Hundred Battles, who in legend was banished from Tara, but returned and brought fertility back to the land.

---

[1] Tadhg Dall Ó Huiginn, *The Bardic Poems of Tadhg Dall Ó Huiginn*, edited and translated by Eleanor Knott, *CELT Database*, https://celt.ucc.ie.

Caluach: Calvagh O'Donnell (1515–66), the father of Conn O'Donnell and king of Tyrconnell.

Conn: Conn of the Hundred Battles.

Cobhthach: Cobhthach Coel Berg a legendary high king of Ireland.

Lugh: Lugh the most important of the pre-Christian gods of Ireland.

Niall, son of Eachaidh: Niall of the Nine Hostages, the semi-legendary founders of the O'Neill dynasty.

Eber: In legend Eber Finn was the son of Míl Espaine and a High King of Ireland.

Brian of Bóroimhe: Brian Boru (c. 941–1014), king of Munster and high king of Ireland.

Sons of Míl: Míl Espáine, or Milesius, is the mythical ancestor of the first inhabitants of Ireland.

It is in store for it that a man shall come to dissolve its enchantments; needs must, then, that he shall one day take possession of the Field of the Gaels.

For thee, Conn, son of the Caluach, many a prophet hath truly foretold thee—it is fitting that you should seek one another—Ireland hath been waiting.

Alas, thou graceful of form, for him who does not give some thing of her desire to the smooth, yew-timbered, bright rampart, first couch of **Conn** and *Cobhthach*.

Look frequently on her bright countenance, bend thine eye upon her in secret; approach her graceful form, speak covertly with Ireland.

Embrace her, go to her couch, thou beautiful yet icy of flesh; take to thee the spouse of *Lugh*, lest Ireland be left unwedded.

Press the lips like berry-bloom, and the shining, snow-white teeth, in a kiss to Bregia of the smooth hill, amidst the welcome of the five provinces.

Great **Niall, son of** *Eachaidh*, from whom thou art sprung, O bright-cheeked countenance, bestowed just such a kiss, whereby he united (under his sway) the fair Dwelling of **Eber**.

Another such kiss gave **Brian of** *Bóroimhe*, by which he gained without dispute, thou white of hand, that stately dwelling place of the **Sons of** *Míl*.

As with other women in manifold enchantments, thou canst procure with a kiss the release of tearful *Banbha*, O white-footed, black-lashed youth.

As with women under enchantments, Ireland, land of rippling waterfalls, plain of great fins, of shallow streams, will be the possession of him who rescues her.

Long ere her time there was a woman even as this country of the Sons of *Míl*, in ancient Africa, sandy, bright, of fertile hills, many-rivered, salmonful.

The man of yore who loved the princess of the wondrous isles changed the white-handed maiden of the soft, shining hair into a great, forbidding she-dragon.

The **daughter of Hippocrates, son of** *Núl*, spent a while in dragon's shape, under many and manifold enchantments, from which it had been difficult to rescue her.

Be the reason what it may, for one day in each year, in order, to rekindle her sorrow, the gift of beauty was granted to her sparkling, youthful countenance.

A merchant's son from the land of the west went to her once upon a time, and found the bright, sweetly-speaking, womanly beauty in her modest maiden's form.

He set the desire of his heart upon the woman, and prayed that the lovely, shining-haired one might be a mate for his own bright figure, though to seek her was a cause of remorse.

The bright-eyed queen replied, "I would be thine were it possible, thou wondrous, comely youth, long-handed, gentle, dark-browed."

"By consent or force thou shalt be mine," said the brown-lashed youth. "I have forsaken the glances of man, it cannot be," returned the maiden.

"At all other times I am in the shape of a fiery dragon, so that my face (*though now*) smooth, modestly blushing, beloved, is horrifying to behold."

"Is help in store for thee in days, to come?" said the youth, "thou bright form, with clear countenance, when dost thou expect thy deliverance?"

"It is destined for me that a knight from the warriors of *Féilim's* **Land** shall come when I am in dragon's shape, with a kiss whereby I shall be delivered."

"The compassionate warrior shall be a husband to me, it is destined for him that he shall be made king over the islands, a thing difficult to accomplish."

"It is destined for me," said the youth, "I am from Ireland, to bestow that kiss which shall quench thy rage, thou curly-haired maiden, so young and noble."

"How could the thing thou sayest be destined for thee, my heart's fruit?" said the stately maiden, "since thou hast never been a knight."

On hearing that, the merchant's son took orders of chivalry; he departed from the rosy maiden of the soft, shining hair to learn a strange calling.

Daughter of Hippocrates: This tale comes from the fourteenth-century book *The Travels of Sir John Mandeville*, which includes this fictional story of the daughter of Hippocrates, the Ancient Greek physician, being turned into a dragon by a jealous goddess.

Son of Núl: Likely another reference to Niall of the Nine Hostages.

Féilim's Land: Fedlimid Rechtmar was a mythical high king of Ireland.

At the break of day he came again to visit the maiden; astonishing was the state in which he found the gracious beauty of the fair, soft tresses.

He found in the early morn the graceful figure with smooth brows, and the smooth, silky, heavy, luxuriant tresses, transformed into an awesome, fiery dragon.

On beholding the terrifying monster he fled in panic; that expedition ended in his death; a case not easy to succour.

The daughter of Hippocrates then returned to her chamber, and the heart of the white-footed, sweet-voiced maiden was full of sorrow.

She vowed that from that day on she would arise for no man until the coming of the prophesied one who was destined to release her from her bonds.

And even yet—long is the suffering—her gray modest-lashed eye, her pleasing form, her rosy countenance await her deliverer.

Ireland is that woman, O silky of hair, thou art the woman who shall deliver Ireland; and the hideous visage of the dragon is the tormenting host of ruthless foreigners.

Draw near to her, thou curly-headed one, do not shrink from the dragon-like aspect which clothes the sweet, beguiling streams of the Boyne; deliver Ireland from her disfigurement.

Conn the Hundredfighter: Conn of the Hundred Battles, a legendary high king of Ireland.

Many say of thee, Conn, descendant of **Conn the Hundredfighter**, thou heedest not that *Cobhthach*'s **Plain** has been for some time in the custody of foreigners.

Cobhthach's Plain: A reference to the territory of Cobthach Coel Berg, mentioned above.

They are right, O bright countenance, not very thankful are the Sons of *Míl* to thee, Conn, son of the Calvach, as regards the famed land of bright apple-trees.

Even though thou mayst not be supreme in the Land of the Gaels, thou thick-haired one, it is in thy power, Conn, to free the country of *Banbha* from its **fetters**.

Fetters: Chains.

It is easy for thee to win triumphs, the Sons of *Míl* are eager for war; it needs few forays, thou man of the Inny, to stir up *Banbha*.

A house takes fire from the one beside it; if thy intention of battle be heard, from thy head of wavy tresses the rest will take it; it is a ready desire that is ignited.

Even as the spreading of a flame, throughout this Plain of *Cobhthach* every territory will have its own **reaver**, from thy raids upon the foreign soldiery.

Reaver: A plunderer or marauder.

And the result, O wondrous form, shall be that the people of every territory, together with thee, O face ruddy as the berry, from which the stream is calm, shall storm the dividing boundaries of Gael and foreigner.

Take command of them, Conn, and lead them to **Frewen**; thou bright-handed warrior of Bregia, revivify the soldiery of the Gael.

Frewen: Frewen Hill a hill in County Westmeath and a site of ancient burial mounds.

Forsake not for **Donegal**, or the **bay of *Eas Dá Éagann***, or ancient **Loch Foyle**, of the sparkling wines, the royal rampart of Tara in the east.

Alas, if anyone found that for the cocket of Sligo Bay, or for bright **Croghan** of the fair equipment thou wouldst abandon ancient Tara of *Tuathal Teachtmhar*.

Donegal: County in the northwest of Ireland, the traditional territory of the O'Donnell dynasty. Ó Huiginn is warning Conn O'Donnell not to sacrifice greater ambitions for the sake of protecting his claim to Donegal.

The words of soothsayers, the utterances of saints, mate her with thee, O wavy tresses; did they not prophesy of yore the salmon from **Frewen's fair harbor**?

Bay of Eas Dá Éagann: Donegal Bay.

Prophets of thy rule, thou lord of *Bearnas*, are the promise of fruit on the green-leafed bough, the fury of the stream bearing its produce, the wave concealed beneath the washed-up treasure.

Loch Foyle: A lake on the north coast of Ireland on the border of the present-day County Donegal.

Croghan: A hill in County Offaly.

Abundance of milk from a small number of cattle, abundance of corn stacks before summer, and—soothsayers through whom thou art most clearly recognized—the ruined buildings of the churches repaired.

Tuathal Teachtmhar: A legendary high king of Ireland; many royal lineages in Ireland claim descent from him.

Thou at the service of all, and all submitting to thee; thou above everyone, and everyone above thee; thou at the pleasure of every man, and for all that, the Gaels at thy mercy.

Frewen's fair harbor: Lough Owel, a lake in the Irish midlands.

The noble Gaels welcome thee to this enterprise, O cheerful heart; as a woman with her unlawful mate, so is Ireland with thy warriors.

Bearnas: An Irish term for a gap in a mountain. An Bearnas Mor or "the big gap" refers to a mountain pass in County Donegal.

From Edmund Spenser, *A View of the Present State of Ireland* (1596)[2]

Edmund Spenser was a poet best known for his epic poem *The Faerie Queene*. Spenser spent years in Ireland in the service of Lord Deputy Arthur Grey and owned estates of his own in County Cork. His time in Ireland also coincided with the Second Desmond Rebellion (1579–83), an event which contributed to the Munster Plantation scheme. Spenser began writing *A View of the Present State* in 1595 or 1596 in response to the beginning of the Nine Years' War (1593–1603). The piece is in the form of a dialogue between two characters, Eudoxus and Irenius. Eudoxus knows relatively little of Ireland while Irenius has recently returned from Ireland and advocates serious military intervention in the country in order to secure English rule.

Accompted: Accounted.

Irenius: Even of a very desire of newfangleness and vanity, for being as they are now **accompted**, the most barbarous Nation in Christendom, they to avoid that reproach would derive themselves from the Spaniards, whom they now see to be a very honorable people, and next bordering unto them....

Iren: Yes, there was an other, and that the last and the greatest, which was by the English, when the Earl Strongbow, having conquered that Land, delivered up the same into the hands of Henry the second, then King, who sent over thither great store of gentlemen, and other warlike people, amongst whom he distributed the Land, and settled such a strong Colony therein, as never since could, with all the subtle practices of the Irish, be rooted out, but abide still a mighty people, of so many as remain English of them.

Eudoxus: What is that you say, of so many as remain English of them? Why are not they that were once English, abiding English still?

Iren: No, for the most part of them are degenerated and grown almost mere Irish, yea, and more malicious to the English than the very Irish themselves....

Iren: Therefore the fault which I find in religion is but one, but the same universal throughout all that country; that is, that they are all Papists by their profession, but in the same so blindly and brutishly informed, for the most

---

2   Edmund Spenser, *A View of the Present State of Ireland*, www.luminarium.org/renascence-editions/veuer.html.

part, as that you would rather think them Atheists or Infidels, for not one amongst a hundred knoweth any ground of religion, and any Article of his faith, but can perhaps, say his **pater noster**, or his **Ave Maria**, without any knowledge or understanding what one word thereof meaneth....

Iren: Then so it is with Ireland continually, for the sword was never yet out of their hand, but when they are weary with wars, and brought down to extreme wretchedness; then they creep a little perhaps, and sue for grace, till they have gotten new breath and recovered strength again: so it is in vain to speak of planting of laws and plotting of policies till they be altogether subdued....

Iren: No; but at the beginning of these wars, and when the garrisons are well planted and fortified, I would wish a proclamation were made generally to come to their knowledge, that what persons soever would within twenty days absolutely submit themselves, excepting only the very principal and ringleaders, should find grace: I doubt not, but upon the settling of these garrisons, such a terror and near consideration of their perilous estate will be stricken into most that they will covett to draw away from their leaders. And again I well know that the rebels themselves (as I saw by proof in the Desmonds wars) will turn away all their rascal people, whom they think unserviceable, as old men, women, children, and **hyndes**, which they call **churls**, which would only waste their victuals, and yield them no aid; but their cattle they will surely keep away: These therefore though policy would turn then back again, that they might the rather consume and afflict the other rebels, yet in a pitiful commiseration, I would wish them to be received; the rather for that this base sort of people doth not for the most part rebell of himself, have no harte thereunto, but is of force drawn by the grand rebels into their action, and carried away with the violence of the stream, ells he should be sure to lose all that he hath, and perhaps his life also, the which now he carrieth with them, in hope to enjoy them their, but he is there by the strong rebels themselves turned out of all, so that the constraint hereof may in him deserve pardon. Likewise if any of their able men or gentlemen shall offer to come away, and to bring there **creete** with them, as some no doubt may steal them away **prevelye**, I wish them also to be received, for the disabling of thenymye, but withall, that good assurance may be taken of their true behavior and absolute submission, and that they then be not suffered to remain any longer in those parts, no nor about the garrison, but sent away into the inner parts of the realme, and dispersed in such sorte as they shall not come together, nor easily return if they would: For if they might be suffered to remain about the garrison, and there inhabit, as shall offer to till the ground, and yield a great part of the profit thereof, and of

Coronell: Literally a small crown or coronet, denoting social rank. In this context likely the head or "colonel" of the garrison

their cattle, to the **coronell**, wherewith they have heretofore tempted many, they would (as I have by experience known) be ever after such a gall and inconvenience to them, as that their profit should not recompense their hurt; for they will privilie relieve their friends that are forth; they will send the enemy secret advertisement of all their purposes and journeys which they mean to make upon them; they will also not stick to draw the enemy upon them, yea and to betray the forte it self, by discovery of all defects and disadvantages if any be, to the cutting of all their throats. For avoiding whereof and many other inconveniences, I wish that they should be carried far from thence into some other parts, so as I said, they come and submit themselves, upon the first summons: but afterwards I would have none received, but left to their fortune and miserable end: my reason is, for that those which afterwards remain without, are stout and obstinate rebels, such as will never be made dutiful and obedient, nor brought to labor or civil conversation, having once tasted the licentious life, and being acquainted with spoil and outrages, will ever after be ready for the like occasions, so as there is no hope of their amendment of recovery, and therefore needful to be cut off.

Eudox: Surely of such desperate persons, as will follow the course of their own folly, there is no comparison to be had, and for the others yee have proposed a merciful means, much more than they have deserved: but what shall be the conclusion of this war? For you have prefixed a short time of their continuance.

Iren: The end I assure yee will be very short, and much sooner than can be, in so great trouble (as it seemeth) hoped for, although there should none of them fall by the sword, nor be slain by the soldier, yet thus being kept from manurance, and their cattle from running abroad, by this hard restraints, they would quickly consume themselves, and devour one another. The proof whereof I saw sufficiently ensampled in those late wars in Munster; for notwithstanding that the same was a most rich and plentiful country, full of corne and cattell, that you would have thought they could have been able to stand longe, yet ere one year and a half they were brought to such wretchedness, as that any stony heart would have renewed the same. Out of every corner of the wood and glens they came creeping forth upon their hands, for their legges could not bear them; they looked Anatomies [of] death, they spake like ghosts, crying out of their graves; they did eat of the carrions, happy where they could find them, yea, and one another soone after, in so much as the very carcasses they spared not to scrape out of their graves; and if they found a plot of water-cresses or shamrocks, there they flocked as to a feast for the time, yet not able long to continue therewithal;

that in a short space there were none almost left, and a most populous and plentiful country suddenly left void of man or beast: yet sure in all that war, there perished not many by the sword, but all by the extremities of famine which they themselves had wrought.

From Tadhg Óg Ó Cianáin, *Departure of the Lords* (1608)[3]

Tadhg Óg Ó Cianáin (died c. 1614) was an Irish writer who entered the service of Hugh O'Neill during the Nine Years' War; in 1607 he left with O'Neill and other Irish lords in what is commonly called the Flight of the Earls. Ó Cianáin kept a detailed diary of the flight from September 1607 to November 1608. The plan was to seek the support of Philip III of Spain in their continued conflicts with England. The plan failed and all remained in permanent exile. Ó Cianáin died in Rome around 1614.

e

In the name of God

Here are some of the adventures and proceedings of Ó Néill from the time that he left Ireland....

They went in on board ship about midday on Friday. Then they hoisted their sails. They moved close to the harbourside. They sent two boats' crews to get water and to search for firewood. The son of Mac Suibhne of Fanaid, and a party of the people of the district came upon them in pursuit. They fought with one another. With difficulty the party from the boats brought water and firewood with them. About the middle of the same night they hoisted their sails a second time. They went out a great distance in the sea. The night was bright, quiet, and calm, with a breeze from the southwest. Then they proposed putting into Ara through need of getting food and drink. An exceeding great storm and very bad weather arose against them, together with fog and rain, so that they were *driven* from proximity to land. They traversed the sea far and wide. That storm and unsettled weather lasted till the middle of the following night. Afterwards, leaving Tir Conaill on the left, they direct their course past the harbour of Sligeach, straight ahead until they were opposite Cruach Padraig in Connacht. Then they feared that the King's fleet, which was in the harbour of Gaillibh, would meet with them. They proceeded out into the sea to make for Spain straight forward if they could. After that they were on the sea for thirteen days with excessive storm and dangerous bad weather. A cross of gold which Ó Néill had, and which contained a portion of the Cross of the Crucifixion and many other relics, being put by them in the sea trailing after the ship, gave them great relief. At the end of that time, much to their surprise, they met in the middle of the sea two small hawks, merlins, which alighted on the ship. The hawks were caught and were fed afterwards.

---

3   Tadhg Óg Ó Cianáin, *The Flight of the Earls*, translated by Paul Walsh, https://celt.ucc.ie.

On Sunday, the thirtieth of September, the wind came right straight against the ship. The sailors, since they could not go to Spain, undertook to reach the harbour of Croisic in Brittany at the end of two days and nights. The lords who were in the ship, in consequence of the smallness of their food-supply, and especially of their drink, and also because of all the hardship and sickness of the sea they had received up to that, gave it as their advice that it was right for them to make straight ahead towards France. Forthwith they directed their course to France. They went on for two days and two nights under full sail. They reached no land at all in that time. Not even did they know well what particular coast was nearest to them.

About midday on Tuesday they saw three very large ships approaching from the south as if coming from Spain. Although they feared that squadron, and though they thought they belonged to the King of England's armament and were in pursuit of them, they considered that it was better for themselves to make for them and imperil their success if they were enemies, or, if they were Catholics, make inquiries and seek direction, than to be in the great danger in which they were in regard to going astray and mistaking the direction and scarcity of drink. They and the squadron came near one another at the end of day. A terrible storm arose at that time so that they and the squadron could not for a time come within speaking distance of one another....

They went next to the Palace. The **Infanta**, the King of Spain's daughter, and the Archduke came to the door of the Palace to meet them. They received them with honour and respect, with welcome and kindliness, and showed them great courtesy. They brought them to their own private apartments. They spent a while in conversation and questioning one another. Afterwards they took their leave. They *the Irish* and the Duke of Ossuna, the Duke of Aumale, and many other illustrious noblemen went to dinner. They set out afterwards, taking coaches and a change of horses from their Highness with them, and returned that night to Nyvel. They were treated with as much honour that night as the first night *they spent there*.

The next day they proceeded to Notre Dame de Hal, and stopped there that night. Early the next morning they went to Brussels, three leagues' journey. Colonel Francisco, with many Spanish, Italian, Irish, and Flemish captains, came out of the city to meet them. They advanced through the principal streets of the town to the door of the Marquis's palace. The Marquis himself, the Papal Nuncio, the Spanish Ambassador, and the Duke of Ossuna came to take them from their coaches. When greetings had been exchanged in abundance, they entered the hall of the Marquis and spent some time in conversation. Afterwards they entered the apartment where the Marquis was accustomed to take food. He himself arranged each one in his place, seating Ó Néill in his own place at the head of the table, the Papal Nuncio to his

Infanta: In Spain "Infanta" is the title given to a daughter of the reigning monarch who is not the heir apparent.

right, the Earl of Tyrconnell to his left, Ó Néill's children and Maguidhir next the Earl, and the Spanish ambassador and the Duke of Aumale on the other side, below the Nuncio. The rest of the illustrious, respected nobles at table, the Marquis himself, and the Duke of Ossuna, were at the end of the table opposite Ó Néill. The excellent dinner which they partook of was grand and costly enough for a king, and nothing inferior was the banquet. Gold and silver plate was displayed inside that no king or prince in Christendom might be ashamed to have. They spent some time in conversation and chatting, and then took leave and returned thanks to one another. They retired that night to Notre Dame de Hal....

It was a wearisome and unusual experience for the Earl of Tyrconnell, the son of Ó Néill, and the son of Ó Domhnaill, to spend so long without moving out of Rome. They proposed and determined that they should leave it for a time, and should go to make holiday and take a change of air. The three set out, taking with them a page and a footman. Alas! Their trip was attended with ill luck and misfortune. They went to a certain town on the sea coast named Ostia, on the bank of the Tiber, fifteen miles from Rome. They stayed for two days and nights on both sides of the river. The Reverend Doctor Domhnall Ó Cearbhaill followed them. These noblemen next returned to Rome. Their journey to Ostia was no source of rejoicing to their friends, for all are agreed that that particular place is one of the worst and most unhealthy for climate in all Italy. Indeed, it was not long until it proved so to them, for the Earl took a hot, fiery, violent fever on the eighteenth of the same month in 1608, the day of the week being Friday. On Saturday, the following day, Cathbharr, the son of Ó Domhnaill, caught the same fever. On the Monday afterwards, the Baron was stricken with it, and Domhnall Ó Cearbhaill in a short time after him. The page and the footman who were with them both got the fever in a very short time. The Earl had a violent sickness and great pain during a period of eleven days. He made a full confession and received the Holy Sacrament. His soul separated from his body and he died, by the grace of God and the Church, after victory over the world and the devil, about midnight on Monday. On the following day, Tuesday the twenty-eighth of July, the feast of Saint Martha, the Earl was buried in the monastery of San Pietro Montorio. A large and splendid funeral in grand procession was ordered by his Holiness the Pope, and on either side of the body there were large numbers of lighted waxen torches and sweet, sad, sorrowful singing. It was enwrapped in the habit of Saint Francis, as he himself had ordered that it should be put about him. Muiris, the Earl's page, died on the third of August. On the *eighth* of the same month Domhnall Ó Cearbhaill, Doctor of Divinity, the son of Uaithne Ó Cearbhaill of Magh Dreithne in Urmhumha, died et cetera.

DOCUMENT 18:

Lochlann Óg Ó Dálaigh, *Where Have the Gaels Gone?* (c. 1608)[4]

Lochlann Óg Ó Dálaigh was a member of a celebrated family of Irish bards, the Ó Dálaigh. He was born in Munster and particularly active in the early seventeenth century. In this poem, written after the Flights of the Earls, he laments the loss of Irish culture during a period which saw the expansion of English rule and the imposition of the plantation system.

Where have the Gaels gone?
What is the fate of the mirthful throngs?
I catch no glimpse of them
within sight of the green land of **Gaoidheal**.
I do not see the dark-eyed throng
around the heights of fortified assembly-places;
their tumult is not audible to me
as I traverse Ireland's plain.
I marvel what can be their condition,
the heroes of the bright, pure fortresses:
I have found the mansions of **Conn's** Ireland,
but I cannot find The Companies of her halls.
They have dispersed from us in all directions,
the young warriors of Leinster, the heroes of Munster,
the fierce-bladed denizens of **Maeve's** plain,
and ancient **Eamhain's** warband of noble race.
It is no ancient faery incantation,
no deceitful mist of magic
that has quite concealed from us the choice scions
from the bright dwelling of the Gaels.
As it turned out the worse,
woe's me for the plain of **Raoile's** protecting band:
the sons of kings from the pleasant green house
of **Breagh** are being made into exiles.
They have been given billeting far and wide,
away from the bright, smooth Ireland;
the palaces of kings of the Eastern lands
are made well-known to the race of **Mil**.

Gaoidheal: The Gaels or the native Irish.

Conn: Conn Cetchathach or Conn of the Hundred Battles, a mythological high king of Ireland from whom many Irish dynasties claimed descent.

Maeve: In Irish legend, Maeve was the powerful Queen of Connaught.

Eamhain: Eamhain Mhaca was the ancient seat of royal power in Ulster, today called Navan Fort.

Raoile: Likely Mullaghreelan Rath, or in Ancient Irish Ráth Mhullach Raoileann, a ring fort in Kildare associated with the ancient kings of Leinster.

Breagh: An ancient Irish kingdom that included parts of Dublin, Meath, and Louth.

Mil: Míl Espáine, or Milesius, is the mythological ancestor of the earliest inhabitants of Ireland.

---

4   Lochlann Óg Ó Dálaigh, "A Poem on the Downfall of the Gaoidhl," translated by William Gillies, *Éigse*, 13 (1969–70): 203–10.

We have in their stead an arrogant, impure crowd,
of foreigners' blood,
of the race of **Monadh**—
there are Saxons there, and Scotch.
They divide it up amongst themselves,
this territory of the children of noble **Niall,**
without a jot of **Flann's** milky plain
that we don't find becoming (mere) acres'.
Here is an analogy for the land of **Banbha:**
a golden chessboard under base chessmen;
for some time our land has been found destitute
of its bright complement of Gaels.
We have witnessed egregious changes upon Ireland—
it is right to enumerate them (or to bewail them)—
which would have been wondrous at any previous
time upon the sparkling-watered land of Laoghaire.
Heavy is the shame! We have come to see
seats of government being made desolate,
the produce wasting in a stream, dark thickets
of the chase become thoroughfares.
A congregation of rustics in the home of Saints,
God's service under the shelter of bright branches;
quilts of clergymen become cattle's bedding,
the hillside is wrenched into fields.
Assemblies (are held) in places of hunting,
hunts upon illustrious streets, belts of the hedges
of cultivation over the plain's face,
without a meet for racing over its cheeks.
They destroy the hostels of noblemen,
they build with despotic vigour
a line of white(washed) multipillared courts
all about the deer-bereft flank of Ireland.
No-one of the blood of Gaoidheal sees anything
at which to rejoice; he hears no voice
he considers full-sweet—och! the extent
of their humiliation I (have to) relate.
They find no sweetness in devotion to poetry, the sound
of harps or the music of an organ, nor the tales of the
kings of **Bregia** of the turreted walls, nor the numbering
of the ancient generations of their forefathers.
The oppressiveness of the judgements passed
upon them, it steals away their souls from them;

the battle-fierce heroes of **Lughaidh's** plain,
they most resemble half-dead corpses.
The expulsion of the Gaels of the field of Banbha,
although its vaunt is claimed for a foreign battalion,
it is the wrath of God scourging them before all—
that is the (real) cause of their expulsion.
They are not the only ones to have been destroyed;
Many's the race for whom there was decreed ill,
as a result of the wrath of God in Heaven,
whereat the shafts of His wrath burst.
The sons of Israel of the bright weapons,
when His wrath was kindled against them,
many's the plague with which He visited His fury
(upon them) to chastise them in the midst of all.
He used to send, moreover—
it is an old tale—much destruction
upon the great race of **Maccabaeus,**
whenever they transgressed against His testament.
However far each of these peoples progressed
towards meriting the wrath of the King on High,
pure repentance for their sins
procured forgiveness for them thereafter.
Repentance now, after that fashion—
alas that the sons of Mil do not do that,
to cast off from them His anger,
to remove the true anger of the King on High.
The stock of the Gaels of the bitter conflicts, till
they may reach the virtuous state of repentance, (let) their protection be
placed in (the hands of) the Creator
of the Elements, in order to avert the wrath of the Lord.
The vengeance of God is the reason for it.
The men of Scotland, the youths of London
have settled in their place.
Where have the Gaels gone?

Lughaidh: Lugh is one of the most powerful gods in Irish mythology. Lugaidh was a popular medieval Irish name and is associated with a number of legendary and semi-legendary Irish kings.

Maccabaeus: Judas Maccabeus was leader of the Maccabees, a group of Jewish rebels in the Old Testament.

DOCUMENT 19:

From John Davies, *Discovery of the True Causes Why Ireland Was Never Entirely Subdued* (1612)

John Davies (1569–1626) was an English lawyer and poet who served as attorney general for Ireland and in the Irish House of Commons. Davies first traveled to Ireland in 1603 to accept Hugh O'Neill's surrender after the Nine Years' War; several years later, following the Flight of the Earls (1607), he travelled to Ulster to help survey the region in advance of the Ulster Plantation. Davies was heavily involved in the Ulster Plantation and was granted land in the region for his service. *Discovery of the True Causes* was written in 1612 as part of an attempt by Davies to explain the challenges of imposing English rule in Ireland. He became Speaker of the House of Commons in Ireland in 1613.

This then I note as a great defect in the Civil policy of this kingdom, in that for the space of 350 years at least after the Conquest first attempted, the English laws were not communicated to the Irish, nor the benefit and protection thereof allowed unto them, though they earnestly desired and sought the same. For, as long as they were out of the protection of the Law; so as every English-man might oppress, spoil, and kill them without controulment, how was it possible they should be other than Outlaws & Enemies to the Crown of England? If the King would not admit them to the condition of Subjects, how could they learn to acknowledge and obey him as their Sovereign? When they might not converse or Commerce with any Civil men, nor enter into any Town or City without peril of their Lives; whither should they fly but into the Woods and Mountains, and there live in a wild and barbarous manner? If the English Magistrates would not rule them by the Law which does punish Treason, and Murder, & Theft with death; but leave them to be ruled by their own Lords and Laws, why should they not embrace their own **Brehon Lawe**, which punnisheth no offence, but with a Fine or **Ericke**? If the Irish be not permitted to purchase estates of Free-holds or Inheritance, which might descend to their Children, according to the course of our Common Law, must they not continue their custom of **Tanistrie** which makes all their possessions uncertain, and brings Confusion, Barbarism, and Incivility? In a word, if the English would neither in peace Govern them by the Law, nor could in War root them out by the sword; must they not need be pricked in their eyes, and thorns in their sides, till the worlds end? and so the Conquest never be brought to perfection.

Brehon Lawe: Brehon Law was the traditional Irish law.

Ericke: A blood fine.

Tanistrie: An Irish system for passing on titles and lands.

But on the other side; If from the beginning, the Laws of *England* had been established, and the *Brehon* or Irish Law utterly abolished, as well in the Irish Countries, as the English Colonies; If there had been no difference made between the Nations in point of Justice and protection, but all had been governed by one Equal, just, and Honourable Law, as *Dido* speaketh in *Virgill; **Tros, Tyriusuè mihi nullo discrimine habetur.*** If upon the first submission made by the Irish Lordes to King *Henry* the second; ***Quem in Regem & Dominum receperunt,*** saith ***Matth. Paris***; or upon the second submission made to King *John* … as the same Author writes; or upon the third general submission made to King Richard the second; when they did not only do homage & fealty, but bound themselves by Indentures and Oaths (as is before expressed) to become and continue loyal subjects to the crown of *England*; If any of these three Kings, who came each of them twice in person into this kingdom, had upon these submissions of the Irishry, received them all, both Lords & Tenants, into their mediate protection, divided their several Countries into Counties; made Sheriffs, Coroners, and Wardens of the peace therein: sent Justices Itinerants half yearly into every part of the Kingdome, as well to punish Malefactors, as to hear and determine causes between party and party, according to the course of the Laws of *England*; taken surrenders of their Lands and territories, & granted estates unto them, to hold by English Tenures; granted them Markets, Fayres, and other Franchises, and erected Corporate Townes among them; all which, hath been performed since his Majesty came to the Crown, assuredly, the Irish Countries had long since been reformed and reduced to Peace, Plenty, and Civility, which are the effects of Laws and good Government: they had built Houses, planted Orchards & Gardens: erected Town-ships, and made provision for their posterities; there had been a perfect Union betwixt the Nations, and consequently, a perfect Conquest of *Ireland*. For the Conquest is never perfect, till the war be at an end; and the war is not at an end till there be peace and unity; and there can never be unity & Concord in any one Kingdom, but where there is but one King, one Allegiance, and one Law....

Lastly, the possessions of the Irishry in the Province of Ulster, though it were the most rude and unreformed part of Ireland, and the *Seat* and *Nest* of the last great Rebellion, are now better disposed and established, then any the Lands in the other Provinces, which have been past and settled upon Surrenders. For, as the occasion of the disposing of those Lands, did not happen without the special providence and finger of God, which did cast out those wicked and ungrateful Traitors, who were the only enemies of the reformation of *Ireland*: so the distribution and plantation thereof, hath been projected & prosecuted, by the special direction and care of the King himself; wherein his Majesty has corrected the Errors before spoken of,

Tros, Tyriusuè mihi nullo discrimine habetur: Latin for "Trojan or Tryian, it shall make no difference to me."

Quem in Regem & Dominum receperunt: Latin for "He received the King and Lord."

Matth. Paris: Matthew Paris (c. 1200–59) was an English monk and author of the *Chronica Majora*, a historical chronicle beginning with creation and continuing until his death.

committed by K. *Henry* 2. & k. *John*, in distributing and planting the first conquered Lands. For, although there were six whole Shires to be disposed, his Majesty gave not an entire Country, or County, to any particular person; much less did he grant **Iura Regalia,** or any extraordinary Liberties. For the best *British Undertaker,* had but a proportion of 3000 acres for himself, with power to create a Manor, and hold a Court Baron: Albeit, many of these Undertakers, were of as great birth & quality, as the best Adventurers in the first conquest. Again, his Majesty did not utterly exclude the Natives out of this plantation, with a purpose to root them out, as the Irish were excluded out of the first English Colonies; but made a mixed plantation of British & *Irish,* that they might grow up together in one Nation: Only, the Irish were in some places transplanted from the Woods & Mountains, into the Plains & open Countries, that being removed (like wild fruit trees) they might grow the milder, and bear the better & sweeter fruit. And this truly, is the Masterpiece, and most excellent part of the work of Reformation, and is worthy indeed of his Majesty's royal pains. For when this Plantation has taken root, and been fixed and settled but a few years, with the favour and blessing of God (for the son of God himself hath said in the Gospel, ***Omnis Plantatio, quam non plantauit pater meus, eradicabitur***) it will secure the peace of *Ireland,* assure it to the Crown of England for ever; and finally, make it a Civil, and a Rich, a Mighty, and a Flourishing Kingdom....

Briefly, the clock of the civil Government, is now well set, and all the wheels thereof do move in Order; The strings of this Irish Harp, which the Civil Magistrate doth finger, are all in tune (for I omit to speak of the State Ecclesiastical) and make a good Harmony in this Commonweale: So as we may well conceive a hope, that *Ireland* (which heretofore might properly be called the *Land of Ire,* because the **Irascible** power was predominant there, for the space of 400 years together) will from henceforth prove a Land of *Peace* and *Concord.* And, though heretofore it hath been like the lean Cow of Egypt, in *Pharaohs* Dream, devouring the fat of *England,* and yet remaining as lean as it was before, it will hereafter be as fruitful as the land of *Canaan*....

And lastly, I have declared & set forth, *How all the said Errors have been corrected, and the Defects supplied under the prosperous Government of his Majesty;* So as I may positively conclude in the same words, which I have used in the *Title* of this Discourse; *That until the beginning of his Majesties Reign, Ireland was never entirely subdued, and brought the Obedience of the Crown of England.* But since the crown of this kingdom, with the undoubted right and Title thereof, descended upon his Majesty; The whole Island from Sea to Sea, hath been brought into his Highness peaceable possession; and all the Inhabitants, in every corner thereof, have been absolutely reduced under his immediate subjection. In which condition of subjects, they will gladly continue, without defection or adhering to any other *Lord* or *King,*

Iura Regalia: Regalia, symbols of power such as robes, swords, crowns, and scepters.

Omnis Plantatio, quam non plantauit pater meus, eradicabitur: Latin for "Every plant that my father hath not planted shall be rooted up."

Irascible: Easy to anger.

as long as they may be *Protected*, and Justly *Governed*, without *Oppression* on the one side, or *Impunity* on the other. For, there is no Nation of people under the sun, that doth love equal and indifferent Justice, better than the Irish; or will rest better satisfied with the execution thereof, although it be against themselves; so as they may have the protection & benefit of the Law, when upon just cause they do desire it.

From Geoffrey Keating, *Foras Feasa ar Éirinn* (1634)[5]

Geoffrey Keating (c. 1569–c. 1644) was an Irish Catholic priest and historian. Little is known of his early life, but Keating had both Irish and Old English ancestry. He studied at the Irish College in Bordeaux and returned to Ireland around 1610. *Foras Feasa ar Éirinn* or *The General History of Ireland* was his most famous work, completed around 1634. The work is primarily a narrative history of Ireland from the creation of the world through the twelfth century. Keating depicts ancient Ireland as an autonomous and united Kingdom under a succession of heroic High Kings. In the preface Keating sets out to refute earlier English writers who had disparaged Ireland.

℘

Whoever undertakes to write the history of any nation or kingdom, ought to give a true and impartial account, not only of the country and the laws, but also of the customs and manners of the people: and therefore, having undertaken to deduce the history of Ireland from the most distant ages, I think myself obliged to remove before hand, those false and injurious representations, which have been published, concerning the ancient Irish, who for above these three thousand years have inhabited this kingdom, as well as what relates to the old English, who have been settled here ever since the reign of King Henry II.

The English historians, who have since that time wrote about the affairs of Ireland, have industriously sought occasion to lessen the reputation of both, as appears by **Giraldus Cambrensis**, **Spencer**, **Stanihurst**, **Morrison**, **Campion**, and others, who, when they write of Ireland, seem to imitate the beetle, which, when enlivened by the influence of the summer heats, flies abroad, and passes over the delightful fields, neglectful of the sweet blossoms or fragrant flowers that are in its way, till at last, directed by its sordid inclination, it settles itself upon some nauseous excrement. Thus the above-mentioned writers proceed, when they write of this kingdom: what was worthy or commendable in the Irish nobility and gentry, they pass over. They take no notice of their piety, learning, and courage; of their charitable disposition to build great churches and religious houses, or of the great privileges and endowments they conferred and settled upon them: they omit to speak of the protection and encouragement they gave to their historiographers, and to other men of learning, to whom their liberality was

Giraldus Cambrensis: Gerald of Wales, author of Documents 7 and 8.

Spencer: Edmund Spenser, author of Document 16.

Stanihurst: Richard Stanihurst (1547–1618), an Anglo-Irish alchemist and historian who wrote contributions on Ireland for Raphael Holinshed's *Chronicles*.

Morrison: Fynes Moryson (1566–1630), an English traveler and writer best known for his multi-volume *Itinerary* of all the places he had traveled, including Ireland.

Campion: Edmund Campion (1540–81), an English Jesuit priest. Executed by Elizabeth I, he was tutor to Richard Stanihurst and wrote *A History of Ireland* during his brief time there.

---

5   Geoffrey Keating, *The General History of Ireland*, translated by Dermod O'Connor (Dublin: James Duffy, 1841).

so abounding, that they not only relieved the indigency of those who made their application to them, but made public invitations to find an opportunity to bestow gratifications upon persons of merit and desert. They forget to mention their virtues and commendable actions; but in their accounts of this kingdom, these authors dwell upon the manners of the lower and baser sort of people, relate idle and fabulous stories, invented on purpose to amuse the vulgar and ignorant, and pass over all that might be said with justice, to the honour of the nobility and gentry of this nation....

The English writers particularly, have never failed to exert their malice against the Irish, and represent them as a base and servile people. I shall here mention some remarkable instances of their falsehoods, as they have been transcribed from that ignorant and malicious writer, Giraldus Cambrensis, the great patron of these mercenary and sordid historians....

It is surprising to me how Spencer could advance such falsehoods, as carry with them their own confutation. He was a writer that was unable to make himself acquainted with Irish affairs, as being a stranger to the language; and besides, being of a poetical genius, he allowed himself an unbounded licence in his compositions. It was the business of his profession, to advance poetical fictions, and clothe them with fine insinuating language, in order to amuse his readers without improving them, and to recommend his fables to the world, when he designed to conceal, or found he could not come at the truth....

What can be the designs of these reflections, but to intimate, that the English, when they got sovereignty of the kingdom into their hands, ought to have extirpated the Irish race, and, like Pagan conquerors, have rooted out the very name and language from off the earth? Whatever people carry their arms into another country, and subdue it, if they are Christians, are contented with the submission of the inhabitants, and with transplanting colonies of their own country among the natives: but the practice of the Pagans was, after they had reduced a country to obedience, to extirpate the native posessors, and compel them to look out for new abodes in foriegn countries. Thus, according to the barbarity of this author, ought the English to have carried on their conquests, to have shaken hands with the principles of humanity and religion, and put all the Irish to the sword. A conqueror, who has any sentiments of Christianity within him, never suppresses the language of the country he overcomes; and in this manner the English were treated by William of Normandy. When he made a conquest of that kingdom, he permitted the people to retain their language, by which means it is continued by the inhabitants with some alterations to this day: but **Hengist the Saxon**, when by the success of his arms he became formidable in England, compelled the inhabitants to forsake the country, and transplanted people of his own in their room; by which means the native

Henigst the Saxon: Hengist and his brother Horsa, according to early sources, led the Germanic invasion of Britain in the fifth century.

language was extirpated, and the new colonies introduced another of their own. This Pagan conqueror acted consistent with the cruel sentiments of Stanihurst, who laments that the Irish language was not banished from the island; which could not have been done unless the inhabitants who used it had been expelled, which had been an act so barbarous and wicked, that no conqueror unless a Pagan would have put it in execution. Such, therefore, we perceive, was the irreconcilable hatred of this writer to the nation of the Irish, that the principles of humanity and religion, and law of nature and nations, are to be violated, to destroy the native Irish, and in general massacre the people and the language are to be rooted out....

The Irish were at length enraged by these insupportable oppressions, for when they observed that the English, instead of propagating the religion of Christ, and reforming the rugged manners of the people, had nothing in view but plunder and booty, and that churches and monasteries were not exempt from their covetous and sacrilegious attempts, they formed a design to free themselves from such merciless auxiliaries, and to drive them out of the island....

It is evident, from what has been hitherto observed, that the tyranny, the oppression, and many cruelties perpetrated by the English upon the native Irish, was the cause of that disaffection which appeared in general throughout the island. The inhabitants were made a sacrifice of upon all occasions, and when the English quarrelled among themselves, whatever party succeeded, the natives were sure to be the sufferers. The pride, ambition, and covetousness of those foreigners was perfectly insupportable, they offered outrageous violence to the law of nations and the received usages of mankind; and therefore it is no wonder that the Irish made frequent attempts to depose their lordly masters, and shake off a yoke that they were unable to bear. The English government in Ireland, had it been administered with discretion and good policy, would have been received by the inhabitants, who naturally are a submissive obedient people, and esteem the authority of the laws as sacred, when they are executed with moderation and prudence. And this character is consistent with what John Davies observes, in the last leaf of his Irish history: "There is no nation or people under the sun that doth love equal and indifferent justice better than the Irish, in case it would proceed against themselves in justice, so as they may have the proportion and benefit of the law, when upon any just occasion they require it." It was the opinion, we perceive, of this author, that the seeds of disobedience were not naturally planted in the people of Ireland; but the oppressions they suffered, by the tyranny of the English commanders, made them desperate, and urged them on to attempts which they would never have thought of, had they been well used, and treated with that tenderness and humanity which the circumstances of their case so justly deserved.

DOCUMENT 21:

The Confederation of Kilkenny, *The Oath of Association* (1642)[6]

Following the 1641 Rebellion and during the period of the civil wars in England there was a brief period of Catholic self-government in Ireland from 1642 to 1649. This period is called the Confederacy because the government was led by an assembly called the Confederation which met in Kilkenny. The government was led by the Catholic nobility of Ireland and issued the Oath of Association in 1642, which they encouraged all Catholics in Ireland to take.

I, A.B., do profess, swear, and protest before God and His saints and angels, that I will, during my life, bear true faith and allegiance to my Sovereign Lord, **Charles**, by the grace of God, King of Great Britain, **France** and Ireland, and to his heirs and lawful successors; and that I will, to my power, during my life, defend, uphold and maintain, all his and their just prerogatives, estates, and rights, the power and privilege of the Parliament of this realm, the fundamental laws of Ireland, the free exercise of the Roman Catholic faith and religion throughout this land; and the lives, just liberties, possessions, estates, and rights of all those that have taken, or that shall take this Oath, and perform the contents thereof; and that I will obey and ratify all the orders and decrees made, and to be made, by the Supreme Council of the Confederate Catholics of this Kingdom, concerning the said public cause; and I will not seek, directly or indirectly, any pardon or protection for any act done, or to be done, touching this general cause, without the consent of the major part of the said Council; and that I will not, directly or indirectly, do any act or acts that shall prejudice the said cause, but will, to the hazard of my life and estate, assist, prosecute and maintain the same.

Charles: Charles I was himself a Protestant, but he was thought to be friendlier towards Catholicism than the rigidly Puritan forces of the English Parliament.

France: It was common for kings of England to also claim to be the king of France dating back to the Hundred Years' War; the last English King to claim this was King George III (1738–1820).

Moreover, I do further swear that I will not accept of, or submit unto any peace, made, or to be made, with the said Confederate Catholics, without the consent and approbation of the General Assembly of the said Confederate Catholics, and for the preservation and strengthening of the association and union of the kingdom. That upon any peace or accommodation to be made, or concluded with the said Confederate Catholics as aforesaid, I will, to the utmost of my power, insist upon and maintain the ensuing propositions, until a peace, as aforesaid, be made, and the matters to be agreed upon in the articles of peace be established and secured by Parliament.

So help me God and His holy gospel.

---

6   C.P. Meehan, *The Confederation of Kilkenny* (Dublin, 1846).

DOCUMENT 22:

From John Temple, *The Irish Rebellion* (1646)

Sir John Temple (1600–77) was an Anglo Irish lawyer and judge who sat in the Irish House of Commons. Temple was in Dublin when the 1641 Rebellion broke out. When civil war broke out in England, Temple supported the side of Parliament; he was suspended from office and imprisoned in Dublin Castle for his activities. In 1646, while living in England, he published *The Irish Rebellion*, a sensationalistic account of the 1641 rebellion. Temple's claims were accepted unquestioningly by English audiences at the time and the book served to inflame English sentiment against the Irish.

ఴ

I have here adventured to present unto public view, the beginnings and first progress of the Rebellion lately raised within this Kingdom of Ireland…. All that I aime at is, that there may remain for the benefit of this present age, as well as posterity, some certain Records and monuments of the first beginnings and fatal progresse of this rebellion, together with the horrid cruelties most unmercifully exercised by the Irish Rebels upon the British, and Protestants within this Kingdom of Ireland. That when Gods time is come of returning it into the bosoms of those who have been the first plotters or present actors therein, and that Kingdom comes to be re-planted with British, and settled in peace again, (which I have even in our lowest condition, with great confidence attended, and do now most undoubtedly believe will ere long be brought to passe) there may be such a course taken, such provisions made, and such a wall of separation set up betwixt the Irish and the British, as it shall not be in their power to rise up (as now and in all former Ages they have done) to destroy and root them out in a moment, before they be able to put themselves into a posture of defence, or to gather together to make any considerable resistance against their bloody attempts….

But to return now to the Northern Rebels, who so closely pursued on their first plot, as they beginning to put it in execution in most of the chief places of strength there, upon the 23 of Octob. the day appointed for the **surprizall** of the Castle of Dublin, had by the latter end of the same month gotten into their possession all the Towns, Forts, Castles, and Gentlemens houses within the Counties of Tyrone, Donegal, Fermanagh, Armagh, Cavan, London Derry, Monaghan, and half the County of Down…. The chief of the Northern Rebels that first appeared in the execution of this Plot within the Province of Ulster were, **Sir Phelim O Neale**, Turlough O Neale, his brother, Roury Mac Guire, brother to the Lord Mac Guire, Philip O Rely, Mulmore O Rely, Sir Conne Mac Gennis, Col. Mac Brian, Mac Mahon; these having

Surprizall: The act of surprising.

Sir Phelim O Neale: (1604–53) Sir Phelim O'Neill an Irish Catholic nobleman who led the rebellion in Ulster.

closely combined together, with several other of their accomplices, the chief of the several **Septs** in the several Counties, divided their forces into several parties; and according to a general assignation made among themselves at one and the same time, surprised by treachery.... This I take to be one main and principal reason that the English were so easily over-run within the Northern Counties, and so suddenly swallowed up, before they could make any manner of resistance in the very first beginnings of this Rebellion. For most of the English having either Irish Tenants, Servants of Landlords, and all of them Irish neighbours their familiar friends.... But these generally either betrayed them into the hands of other Rebels, or most perfidiously destroyed them with their own hands. The Priests had now charmed the Irish, and laid such bloody impressions in them, as it was held, according to the maxims they had received, a mortal sin to give any manner of relief or protection to any of the English.... For they living promiscuously among the British, in all parts having from their priests received the Watchwords both for time and place, rose up, as it were actuated by one and the same spirit, in all places of those Counties before mentioned at one and the same point of time; and so in a moment fell upon them, murdering some, stripping only, or expelling others out of their habitations....

Septs: Clans.

Besides these, we have very many other presumptions that the Irish since they found their own strength, and that they were able to draw together so great numbers of men, as their several Septs so strangely multiplied during the late peace can now afford, have long had it in design to shake off the English government, to settle the whole power of the State in the hands of the Natives, and to re-possess them of all the Lands now enjoyed by the British throughout the Kingdom: And that in this plot they did but go about to actuate those confused general notions, and to put them in a way of execution. Now they supposed there could never be offered unto them a fairer opportunity than this most unhappy conjecture of the affairs of great Britain, when **Scotland lately in Arms**, had by their own power and wise managements, drawn his Majesty to condescend to their entire satisfactions, as well in their Church discipline, as the liberties of that Kingdom. And in England, the distractions being grown up to some height, through the great misunderstanding betwixt the King and his parliament, Ireland was at this time left naked and unregarded, the Government in the hands of Justices, the old Army dispersed in places of so great distance, as it could be of little advantage, the common Soldiers most of them Irish, and all the old Commanders and Captains, except some few worn out and gone: This, as the first plotters thought, was the time to work out their own ends, and masking their perfidious designs under the public pretenses of Religion, and the defense of his Majesties Prerogative, they let loose the reins of their own vindictive humour and irreconcilable hatred to their British Neighbours....

Scotland lately in Arms: The Bishops' Wars in 1639 and 1640 were fought between Scottish Presbyterians (Covenanters) and King Charles I over the king's attempt to impose new religious practices in Scotland.

... The people being now set at liberty, and prepossessed by their Priests with a belief that it was lawful for them to rile up and destroy all the Protestants, who, they told them, were worse than Dogs; that they were Devils, and served the Devil; assuring them the killing of such was a meritorious act, and a rare preservative against the pains of Purgatory, gathered themselves together in great numbers, assembling in several companies through the several parts of the Northern counties, with **staves**, scythes and pitch-forks, for at first they had not many better weapons: And so in a most confused manner, they began tumultuously to drive away at the first only the Cattle belonging to the English, and then to break into their houses, and seize upon their goods. It is true, there were some murders committed the very first day of their riling, and some houses set on fire, but these as I conceive, were for the most part out of private spleen, or where they had particular instructions so to do, as they had from the Lord MacGuire, to kill Master Arthur Champion, a Justice of Peace in the County of Fermanagh, who with several other of his neighbours were murdered at his own house upon the 23. of October in the morning. But certainly that which they mainly intended at first, and which they most busily employed themselves about, was driving away the Englishmens Cattle, and possessing their goods: Wherein the common people were not the only actors, but even the chief Gentlemen of the Irish in many places, most notoriously appeared, and under plausible pretences of securing their goods from the rapine and spoile of the common sort, got much peaceably into their hands: And so confident were the English of their good-dealing at first, as many delivered their goods by retail unto them, gave them particular Inventories of all they had, nay digged up such of their best things as they had hidden underground, to deposit in their custody. Much likewise they got by fair promises and deep engagements to do them no further mischief, to suffer them, their wives and children quietly to retire and leave the country: But others, and especially the meaner sort of people fell more rudely to work, at the very first, breaking up their houses, and using all manner of force and violence, to make themselves masters of their goods....

Staves: A stick of wood.

DOCUMENT 23:

Oliver Cromwell, *Letters from Ireland* (1649)[7]

Oliver Cromwell (1599–1658) first rose to prominence as a general in the **New Model Army** during the English Civil Wars. Following parliament's victory over King Charles I, he was sent to Ireland in 1649 to defeat the military threat posed by the Irish Catholic Confederation. During the course of his campaign Cromwell adopted a very harsh policy towards both his military enemies and Irish civilians. He left Ireland in 1650 but the military campaign continued under Generals Henry Ireton and Edmund Ludlow until 1652. Cromwell would go on to become Lord Protector of England, Scotland, and Ireland until his death in 1658.

New Model Army: Standing army formed by parliamentary forces during the English Civil War.

e

Letter: 'To the Honorable John Bradshaw, Esquire, President of the Council of State: These.'

Dublin, 16th September, 1649

Sir,
It hath pleased God to bless our endeavours at Drogheda. After battery, we stormed it. The Enemy were about 3,000 strong in the Town. They made a stout resistance; and near 1,000 of our men being entered, the Enemy forced them out again. But God giving a new courage to our men, they attempted again, and entered; beating the Enemy from their defences.

The Enemy had made three retrenchments, both to the right and left 'of' where we entered; all which they were forced to quit. Being thus entered, we refused them quarter; having the day before summoned the Town. I believe we put to the sword the whole number of the defendants. I do not think Thirty of the whole number escaped with their lives. Those that did, are in safe custody for the **Barbadoes**. Since that time, the Enemy quitted to us Trim and Dundalk. In Trim they were in such haste that they left their guns behind them.

This hath been a marvellous great mercy. The Enemy, being not willing to put an issue upon a field-battle, had put into this Garrison almost all their prime soldiers, being about 3,000 horse and foot, under the command of their best officers; Sir Arthur Ashton being made Governor. There were some seven or eight regiments, Ormond's being one, under the command

Barbadoes: England first colonized Barbados in 1627; the prisoners that Cromwell refers to are being sent there as indentured servants to work on sugar-cane plantations.

---

7 Thomas Carlyle, ed., *Oliver Cromwell's Letters and Speeches* (New York: Scribner, Welford, and Company, 1871).

of Sir Edmund Varney. I do not believe, neither do I hear, that any officer escaped with his life, save only one Lieutenant, who, I hear, going to the Enemy said, That he was the only man that escaped of all the Garrison. The Enemy upon this were filled with much terror. And truly I believe this bitterness will save much effusion of blood, through the goodness of God....

Letter: To the Honourable William Lenthall, Speaker of the Parliament of England

Dublin, 17th September 1649

Pallisadoed: Enclosed by wooden stakes.

Sir Arthur Ashton: An English soldier (1590–1649) who supported King Charles I in the English Civil War, he was killed at the Siege of Drogheda, described in this letter.

... Divers of the Enemy retreated into the Mill-Mount; a place very strong and of difficult access; being exceedingly high, having a good graft, and strongly **pallisadoed**. The Governor, **Sir Arthur Ashton**, and divers considerable Officers being there, our men getting up to them, were ordered by me to put them all to the sword. And indeed, being in the heat of action, I forbade them to spare any that were in arms in the Town: and, I think, that night they put to the sword about 2,000 men;—divers of the officers and soldiers being fled over the Bridge into the other part of the Town, where about 100 of them possessed St. Peter's Church-steeple, some the west Gate, and others a strong Round Tower next the Gate called St. Sunday's. These, being summoned to yield to mercy, refused. Whereupon I ordered the steeple of St. Peter's Church to be fired, when one of them was heard to say in the midst of the flames: "God damn me, God confound me: I burn, I burn."

The next day, the other two Towers were summoned; in one of which was about six or seven score: but they refused to yield themselves: and we knowing that hunger must compel them, set only good guards to secure them from running away until their stomachs were come down. From one of the said Towers, notwithstanding their condition, they killed and wounded some of our men. When they submitted, their officers were knocked on the head; and every tenth man of the soldiers killed; and the rest shipped for the Barbadoes. The soldiers in the other Tower were all spared, as to their lives only; and shipped likewise for the Barbadoes.

I am persuaded that this is a righteous judgment of God upon these barbarous wretches, who have imbrued their hands in so much innocent blood; and that it will tend to prevent the effusion of blood for the future. Which are the satisfactory grounds to such actions, which otherwise cannot but work remorse and regret. The officers and soldiers of this Garrison were the flower of their Army. And their great expectation was, that our attempting this place would put fair to ruin us: they being confident of the resolution of their men, and the advantage of the place....

DOCUMENT 24:

Anthony O'Connor, *Ireland's Lamentation* (1659)[8]

Déorchaóineadh na hEírionn or *Ireland's Lamentation* was written around
1659 by Anthony O'Connor, an Irish Franciscan at the Franciscan College in
Prague. The poem was written in the aftermath of Oliver Cromwell's military
campaign in Ireland, which concluded in 1653. The Act for the Settlement of
Ireland in 1652 imposed severe penalties for Irish who were associated with
the 1641 Rebellion.

❧

My sense benumbed, my spirits dead, I swim in seas of grief;
My tears are made my daily bread, affliction is my life.
My heart doth groane, my thoughts bemoan poor Ireland's rueful state;
No earthly joy doth she enjoy: such is her cursed fate.

Her pomp and state reduced to naught, her *chieftains* all exiled;
The ruins of her churches mourn, polluted and defiled.
Since Israel a thrall befell unto her cruell foes,
Could any see such misery? No tongue can tell our woes.

Our pastors fled, the flock disused, and none to feed but Thou.
The wolves devour and slaughter all. Come, come! redeem us now.
Contain, o God, thy smarting rod, or else we all decaye.
Come, cure with speed our wounds that bleed; they wrath, o Lord, allay.

Our Vestalls *stand* amazed to see their cloisters all defaced
And lechery usurping roome, where chastity was placed.
No sacrifice or edifice unspotted doth appear.
Our monuments and ornaments destroyed, and what is dear.

Our aged folke, our women, maydes, our youths *are* captives made,
Our wealth consumd, our orphans starve and wither in the blade.
Our lands are waste, and none do taste the fruit thereof with joy.
Plague, famine, war gave us a scarre and all that could annoy.

And yet, o Lord, thy bow is bent; thy arrows pierce our heart.
From top to toe no place is sound, each limb hath felt a smart.

---

8   Rudolf Thurneysen, *La lamentation d'Irlande in Revue Celtique* Volume 14 (Paris: Émile Bouillon,
      1893), 153–62.

The rich, the poore, the lord, the boore, the weake, the stout, the strong,
The church, the state, and all of late, doe beare their cros along.

The sea alone doth favour us, as feeling some increase
By our sad tears that drop to her; our sighs with wind made peace.
The heavens seem not to redeem our woes, denying aide;
The rocks and dens, the woods and fennes to shade us are afraid.

Our quire is mute, our organs dumb, our notes both shrill and sharp;
Our instruments no consort keep, for sorrow tunes our harp.
Until again our men from Spain unto soil return,
In endless grief without relief we'll never cease to mourn.

Thy sinnes, poor Ireland, wrought thy woe; affliction is thy cure,
The fire whereof consumed thy drosse, I hope, and made thee pure
Repent, repent! God will relent and save thee in the end
And deale with thee in piety, thy faults.

These were thy hideous, monstrous sinnes: oppression, rapine, stealth;
Thy pride exceeded farre thy strength; thy score surpassed thy wealth.
Thy treacherous heart increased thy smart, unto thee selfe untrue.
Unjustice crept, thy widdowes wept and orphans weak did rue.

No law could yett unite our hearts; obedient none was found;
All power **contemned**, no orders kept; confusion walked the round.
Thy riotous life, contention, strife intestine broyles and jarres,
Hath made thy state unfortunate: thus ended Ireland's wars.

Repent, repent! Return, return again unto thy God!
Lament with tears thy sinful days, and He will spare the rod.
O Lord of hosts, accept our votes! From dust thy people raise!
And we will tell like Israel thy wonders, sing the praise.

Awake, awake, yee Irish saints! O patrons, now arise!
Let faithless know your power with God, give ears unto our cries!
Such as deny and doe defye your favours, beare the sway;
And wee that pray to you each day, are banished all away.

Recall, o Lord, our pastors backe; give us true charity;
Confirm us in thy heavenly grace; give hope, o Deity;
If Thou forgive, then we shall live; if dead? Thou wilt revive.
If God for us and man against us, all our affairs shall thrive!—

Contemned: Treated with contempt.

DOCUMENT 25:

The Treaty of Limerick (1691)[9] and the Penal Laws[10]

The Treaty of Limerick, signed in 1691, brought an end to the Williamite War in Ireland, fought between King William III, who had taken the throne of England in the Glorious Revolution, and his father-in-law the Catholic King James II who had fled England but later tried to reclaim his throne with the support of Irish Catholics and the King of France. In the years that followed, a Protestant ruling elite in Ireland passed a series of legislations, called the Penal Laws, which sought to regulate and control the Catholic population of Ireland.

The Treaty of Limerick

1. The Roman Catholics of this kingdom shall enjoy such privileges in the exercise of their religion as are consistent with the laws of Ireland, or as they did enjoy in the reign of king Charles the second: and their majesties, as soon as their affairs will permit them to summon a parliament in this kingdom, will endeavour to procure the said Roman Catholics such farther security in that particular, as may preserve them from any disturbance upon the account of their said religion.

2. All the inhabitants or residents of Limerick, or any other garrison now in the possession of the Irish, and all officers and soldiers now in arms, under any commission of king James, or those authorized by him to grant the same, in the several counties of Limerick, Clare, Kerry, Cork, and Mayo, or any of them; and all the commissioned officers in their majesties' quarters that belong to the Irish regiments now in being, that are treated with, and who are not prisoners of war, or have taken protection and who shall return and submit to their majesties' obedience, and their and every of their heirs, shall hold, possess, and enjoy all and every their estates of freehold and inheritance, and all the rights, titles and interests, privileges and immunities, which they and every or any of them held, enjoyed, or were rightfully and lawfully entitled to in the reign of king Charles II., or at any time since, by the laws and statutes that were in force in the said reign of king Charles II., and shall be put in possession, by order of the government, of such of them as are in the king's hands, or the hands of his tenants, without

9 *The Treaty of Limerick*, https://celt.ucc.ie.
10 Irish Penal Law—Statutes by Subject, https://www.law.umn.edu/library/irishlaw/subjectlist.

being put to any suit or trouble therein; and all such estates shall be freed and discharged from all arrears of crown-rents, quit-rents, and other public charges incurred and become due since Michaelmas, 1688, to the day of the date hereof: and all persons comprehended in this article shall have, hold, and enjoy all their goods and **chattels**, real and personal, to them or any of them belonging and remaining, either in their own hands or the hands of any persons whatsoever, in trust for or for the use of them or any of them: and all and every the said persons, of what profession, trade or calling soever they be, shall and may use, exercise, and practise their several and respective professions, trades, and callings as freely as they did use, exercise, and enjoy the same in the reign of king Charles II., provided that nothing in this article contained be construed to extend to or restore any forfeiting person now out of the kingdom, except what are hereafter comprized: provided also, that no person whatsoever shall have or enjoy the benefit of this article, that shall neglect or refuse to take the oath of allegiance, made by act of parliament in England, in the first year of the reign of their present majesties, when thereunto required....

Penal Laws (selected examples)

3 Will & Mary c.2 (1691): An Act for the Abrogating the **Oath of Supremacy** in Ireland and Appointing Other Oaths

Sec. 4. Every person that shall become a barrister at law, attorney, clerk, or other officer of the court in Ireland shall take the oaths of allegiance and abhorrence and make the declaration against **transubstantiation** in open court between nine and twelve in the forenoon, and said fact shall be recorded, before he shall be admitted to practice.

And all persons that shall be admitted into any office or employment, ecclesiastical or civil, who should have taken the oaths required by 1 Eliz. c. 1, shall take the said oaths and make said declaration.

7 Will III c.4 (1695): An Act to Restrain Foreign Education

Sec. 1. In case any of his Majesty's subjects of Ireland shall go or send any child or other person beyond the seas to be trained in any popish university, college or school, or in any private popish family, or shall send any money for the support of any such person, then the person sending and the person sent shall, upon conviction, be disabled to prosecute any action in a court of law, or be a guardian or executor, or receive any legacy or gift, or bear any public office, and shall forfeit all their lands and estates during their lives.

Chattels: Personal property.

Oath of Supremacy: An oath requiring anyone taking public office to swear that William and Mary were the monarchs of Ireland and also heads of the Church of Ireland.

Transubstantiation: Fundamental belief of the Roman Catholic Church that during communion the bread and wine become the true body and blood of Christ.

7 Will III c.5 (1695): An Act for the Better Securing the Government, by Disarming Papists

Sec. 1. All papists within this kingdom of Ireland shall before the 1st day of March, 1696, deliver up to some justice of the peace or corporation officer where such papist shall dwell, all their arms and ammunition, notwithstanding any licence for keeping the same heretofore granted. Justices of the peace, mayors, sheriffs, and chief officers of cities and towns and persons under their warrants, may search and seize all arms and ammunition of papists, or in the hands of any persons in trust for them, wherever they shall suspect they may be concealed. And such arms shall be preserved for the use of his Majesty.

9 Will III c.1 (1697): An Act for Banishing all Papists Exercising Any Ecclesiastical Jurisdiction and All Regulars of the Popish Clergy....

Sec. 1. Whereas it is notoriously known, that the late rebellions in this kingdom have been promoted by popish bishops and other ecclesiastical persons of the popish religion, and forasmuch as the peace and publick safety of this kingdom is in danger by the great number of said the clergy now residing here, and settling in fraternities contrary to law, and to the great impoverishing of his Majesty's subjects who are forced to maintain them, and said the clergy do not only endeavour to withdraw his Majesty's subjects from their obedience, but do daily stir up and move sedition and rebellion, all popish archbishops, bishops, vicars-general, deans, jesuits, monks, friars, and all other regular popish clergy shall depart out of this kingdom before the 1st day of May, 1698, and if any of said ecclesiastical persons shall after that day be in this kingdom, they shall suffer imprisonment, and remain in prison until transported out of his Majesty's dominions, wherever his Majesty or the chief governors of this kingdom shall see fit, and if any person so transported shall return, he shall be guilty of high treason.

9 Will III c.3 (1697): An Act to Prevent Protestants Intermarrying with Papists

Sec. 1. Whereas many protestant women, heirs or heirs apparent to lands or other great substances in goods or chattels, or having considerable estates for life, or guardianship of children intitled to such estates, by flattery and other crafty insinuations of popish persons, have been seduced to contract matrimony with and take to husband, papists, to the great ruin of such estates, to the great loss of many protestant persons to whom the same might descend, and to the corrupting such protestant women that they forsake their religion and become papists, to the great dishonour of Almighty God, the great prejudice of the protestant interest, and the heavy sorrow of all their protestant friends, if any Protestant woman having any estate or interest real or, if personal of a value of 500 pounds, shall take to husband any person without first having a certificate from the minister of the parish, bishop, and justice of the peace living near the place where such person shall be resident at the time of such marriage, that he is a known protestant, which certificate shall also be attested under the hands of 2 credible witnesses, that protestant woman, and the person she shall so marry, shall be incapable of holding or enjoying any of her aforesaid estates or interests.

And by such marriage all said estates and interests shall be vested in the next protestant of kin to whom such estate or interests would descend were such protestant woman dead. And such protestant person may sue for and recover such estates or interests at any time after such marriage.

1 Ann c.26 (1702): An Act for the Relief of the Protestant Purchasers of the Forfeited Estates in Ireland

Sec. 7: To the end that none of the aforesaid purchased forfeited estates may ever descend to any Papist but shall remain to be held and enjoyed by Protestants for the strengthening of the English interest and Protestant religion, if any person educated in the popish religion, or professing the same, and being under the age of 18, shall not, within 6 months of attaining the age of 18, take the oaths of allegiance and supremacy, and the declaration against transubstantiation in the courts of Chancery or Kings-bench in England or Ireland, or in the quarter-sessions where such person shall reside, and continue to be a protestant such person in respect of himself only, and not his heirs or posterity, shall be disabled to take by decent, devise, or limitation, any of the forfeited estates purchased in Ireland, and during the life of such person, or until he shall take the oaths etc., the protestant next of kin shall enjoy the premises.

2 Ann c.6 (1703): An Act to Prevent the Further Growth of Popery

Sec. 3. The Protestant child of popish parents may bring a complaint in the Court of Chancery, which court may order such popish parent to maintain such child suitable to the degree and ability of such popish parent and the age of such child, and order an appropriate portion for every such Protestant child to be paid at the decease of such popish parent.

If the eldest son and heir of a popish parent shall become protestant, such popish parent shall, from the time of inrolment in chancery of a certificate of the bishop of the diocese testifying the son's being a protestant, become only tenant for life of any real estate which the popish parent shall then own, and the reversion vested in such protestant eldest son, subject to maintenances and portions for the other children, as the court shall order, not to exceed one third of the estate, and free of all settlements, sales and incumbrances made by the popish parent after conversion of the son. And rolls shall be kept in a publick place of such certificates, where all persons may at seasonable times resort to and peruse this same without fee.

Sec. 10. All lands owned by a papist, and not sold during his lifetime for valuable consideration, really and bona fide paid, shall descend in **gavelkind**, that is to all of his sons, share and share alike, and not to the eldest son only, and lacking sons, to all his daughters, and lacking issue, to all kin of the papist's father in equal degree, etc.; notwithstanding any grant, settlement or disposition made by such papist, by will or otherwise, subject however to all debts and incumbrances charging such estate.

Gavelkind: A system of inheritance in which a deceased person's land and property is equally divided among all male heirs, as opposed to primogeniture where only the eldest son inherits. The purpose is to prevent Catholic families from accumulating generational wealth.

1 Geo II c.9 (1727): An Act for the Further Regulating the Election of Members of Parliament; ...

Sec. 7. No papist, though not convicted as such, shall be intitled to vote at the election of any member to serve in parliament, or at the election of any magistrate for any city or other town corporate.

DOCUMENT 26:

From William Petty, *The Political Anatomy of Ireland* (1691)

William Petty (1623–87) was an English economist and scientist. He first traveled to Ireland in 1652 with Cromwell's army. He remained prominent after the restoration of the monarchy: he returned to Ireland in 1666 and was granted several estates there. He wrote *The Political Anatomy of Ireland* in 1672 although it was not published until after his death. In it he provides a rough estimate of the Irish population and the impact of the recent wars in Ireland.

✑

The number of the People being now Anno 1672 about 1100,000 and Anno 1652 about 850 **M.** because I conceive that 80 M. of them have in 20 years encreased by Generation 70 M. by return of banished and expelled English; as also by the access of new ones, 80 M. of New Scots, and 20 M. of returned Irish, being all 250 M.

M: One thousand in Roman numerals.

Now if it could be known what number of people were in Ireland, Ann. 1641 then the difference between the said number, and 850, adding unto it the encrease by Generation, in 11 years will shew the destruction of people made by the Wars, viz. by the Sword, Plague, and Famine occasioned thereby.

I find, by comparing superfluous and spare Oxen, Sheep, Butter and Beef, that there was exported above ⅓ more Ann. 1664 than in 1641 which shews there were ⅓ more of people, viz. 1466,000; Out of which Sum take what were left Ann. 1652 there will remain 616,000 destroyed by the Rebellion.

Whereas the present proportion of the British is as 3 to 11; But before the Wars the proportion was less, viz. as 2 to 11 and then it follows that the number of British slain in 11 years was 112 thousand Souls; of which I guess ⅔ to have perished by War, Plague and Famine. So as it follows that 37,000 were massacred in the first year of Tumults: So as those who think 154,000 were so destroyed, ought to review the grounds of their Opinion.

It follows also, that about 504 M of the Irish perished, and were wasted by the Sword, Plague, Famine, Hardship and Banishment, between the 23 of October 1641 and the same day 1652.

Wherefore those who say, That not ⅙ of them remained at the end of the Wars, must also review their opinions; there being by this Computation near ⅔ of them; which Opinion I also submit....

The Number of Landed Irish-Papists, or Freeholders before the Wars, was about 3000; whereof, as appears by 800 Judgments of the Court of Claims, which fate Ann. 1663 upon the Innocence and Effects of the Irish, there were not above ⅐ part or 400 guilty of the Rebellion, unto each of whom I allow 20 Followers, which would have made up an Army of 8000: But by the 49 Officers account, the British Army before 1649 must have been about 40 M. men; upon whom the said 8000 **Nocent** Irish so prevail'd, as that the Peace ended in the Articles of 1648. By which the Irish were made at least equal Partners with His Majesty in the Government of Ireland; which sheweth, that the Irish were men of admirable Success and Courage: Unless we should rather think, that the said Court of Claims were abused by their Perjuries and Forgeries, which one would think, that a Nation, who caus'd the destruction of so many thousand Lives, for the sake of God and Religion, should not be so guilty of.

Nocent: Not innocent.

The Estates of the Irish before the Wars, was double to that of the English; but the number and natural force of the Irish quintuple to that of the English.

The Cause of the War was a desire of the Romists, to recover the Church-Revenue, worth about 110 M. *l.* per Ann. and of the Common Irish, to get all the Englishmens Estates; and of the 10 or 12 Grandees of Ireland, to get the Empire of the whole. But upon the playing of this Game or Match upon so great odds, the English won and have (among, and besides other Pretences) a Gamester's Right at least to their Estates. But as for the Bloodshed in the Contest, God best knows who did occasion it....

The English invaded Ireland about 500 years since; at which time, if the Irish were in number about 1,200,000. Anno 1641 they were but 600 M. in number, 200 years ago, and not above 300,000 M. at the said time of their Invasion; for 300,000 people will, by the ordinary Course of Generation, become 1200 M. in 500 years; allowance being made for the Extraordinary Effects of Epidemical Diseases, Famines, Wars, &c.

There is at this Day no Monument or real Argument that, when the Irish were first invaded, they had any Stone-Housing at all, any Money, any Foreign Trade, nor any Learning but the Legend of the Saints, Psalters; Missals, Rituals, &c. viz. nor Geometry, Astronomy, Anatomy, Architecture, Enginery, Painting, Carving, nor any kind of Manufacture, nor the least use of Navigation, or the Art Military.

Sir John Davys hath expressed much Wit and Learning, in giving the Causes why Ireland was in no measure reduced to English Government, till in Queen Elizabeths Reign, and since; and withal offers several means, whereby what yet remains to be done, may be still effected.

Sir John Davys: A reference to Document 19.

The Conquest made by the English, and described in the Preamble of the Act of Parliament past Ann. 1662 for the Settlement of Ireland, gave means for any thing that had been reasonable of that kind; but their Forfeiters being abroad, and suffering with His Majesty from the same usurping hands, made some diversion.

Wherefore (**Rebus sic stantibus**) what is now to be done is the Question, viz. What may be done by natural possibility, if Authority saw it fit?

Rebus sic stantibus: Latin for "matters standing."

Some furious Spirits have wished, that the Irish would rebel again, that they might be put to the Sword. But I declare, that motion to be not only impious and inhumane, but withal frivolous and pernicious even to them who have rashly wish'd for those occasions.

That the Irish will not easily rebel again, I believe from the memory of their former Successes, especially of the last, had not many Providences interpos'd; and withal from the consideration of these following Particulars, viz.

1. That the British Protestants and Church have ¾ of all the Lands; ⅚ of all the Housing; of all the Housing in wall'd Towns, and Places of strength ⅔ of the Foreign Trade. That 6 of 8 of all the Irish live in a brutish nasty Condition, as in Cabins, with neither Chimney, Door, Stairs nor Window; feed chiefly upon Milk and Potatoes, whereby their Spirits are not dispos'd for War. And that although there be in Ireland 8 Papists for 3 others; yet there are far more Soldiers, and Soldierlike-Men of this latter and lesser Number, than of the former.

That His Majesty, who formerly could do nothing for, and upon Ireland, but by the help of England, hath now a Revenue upon the Place, to maintain, if he pleases, 7000 Men in Arms, besides a Protestant Militia of 25000 more, the most whereof are expert in War.

That the Protestants have Housing enough within Places of strength within 5 Miles of the Sea-side; to receive and protect, and harbour every Man, Woman and Child belonging to them, and have also places of strength of their own properly, so situate in all parts of Ireland, to which they can easily travel the shortest day of the year.

That being able so to secure their Persons, even upon all sudden Emergencies, they can be easily supplied out of England with Food sufficient to maintain them, till they have burnt 160 M. of their afore-described Cabins, not worth 50 M. *l.* destroy'd their Stacks and Haggards of Corn, and disturbed their Tillage, which the embody'd British can soon and easily achieve.

That a few Ships of War, whereof the Irish have none, nor no Skill or Practice of Navigation, can hinder their relief from all Foreign help.

That few Foreigners can help them if they would. But that none, not the King of France, can gain advantage by so doing, even tho he succeeded. For England hath constantly lost these 500 years by their medling with Ireland. And at this day, than when Ireland was never so rich and splendid, it were the advantage of the English to abandon their whole Interest in that Country; and fatal to any other Nation to take it, as hath been elsewhere (as I think) demonstrated; and the advantage of the Landlords of England, to give them the Equivalent of what they should so quit out of their own Estates in England.

Lastly, Let the Irish know, That there are, ever were, and will be men discontented with their present Conditions in England, and ready for any Exploit and Change, more than are sufficient to quell any Insurrection they can make and abide by.

Wherefore, declining all Military means of setling and securing Ireland in peace and plenty, what we offer shall tend to the transmuting one People into the other, and the thorough union of Interests upon natural and lasting Principles; of which I shall enumerate several, tho seemingly never so uncouth and extravagant.

1. If Henry the II had or could have brought over all the people of Ireland into England, declining the Benefit of their Land; he had fortified, beautified and enrich'd England, and done real Kindness to the Irish. But the same Work is near four times as hard now to be done as then; but it might be done, even now, with advantage to all Parties.

Whereas there are now 300 M. British, and 800 M. Papists, whereof 600 M. live in the wretched way above mentioned: If an Exchange was made of but about 200 M. Irish, and the like number of British brought over in their rooms, then the natural strength of the British would be equal to that of the Irish; but their Political and Artificial strength three times as great; and so visible, that the Irish would never stir upon a National or Religious Account.

3. There are among the 600 M. above mentioned of the poor Irish, not above 20 M. of unmarried marriageable Women; nor would above two thousand per Ann. grow and become such. Wherefore if ½ the said Women were in one year, and ½ the next transported into England, and disposed of one to each Parish, and as many English brought back and married to the Irish, as would improve their Dwelling but to an House and Garden of 3 l. value, the whole Work of natural **Transmutation** and Union would in 4 or 5 years be accomplished.

Transmutation: The changing of one substance to another, usually of a higher form; in alchemy the transmutation refers to the changing of base metals into gold.

The charge of making the exchange would not be 20,000 *l.* per Ann. which is about 6 Weeks Pay of the present or late Armies in Ireland.

If the Irish must have Priests, let the number of them, which is now between 2 and 3 thousand Secular and Regulars, be reduced to the competent number of 1000, which is 800 Souls to the pastorage of each Priest; which let be known persons, and English-men, if it may be. So as that when the Priests, who govern the Conscience, and the Women, who influence other powerful Appetites, shall be English, both of whom being in the Bosom of the Men, it must be, that no massacring of English, as heretofore, can happen again. Moreover, when the Language of the Children shall be English, and the whole **Oeconomy** of the Family English, viz. Diet, Apparel, &c. the Transmutation will be very easy and quick.

Oeconomy: Archaic spelling of economy.

Add hereunto, That if both Kingdoms, now two, were put into one, and under one Legislative Power and Parliament, the Members whereof should be in the same proportion that the Power and Wealth of each Nation are, there would be no danger such a Parliament should do any thing to the prejudice of the English Interest in Ireland; nor could the Irish ever complain of Partiality, when they shall be freely and proportionably represented in all Legislatures.

DOCUMENT 27:

From William Molyneux, *The Case of Ireland Being Bound by Acts of Parliament in England, Stated* (1698)

William Molyneux (1656–98) was an Anglo-Irish writer on science and politics. He was born to a landowning Protestant family. In 1683 he founded the Dublin Philosophical Society, a scientific society. In 1698 he published *The Case of Ireland Being Bound by Acts of Parliament in England, Stated* which sought to address the then contentious constitutional issue of English Parliament legislating for Ireland, despite Ireland having an independent Parliament.

૭

I could never Imagine that those Great Assertors of their Own Liberties and Rights, could ever think of making the least Breach in the Right's and Liberties of their Neighbours, unless they thought that they had Right so to do; and this they might well surmise, if their Neighbours quietly see their Inclosures Invaded, without Expostulating the Matter at least, and shewing Reasons, why they may think that Hardships are put on them therein....

The last thing I shall take Notice of, that some raise against us, is, That Ireland is to be look'd upon only as a Colony from England: And therefore as the Roman Colonies were subject to, and bound by, the Laws made by the Senate at Rome, so ought Ireland by those made by the Great Council at Westminster. Of all the Objections raised against us, I take this to be the most Extravagant; it seems not to have the least Foundation or Colour from Reason or Record: Does it not manifestly appear by the Constitution of Ireland, that 'tis a Compleat Kingdom within it self? Do not the Kings of England bear, the Stile of Ireland, amongst the rest of their Kingdoms? Is this agreeable to the nature of a Colony? Do they use the Title of Kings of Virginia, New-England, or Mary-Land? Was not Ireland given by Henry the Second in a Parliament at Oxford to his son John, and made thereby an Absolute Kingdom, separate and wholly Independent on England, till they both came United again in him, after the Death of his Brother Richard, without Issue? Have not multitudes of Acts of Parliament both in England and Ireland, declared Ireland a Compleat Kingdom? Is not Ireland stiled in them All, the Kingdom, or Realm of Ireland? Do these Names agree to a Colony? Have we not a Parliament, and Courts of Judicature? Do these things agree with a Colony? This on all hands involves so many Absurdities, that I think it deserves nothing more of our Consideration....

It is against the Practice of all former Ages. Wherein can it appear, that any Statute made in England, was at any time since the Reign of Henry the Third, allowed and put in practice in the Realm of Ireland, without the Authority of the Parliament of Ireland. Is it not manifest by what forgoes, that from the Twentieth of King Henry the Third, to the Thirteenth of Edward the Second, and from thence to the Eighteenth of Henry the Sixth, and from thence, to the Thirty-Second of Henry the Sixth, and from thence, to the Eight of Edward the Fourth, and from thence, to the Tenth of Henry the Seventh, there was special care taken to Introduce the Statutes of England (such of them as were necessary or convenient for this Kingdom) by degrees, and always with Alowance, and Consent of the Parliament and People of Ireland. And since the General Allowance, of all the English Acts and Statutes in the Tenth of Henry the Seventh, there have several Acts of Parliament, which were made in England in the Reigns of all the Kings from that Time, successively to this very Day, been particularly Recieved by Parliament in Ireland, and so they become of force here, and not by reason of any General Comprehensive words, as some Men have lately fancied. For if by General Comprehensive Words, the Kingdom of Ireland could be bound by the Acts of Parliament of England, what needed all the former Receptions in the Parliament of Ireland, or what use will there be of the Parliament of Ireland at any time? If the Religion, Lives, Liberties, Fortunes, and Estates of the Clergy, Nobility, and Gentry of Ireland, may be disposed of, without their Privity and Consent, what Benefit have they of any Laws, Liberties, or Privileges granted unto them by the Crown of England: I am loth to give their Condition an hard Name; but I have no other Notion of Slavery, but being Bound by a Law to which I do not Consent ...

Lastly, The People of Ireland are left by this Doctrine in the greatest Confusion and Uncertainty Imaginable. We are certainly bound to Obey the Supream Authority over us; and yet hereby we are not permitted to know who or what the same is; whether the Parliament of England, or that of Ireland, or both; And in what Cases the One; and in what the other: Which Uncertainty is or may be made a Pretence at any time for Disobedience. It is not impossible but the Different Legislatures we are subject to, may Enact Different or Contrary Sanctions: Which of these must we obey?

To conclude all, I think it highly Inconvenient for England to Assume this Authority over the Kingdom of Ireland. I believe there will need no great Arguments to convince the Wise Assembly of English Senators, how inconvenient it may be to England, to do that which may make the Lords and People of Ireland that they are not well used, and may drive them into Discontent. The Laws and Liberties of England were granted above five hundred years ago to the People of Ireland, upon their Submissions to the Crown of England, with a Design to make them Easie to England, and to keep them in the Allegiance of the King of England. How Consistent it may be with True Policy, to do that which the People of Ireland may think is an Invasion of their Rights and Liberties, I do most humbly submit to the Parliament of England to Consider. They are Men of Great Wisdom, Honour and Justice, and know how to prevent all future Inconveniencies. We have heard great Out-cries, and deservedly, on breaking the Edict of Nantes and other Stipulations; how far the Breaking our Constitution, which has been of Five Hundred years standing exceeds that, I leave the World to judge. It may perhaps be urged, That tis convenient for the State of England, that the Supream Council thereof should make their Jurisdiction as Large as they can. But with Submission, I conceive that if this Affirmed Power be not Just. Nor do I think, that tis any wise necessary to the Good of England to Assert this High Jurisdiction over Ireland. For since the Statutes of this Kingdom are made with such Caution, and in such Form, as is prescribed by **Poyning's Act** 10.H.7: and by the 3d and 4th of Phil. and Mar. and whilst Ireland is in English hands, I do not see how tis possible for the Parliament of Ireland to do any thing that can be in the least prejudicial to England. But on the other hand, if England assume a Jurisdiction over Ireland, whereby they think their Rights and Liberties are taken away; That their Parliaments are rendred meerly nugatory, and that their Lives and Fortunes Depend on the Will of a Legislature wherein they are not parties; there may be ill Consequences of this. Advancing the Power of the Parliament of England by breaking the Rights of an other, may in time have ill Effects. The Rights of Parliament should be preserved Sacred and Inviolable, wherever they are found. This kind of Government, once so Universal all over Europe, is now almost Vanished, from amongst the Nations thereof. Our Kings Dominions are the only Supporters of this noble Gothick Constitution, save only what little remains may be found thereof in Poland. We should not therefore make so light of that fort of Legislature, and as it were Abolish it in One Kingdom of the Three, wherein it appears; but rather Cherish and Encourage it wherever we meet it.

Poynings' Act: See Document 12.

DOCUMENT 28:

From *Bogg-Witticisms: or, Dear Joy's Common-Places* (1698)

The full title of this humorous pamphlet is *Bogg-Witticisms: or, Dear Joy's Common-Places. Being a Compleat Collection of the Most Profound Punns, Learned Bulls, Elaborate Quibbles, and Wise Sayings of Some of the Natives of Teague-Land.* Teague is the anglicized version of the Irish male name Tadhg, then quite popular in Ireland. In the late seventeenth century "Teague" began to be used as an ethnic slur to refer to Irish men. The stories in pamphlets such as this reinforced the image of the "stage Irishman" as an object of humor and contempt rather than fear.

To the Reader

The Bulls and Witticisms, that have too frequently dropt from the Mouths of Dear Joys, have made them so Famous, that they are become the Discourse and Entertainment of almost all sorts of Companies: And in troth, they are generally so full of Diversion, that they would almost force a Smile from **Heraclitus**. Nothing more recommends them, than the natural Stupidity or Simplicity of the Natives; so that they do not appear like little Contrivances, but purely the Effects of their Notions and Mistakes of Things.

The Welchmen and Scots had a long time Engrossed all the Table-Talk of the Town; and the Jests and Stories that were Related concerning them, passed instead of a Song, or a Fidle. But Teague and his Countrymen have clearly Baffled **Saint Taffy** and **Saint Andrew**, for down-right Dunstable, Blunder, and Punn; who are no more to be compared to them, than the little Sooty Lanthorns in Smithfield, to the Radiant Magnifying Lights in Cheapside. The following Collection presents you with a great variety of the most Novel and Facetious; which may serve as Wallnuts with a Glass of Wine, and be an excellent Relief against an uneasie and sullen Melancholy....

A certain Lord having a Nimble **Bog-Trotter** to his servant which use to travell with him when he rode and wou'd make as quick speed as his Horse let him ride never so hard, This Nobleman having occasion to send his servant to a Gentleman of his acquaintance who lived about a dozen Miles from him, he call'd his Man to him over Night, and said Teague (for so the fellow was named) I must send you morrow very early in the morning to Mr ... pray remember, to which Teague reply'd au my shoul Joy I saul remember very well, In the morning Teague rose very Early and away he trots to this Gentlemans house leaving his Master (as supposed) asleep, and being come Teague knocked at the Door, and was let in, Who presently ask'd

---

Heraclitus: An Ancient Greek philosopher, known for being something of a misanthrope.

Saint Taffy: A reference to St. David, the patron saint of Wales; Taffy is a derivation of David in Welsh.

Saint Andrew: The patron saint of Scotland.

Bog-Trotter: An Irishman, a derisive reference to Ireland's numerous bogs.

for the Gentleman, the Master of the House, to which the Servant answered he was not stirring; Teague said "be Chreesht I must speake with him I did come from the Lord … my Master." The Servant went & acquainted his Master thereof, (thinking it had been some Urgent affair that Teague should come 12 miles so soon in the morning). Whereupon his Mr. having a great respect for the Lord (and believing it business of Moment) ordered Teague to come up to his Chamber, And the Gentleman said "how now Teague, what news doe you bring from My Lord your Mr. that you are here so Early," to which Teague answered, "be Chrest I cano tell," "how does my Lord" quoth the Gent. "Indeed very well," said Teague, "what is your Errant or business with me Teague," (quoth the Gent). Quoth Teague "be Chrest & St. Patrick I cannot tell, My Lord did call me to him over night and said I must come to thee this morning, yes indeed, & he did charge me to remember it, and be Christ thou canst witness I have not forgat it for thou seest I am here with thee," quoth the Gent. "is this all," quoth Teague "au my shaul I doe not know any more, and so I will goe home (Dear Joy) to my Master and tell him I did remember to come to thee" (quoth the Gentleman) "now I think on't Teague, you must stay a little while, I have something to send to your Master, which you come for," "be Chreest (quoth Teague) I cano tell": Then the Gentleman began to think how he should be reveng'd of this Rogue that had thus disturb'd him to no purpose, at length he Considered he had an ugly stone Mortar which he did not value, which Mortar he gave Teague and told him, he came for that Mortar, and that his Master had sent him purposely for it; The Mortar weighed about 80 l. which Teague gott upon his Back, and took his leave of the Gentleman, many a face and many a Curse he did make at the Mortar, for it did hurt his back and shoulders, and almost grippled poor Teague, but he was bound to endure it with Patience, having brought it home, he had some help to get it off his back; And the rest of his Servants asked him where he had been, for his Lord miss'd him; To which he was Dumb and would not answer any thing for a long while, at last My Lord being at a Bouling Green near, sent to see for Teague, and to command him to come to him, who came to the Green to My Lord, said the Lord to Teague "ye plaguy Rogue where have you been all this day," Teague made ugly faces and points to his back and shoulders being sore and gauld by the stone Mortar and as often as My Lord ask'd him where he had been, My Lord received no other answer but wretched wry faces and pointing to his shoulders & back, till at length my Lord grew a little angry, "Sirra," said he, "tell me where you have been & the meaning of your Pointings and wry Mouth, or else I will Cudgel your bones," Then Teague answered, "didst thou not say I must goe to Mr … this morning, and be Chrest I have been with him," "you dam'd Rogue," said My Lord, "I told you overnight you should goe to him in the morning but you should have come to me and taken my Errant along with you," "A plague take thee, and they Errant to, I did bring they Errant upon my back be Chreest, till I did bruise my shoulders, and au my shoul I shal goe no more of thy Errants," "nay Teague" (quoth my Lord, doe not say so) "what is it you brought from the Gentleman," "be Chreest thou may'st see it if thou wilt go home," "no Teague," said the Lord being willing that some should share the mirth that this fellow was like to make among them "goe you home and fetch this Errant that has so mortifyed your shoulders and let me see it," Teague goes home and takes up the Mortar and brings it to his Master upon the Green, and throwes it down there, at which they all laughed heartily that this fellow should be so sordid as to goe to the Gentleman without his Errant, and commended the Gentlemans ingenuity to punish the fool with such a burthen. To be short, his Master and the Company having had sport enough with his sowr faces, his pointings and his Errant, his Master bid him carry the Mortar home but withall to goe to the Gentleman again and fetch the Pestell to the Mortar, he having forgot it.

DOCUMENT 29:

From Jonathan Swift, *Drapier's Letters* (1724–25)[11]

Jonathan Swift was an Anglo-Irish clergyman most famous for his work as a writer and satirist. In 1724 he began anonymously publishing a series of pamphlets under the pseudonym M.B. Drapier, with each work addressing the Wood's halfpence controversy. William Wood, an English ironmaster, was given a patent to produce small value coins for Ireland and the American colonies. The copper coins minted by Wood were extremely unpopular in Ireland with many arguing they were inferior to existing coins, that they might damage the Irish economy, and also objecting to the patent being granted to Wood secretly and without the consultation of any Irish authorities. Swift in particular saw the patent granted to Wood as evidence of corruption and argued that Ireland should be constitutionally and financially independent of England.

e

But to go on. To remove our "direful apprehensions that he will drain us of our gold and silver by his coinage": This little arbitrary mock-monarch most graciously offers to "take our manufactures in exchange." Are our Irish understandings indeed so low in his opinion? Is not this the very misery we complain of? That his cursed project will put us under the necessity of selling our goods for what is equal to nothing. How would such a proposal sound from France or Spain or any other country we deal with, if they should offer to deal with us only upon this condition, that we should take their money at ten times higher than the intrinsic value? Does Mr. Wood think, for instance, that we will sell him a stone of wool for a parcel of his counters not worth sixpence, when we can send it to England and receive as many shillings in gold and silver? Surely there was never heard such a compound of impudence, villainy and folly.

His proposals conclude with perfect high treason. He promises, that no person shall be *obliged* to receive more than **fivepence halfpenny** of his coin in one payment: By which it is plain, that he pretends to *oblige* every subject in this kingdom to take so much in every payment, if it be offered; whereas his patent obliges no man, nor can the prerogative by law claim such a power, as I have often observed; so that here Mr. Wood takes upon him the entire legislature, and an absolute dominion over the properties of the whole nation.

Fivepence halfpenny:
Five pence in halfpennies would be eleven of Wood's halfpence coins.

---

11   *The Prose Works of Jonathan Swift*, Temple Scott, ed., vol. VI (London: George Bell and Sons, 1903).

Good God! Who are this wretch's advisers? Who are his supporters, abettors, encouragers, or sharers? Mr. Wood will *oblige* me to take fivepence halfpenny of his brass in every payment! And I will shoot Mr. Wood and his deputies through the head, like highwaymen or housebreakers, if they dare to force one farthing of their coin upon me in the payment of an hundred pounds. It is no loss of honour to submit to the lion, but who, with the figure of a man, can think with patience of being devoured alive by a rat. He has laid a tax upon the people of Ireland of seventeen shillings at least in the pound; a tax I say, not only upon lands, but interest-money, goods, manufactures, the hire of handicraftsmen, labourers, and servants. Shopkeepers look to yourselves. Wood will *oblige* and force you to take fivepence halfpenny of his trash in every payment, and many of you receive twenty, thirty, forty payments in a day, or else you can hardly find bread: And pray consider how much that will amount to in a year: Twenty times five-pence halfpenny is nine shillings and twopence, which is above an hundred and sixty pounds a

You will be losers: Swift's argument here is that Wood's coin is debased, it is not actually worth a halfpence so merchants will lose money when they have to accept payment in it.

year, whereof **you will be losers of at least one hundred and forty pounds by taking your payments in his money**. If any of you be content to deal with Mr. Wood on such conditions they may. But for my own particular, "let his money perish with him." If the famous Mr. Hampden rather chose to go to prison, than pay a few shillings to King Charles 1st. without authority of Parliament, I will rather choose to be hanged than have all my substance taxed at seventeen shillings in the pound, at the arbitrary will and pleasure of the venerable Mr. Wood....

In my humble opinion, the committee of council, hath already prejudged the whole case, by calling the united sense of both Houses of Parliament in Ireland an "universal clamour." Here the addresses of the Lords and Commons of Ireland against a ruinous destructive project of an "obscure, single undertaker," is called a "clamour." I desire to know how such a style would be resented in England from a committee of council there to a Parliament, and how many impeachments would follow upon it. But supposing the appellation to be proper, I never heard of a wise minister who despised the universal clamour of a people, and if that clamour can be quieted by disappointing the fraudulent practice of a single person, the purchase is not exorbitant....

Were not the people of Ireland born as free as those of England? How have they forfeited their freedom? Is not their Parliament as fair a representative of the people as that of England? And hath not their Privy-council as great or a greater share in the administration of public affairs? Are they not subjects of the same King? Does not the same sun shine on them? And have they not the same God for their protector? Am I a freeman in England, and do I become a slave in six hours by crossing the Channel? No wonder then, if the boldest persons were cautious to interpose in a matter already determined by the whole voice of the nation, or to presume to represent the representatives of the kingdom, and were justly apprehensive of meeting such a treatment as they would deserve at the next session. It would seem very extraordinary if an inferior court in England, should take a matter out of the hands of the high court of Parliament, during a prorogation, and decide it against the opinion of both Houses....

Among other clauses mentioned in this patent, to shew how advantageous it is to Ireland, there is one which seems to be of a singular nature, that the patentee shall be obliged, during his term, "to pay eight hundred pounds a year to the crown, and two hundred pounds a year to the comptroller." I have heard indeed that the King's council do always consider, in the passing of a patent, whether it will be of advantage to the crown, but I have likewise heard that it is at the same time considered whether the passing of it may be injurious to any other persons or bodies politic. However, although the attorney and solicitor be servants to the King, and therefore bound to consult His Majesty's interest, yet I am under some doubt whether eight hundred pounds a year to the crown would be equivalent to the ruin of a kingdom. It would be far better for us to have paid eight thousand pounds a year into His Majesty's coffers, in the midst of all our taxes (which, in proportion, are greater in this kingdom than ever they were in England, even during the war) than purchase such an addition to the revenue at the price of our *utter undoing*.

But here it is plain that fourteen thousand pounds are to be paid by Wood, only as a small circumstantial charge for the purchase of his patent, what were his other visible costs I know not, and what were his latent, is variously conjectured. But he must be surely a man of some wonderful merit. Hath he saved any other kingdom at his own expense, to give him a title of reimbursing himself by the destruction of ours? Hath he discovered the longitude or the universal medicine? No. But he hath found out the philosopher's stone after a new manner, by debasing of copper, and resolving to force it upon us for gold.

When the two Houses represented to His Majesty, that this patent to Wood was obtained in a clandestine manner, surely the Committee could not think the Parliament would insinuate that it had not passed in the common forms, and run through every office where fees and perquisites were due. They knew very well that persons in places were no enemies to grants, and that the officers of the crown could not be kept in the dark. But the late Lord Lieutenant of Ireland affirmed it was a secret to him (and who will doubt of his veracity, especially when he swore to a person of quality; from whom I had it, that Ireland should never be troubled with these halfpence). It was a secret to the people of Ireland, who were to be the only sufferers, and those who best knew the state of the kingdom and were most able to advise in such an affair, were wholly strangers to it....

Lastly, it is added that "such patents are in no manner derogatory or invasive of any liberty or privilege of the King's subjects of Ireland." If this proposition be true, as it is here laid down, without any limitation either expressed or implied, it must follow that a King of England may at any time coin copper money for Ireland, and oblige his subjects here to take a piece of copper under the value of half a farthing for half-a-crown, as was practiced by the late King James, and even without that arbitrary prince's excuse, from the necessity and exigences of his affairs. If this be in no manner "derogatory nor evasive of any liberties or privileges of the subjects of Ireland," it ought to have been expressed what our liberties and privileges are, and whether we have any at all, for in specifying the word *Ireland*, instead of saying "His Majesty's subjects," it would seem to insinuate that we are not upon the same foot with our fellow-subjects in *England*; which, however the practice may have been, I hope will never be directly asserted, for I do not understand that **Poining's act** deprived us of our liberty, but only changed the manner of passing laws here (which however was a power most indirectly obtained) by leaving the negative to the two Houses of Parliament. But, waiving all controversies relating to the legislature, no person, I believe, was ever yet so bold as to affirm that the people of Ireland have not the same title to the benefits of the common law, with the rest of His Majesty's subjects, and therefore whatever liberties or privileges the people of England enjoy by common law, we of Ireland have the same; so that in my humble opinion, the word *Ireland* standing in that proposition, was, in the mildest interpretation, *a lapse of the pen.*

The Report farther asserts, that "the precedents are many, wherein cases of great importance to Ireland, and that immediately affected the interests of that kingdom, warrants, orders, and directions by the authority of the King and his predecessors, have been issued under the royal sign manual, without any previous reference or advice of His Majesty's officers of Ireland, which have always had their due force, and have been punctually complied with, and obeyed." It may be so, and I am heartily sorry for it, because it may prove an eternal source of discontent. However among all these precedents there is not one of a patent for coining money for Ireland.

Poining's Act: Poynings' Law, Document 12.

DOCUMENT 30:

From Charles O'Conor, *The Case of the Roman-Catholics of Ireland* (1755)

Charles O'Conor (1710–91) was an Irish writer and historian. His work collecting Irish manuscripts was influential in the preservation of Gaelic culture and writing. He also spent much of his time campaigning for Catholic civil rights. In 1757 he co-founded the Catholic Committee, an organization that sought the repeal of the penal laws. The Committee dissolved itself in 1793 after many of the penal laws were repealed by the Catholic Relief Act of 1793.

In the Beginning of this Century, a Multiplicity of **Penal Laws** were enacted against the Roman Catholics. One Half of the People were put under the greatest Discouragements, in a Country extremely thin of inhabitants; and those Discouragements created that Sloth and Lowness of Spirits, which ever was, and ever must be, the Consequence of great and many legal Restraints. In Party-Justice, it was, perhaps, proper to exclude Papists from that Share of Landed Property, which might, possibly, in Course of Time, produce something like an Equality of Power: The Mistake lay in allowing them no Title at all, or a precarious one. Thus hath this Kingdom, more than fifty years past, been deprived of the Activity and Industry of near a Million of its People.

> **Penal laws:** See examples in Document 25.

The following Tract is written to shew, That Popery is not so dangerous to the Protestant Interest here as it was then imagined. While this Kingdom is knit, as it now is, with the Imperial Crown of Great-Britain, no Country in Europe hath less to apprehend on that Score; a Consideration which alone should remove all Jealousies, except of those real Dangers which surround us: Popery is not of the Number. The political Faith of the Roman-Catholics is here shewn to be Orthodox to our Constitution, and a TEST is offered to demonstrate it. What more can Government require to intitule loyalty to its proper Reward in a Land of Liberty? Their Declarations (it may be said) cannot be depended upon, and their Good conduct is a mere Act of Necessity: But what hated Party can ever be reputed Innocent upon such a Principle? If the Suggestion be groundless, how much doth the Public suffer? If it were, in Fact, true; yet, even in that Idea, it would be easy to shew, That, in our present Circumstances, it may be expedient to take off many Restraints: To limit the Possession; but at the same Time to grant every Constitutional Security to what is possessed. Powers may be granted to Parties, apparently loyal, for the Good of the Whole: Penalties may be inflicted on them to its Detriment. There are certain Bounds to be preserved in such Cases, as in all others; and beyond them, political Wisdom cannot exist....

It will cease the more, when those Interests and Notions are combated by active Violence, or false Reasoning; especially by Persons in Authority, who take the Lead, and pretend to speak the Sense of those Numbers who join with them. In such a Case, I say, we will not wonder, that the Principles of any religious Party, should be mistaken by Persons who are in a State of spiritual Warfare with it. And all this will, in Part, account for the penal Laws and Persecutions on the Score of Religion, in every Country; more particularly for those inflicted on the People called Papists; some of whom, and some in the highest Authority too, have, in certain, Conjunctures, maintained Principles, as well as held a Conduct, which the Catholic Religion never warranted: What brings us home to our principal Position; that most of the Disorders of these latter Ages are not owing to the Religion which forbids, but the Passions which excite, all Deviations from the Line of true Theology and true Subjection....

It is Time, God knows, we should grow wise, by all this dear-bought Experience, since so great a Part of our Happiness, as Members of Society, and of our Peace, as Fellow-Citizens, must result from it. The Causes of former Disturbances in Ireland are now no more. Let not the Effects, when such Causes are removed, remain; to prey upon our good Sense, our Industry, and our Morals. The Protestant Religion is long established by Law among us, with all the Power and Property in the Kingdom on its Side. The Roman Catholics revere our Constitution, and have long been obedient to this Government by Principle as well as Practice; or, if there be any among them in Enmity to either, a legal TEST may be framed, to distinguish the Elect of Government from the Reprobate. What more can the Legislature require? If the Roman-Catholics of this Land warred originally on the Reformation, with the Constitution and a safe Conscience on their Side, can they be supposed (without a Degree of Infatuation, hitherto unknown among Men) to do so now, with both consciously against them? May not Circumstances and Conjunctures concur to justify any Resistance, which, in other and settled Times, would be unjustifiable to all Law, Reason, and Religion? Is there no Difference between receiving and giving the Attack? between a controverted and a recognized Establishment? in Fact, although a different Religion may render the Roman-Catholics of Ireland a more favored, yet none can render them a more obedient Party of Subjects, than that they now profess: a Consideration which alone should recommend their CASE to the Attention of the present Parliament, on whom alone it rests to render them, by one short Bill, as useful as they are obedient to this Government. In the present Temper (aided by Knowledge, and formed by Experience) so much Loyalty cannot be rewarded with a State of Servitude; nor will the Prosperity of this Nation be suspended, for the Sake of any theological Disputes which interfere not with it; for the Sake of Doctrines which chiefly regard the private, not the political Morals of Mankind....

The Resistance of the Irish-Catholics, in the Beginning of King William's Reign, was, perhaps, more their Weakness than their Crime; considering the Circumstances of the Time, and the natural Hopes as well as Panics of Men, on the Commencement of all great Revolutions. But, admitting the criminal Charge on this Account, was it not remitted, on their Submission, by the Monarch on the Throne? Is this the Time to punish for the Actions, when the Actors are no longer in Being? Shall it be deemed impossible for Faction to reclaim? Or shall it be forbid to Religion and Reason to resume their Influence on Men, wounded and humbled by their Deviations from both? God forbid, that this should be the Judgment or Charity of any considerable Party among us! Sure I am, that it can not be the Judgment of those Members of the Legislature, who have the Rewards and Punishments of the Constitution in their Hands, and who are sufficiently wise to find out the proper Objects of them....

Whatever the Event be, the Roman-Catholics of Ireland should, out of Tenderness to the Public (so long deceived on their Account) and out of Tenderness to themselves (so long excluded from the Immunities of the Constitution) come to the Explanation recommended to them in the foregoing Pages. Let them acquit themselves, not of Guilt indeed, (for they have none to answer for) but of the most distant Suspicion of Guilt, with Regard to our political Government; and let them not incur the Blame of such an Omission in this Reign, the mildest, the happiest, and the longest we enjoyed, since the Commencement of the sixteenth Century. The Relief destined for them may be suspended: By such Suspension the Importance of it will be the more considered; the Necessity of it the more acknowledged; and the Objects of it, the more worthy of Favor and Confidence.

DOCUMENT 31:

From Arthur Young, *A Tour in Ireland* (1780)

Arthur Young (1741–1820) was an English writer who wrote primarily on
agricultural improvement. He was also widely known as a travel writer,
and his *Tour in Ireland* was based on his travels in the country from 1776
to 1777. Young's work on Ireland contains many discussions of the land and
agriculture as well as the economic, political, and social conditions of the
country.

e

In conversation upon the subject of a union with Great Britain, I was
informed that nothing was so unpopular in Ireland as such an idea; and that
the great objection to it was increasing the number of absentees. When it
was in agitation, twenty peers and sixty commoners were talked of to sit in
the British Parliament, which would be the resident of eighty of the best
estates in Ireland. Going every year to England would, by degrees, make
them residents; they would educate their children there, and in time become
mere absentees: becoming so they would be unpopular, others would be
elected, who, treading in the same steps, would yield the place still to others;
and thus by degrees, a vast portion of the kingdom now resident would be
made absentees, which would, they think, be so great a drain to Ireland,
that a free trade would not repay it.

I think the idea is erroneous, were it only for one circumstance, the
kingdom would lose, according to this reasoning, an idle race of country
gentlemen, and in exchange their ports would fill with ships and commerce,
and all the consequences of commerce, an exchange that never yet proved
disadvantageous to any country....

Before I conclude this article of the common labouring poor in Ireland,
I must observe, that their happiness depends not merely upon the payment
of their labour, their clothes, or their food; the subordination of the lower
classes, degenerating into oppression, is not to be overlooked. The poor in
all countries, and under all governments, are both paid and fed, yet there is
an infinite difference between them in different ones. This inquiry will by
no means turn out so favourable as the preceding articles. It must be very
apparent to every traveller through that country, that the labouring poor are
treated with harshness, and are in all respects so little considered that their
want of importance seems a perfect contrast to their situation in England, of
which country, comparatively speaking, they reign the sovereigns. The age has
improved so much in humanity, that even the poor Irish have experienced its
influence, and are every day treated better and better; but still the remnant

of the old manners, the abominable distinction of religion, united with the oppressive conduct of the little country gentlemen, or rather vermin of the kingdom, who never were out of it, altogether bear still very heavy on the poor people, and subject them to situations more mortifying than we ever behold in England. The landlord of an Irish estate, inhabited by Roman Catholics, is a sort of despot who yields obedience, in whatever concerns the poor, to no law but that of his will. To discover what the liberty of the people is, we must live among them, and not look for it in the statutes of the realm: the language of written law may be that of liberty, but the situation of the poor may speak no language but that of slavery. There is too much of this contradiction in Ireland; a long series of oppressions, aided by many very ill-judged laws, have brought landlords into a habit of exerting a very lofty superiority, and their vassals into that of an almost unlimited submission: speaking a language that is despised, professing a religion that is abhorred and being disarmed, the poor find themselves in many cases slaves even in the bosom of written liberty. Landlords that have resided much abroad are usually humane in their ideas, but the habit of tyranny naturally contracts the mind, so that even in this polished age there are instances of a severe carriage towards the poor, which is quite unknown in England.

A landlord in Ireland can scarcely invent an order which a servant, labourer, or **cottar** dares to refuse to execute. Nothing satisfies him but an unlimited submission. Disrespect, or anything tending towards sauciness, he may punish with his cane or his horsewhip with the most perfect security; a poor man would have his bones broke if he offered to lift his hands in his own defence....

Cottar: A farm laborer who occupies a cottage in return for labor.

Our own service both by sea and land, as well as that (unfortunately for us) of the principal monarchies of Europe, speak their steady and determined courage. Every unprejudiced traveller who visits them will be as much pleased with their cheerfulness, as obliged by their hospitality; and will find them a brave, polite, and liberal people.

DOCUMENT 32:

Seághan Ó Coileáin, *Lament over the Ruins of the Abbey of Teach Molag* (late 18th century)[12]

Seághan Ó Coileáin (1754–1817) was an Irish-language poet and schoolmaster in County Cork. During his life he was known as "The Silver Tongue of Munster." Teach Molag or Timoleague Abbey was a Franciscan friary in County Cork founded in 1240. The abbey was dispersed during the Reformation, although some friars remained. It was sacked by English soldiers in 1612 and later burnt by English soldiers in 1642. This particular poem was translated in 1846 and appeared in the Irish nationalist newspaper *The Nation*.

I wandered forth at night alone
Along the dreary, shingly, billow-beaten shore;
Sadness that night was in my bosom's core,
My soul and strength lay prone.
The thin wan moon, half overveiled
By clouds, shed her funereal beams upon the scene;
While in low tones, with many a pause between,
The mournful night-wind wailed.
Musing of Life, and Death, and Fate,
I slowly paced along, heedless of aught around,
Till on the hill, now, alas! ruin-crowned,
Lo! the old Abbey-gate!
Dim in the pallid moonlight stood,
Crumbling to slow decay, the remnant of that pile
Within which dwelt so many saints erewhile
In loving brotherhood!
The memory of the men who slept
Under those desolate walls—the solitude—the hour—
Mine own lorn mood of mind—all joined to o'erpower
My spirit—and I wept!
In yonder Goshen once—I thought—
Reigned Piety and Peace: Virtue and Truth were there;
With Charity and the blessed spirit of Prayer
Was each fleet moment fraught!
There, unity of Work and Will

---

12   J.C. Mangan, "Lament over the Ruins of the Abbey of Teach Molaga," *The Nation*, 8 August 1846.

Blent hundreds into one: no jealousies or jars
Troubled their placid lives: their fortunate stars
Had triumphed o'er all Ill!
There, knolled each morn and even
The Bell for Matin and Vesper: Mass was said or sung.—
From the bright silver censer as it swung
Rose balsamy clouds to Heaven.
Through the round cloistered corridors
A many a midnight hour, bareheaded and unshod,
Walked the **Grey Friars**, beseeching from their God
Peace for these western shores!
The weary pilgrim bowed by Age
Oft found asylum there—found welcome, and found wine.
Oft rested in its halls the Paladine,
The Poet and the Sage!
Alas! alas! how dark the change!
Now round its mouldering walls, over its pillars low,
The grass grows rank, the yellow **gowans** blow,
Looking so sad and strange!
Unsightly stones choke up its wells;
The owl hoots all night long under the altar-stairs;
The fox and badger make their darksome lairs
In its deserted cells!
Tempest and Time—the drifting sands—
The lightnings and the rains—the seas that sweep around
These hills in winter-nights, have awfully crowned
The work of impious hands!
The sheltering, smooth-stoned massive wall—
The noble figured roof—the glossy marble piers—
The monumental shapes of elder years—
Where are they? Vanished all!
Rite, incense, chant, prayer, mass, have ceased—
All, all have ceased! Only the whitening bones half sunk
In the earth now tell that ever here dwelt monk,
Friar, acolyte, or priest.
Oh! woe, that Wrong should triumph thus!
Woe that the olden right, the rule and the renown
Of the Pure-souled and Meek should thus go down
Before the Tyrannous!
Where wert thou, Justice, in that hour?
Where was thy smiting sword? What had those good men done,
That thou shouldst tamely see them trampled on

Grey Friars: A term for Franciscans; a reference to the gray robes they wore.

Gowans: A type of white or yellow wild flower.

By brutal England's Power?
Alas! I rave! ... If Change is here,
Is it not o'er the land? Is it not too in me?
Yes! I am changed even more than what I see.
Now is my last goal near!
My worn limbs fail—my blood moves cold—
Dimness is on mine eyes—I have seen my children die;
They lie where I too in brief space shall lie—
Under the grassy mould!
I turned away, as toward my grave,
And, all my dark way homeward by the Atlantic's verge,
Resounded in mine ears like to a dirge
The roaring of the wave.

DOCUMENT 33:

Henry Grattan, Speech in the Irish Parliament (16 April 1782)[13]

Henry Grattan (1746–1820) was an Irish politician; he served as a member of the Irish Parliament and later a member of the Parliament of the United Kingdom. He spent the bulk of his career campaigning for legislative independence for Ireland's Parliament. A goal which he largely achieved in 1782 when a series of legal changes meant that Ireland's Parliament was no longer legally subordinate to England. This speech was given to celebrate that achievement.

Mr. Grattan rose, and spoke as follows:

I am now to address a free people: ages have passed away, and this is the first moment in which you could be distinguished by that appellation.

I have spoken on the subject of your liberty so often, that I have nothing to add, and have only to admire by what heaven-directed steps you have proceeded until the whole faculty of the nation is braced up to the act of her own deliverance.

I found Ireland on her knees, I watched over her with an eternal solicitude; I have traced her progress from injuries to arms, and from arms to liberty. Spirit of **Swift**! Spirit of **Molyneux**! your genius has prevailed! Ireland is now a nation! in that new character I hail her! and bowing to her august presence, I say, **Esto perpetua**!

She is no longer a wretched colony, returning thanks to her governor for his rapine, and to her king for his oppression; nor is she now a squabbling, fretful sectary, perplexing her little wits, and firing her furious statutes with bigotry, sophistry, disabilities, and death, to transmit to posterity insignificance and war.

Look to the rest of Europe, and contemplate yourself, and be satisfied. Holland lives on the memory of past achievement; Sweden has lost her liberty; England has sullied her great name by an attempt to enslave her colonies. You are the only people, you, of the nations in Europe, are now the people who excite admiration, and in your present conduct you not only exceed the present generation, but you equal the past. I am not afraid to turn back and look antiquity in the face: the revolution, that great event, whether you call it ancient or modern I know not, was tarnished with

Swift: Jonathan Swift, author of Document 29.

Molyneux: William Molyneux, author of Document 27.

Esto perpetua: Latin for "let it be perpetual."

---

13 *The Speeches of the Right Honourable Henry Grattan*, ed. Henry Grattan (son) (London: Longman, Hurst, Rees, Orme, and Brown, 1822).

bigotry: the great deliverer (for such I must ever call the Prince of Nassau,) was blemished with oppression; he assented to, he was forced to assent to acts which deprived the Catholics of religious, and all the Irish of civil and commercial rights, though the Irish were the only subjects in these islands who had fought in his defence. But you have sought liberty on her own principle: see the Presbyterians of Bangor petition for the freedom of the Catholics of Munster. You, with difficulties innumerable, with dangers not a few, have done what your ancestors wished, but could not accomplish; and what your posterity may preserve, but will never equal: you have moulded the jarring elements of your country into a nation, and have rivalled those great and ancient commonwealths, whom you were taught to admire, and among whom you are now to be recorded: in this proceeding you had not the advantages which were common to other great countries; no monuments, no trophies, none of those outward and visible signs of greatness, such as inspire mankind and connect the ambition of the age which is coming on with the example of that going off, and forms the descent and concatenation of glory: no; you have not had any great act recorded among all your misfortunes, nor have you one public tomb to assemble the crowd, and speak to the living the language of integrity and freedom.

Your historians did not supply the want of monuments; on the contrary, these narrators of your misfortunes, who should have felt for your wrongs, and have punished your oppressors with oppressions, natural scourges, the moral indignation of history, compromised with public villany and trembled; they excited your violence, they suppressed your provocation, and wrote in the chain which entrammelled their country. I am come to break that chain, and I congratulate my country, who, without any of the advantages I speak of, going forth as it were with nothing but a stone and a sling, and what oppression could not take away, the favour of Heaven, accomplished her own redemption, and left you nothing to add and every thing to admire.

You want no trophy now; the records of Parliament are the evidence of your glory: I beg to observe, that the deliverance of Ireland has proceeded from her own right hand; I rejoice as it, for the great requisition of your freedom proceeded from the bounty of England, that great work would have been defective both in renown and security: it was necessary that the soul of the country should have been exalted by the act of her own redemption, and that England should withdraw her claim by operation of treaty, and not of mere grace and condescension; a gratuitous act of parliament, however express, would have been revocable, but the repeal of her claim under operation of treaty is not: in that case, the legislature is put in covenant, and bound by the law of nations, the only law that can legally bind Parliament: never did this country stand so high; England and Ireland treat **ex aequo**. Ireland transmits to the King her claim of right, and requires of

Ex aequo: Latin for "equally placed."

the Parliament of England the repeal of her claim of power, which repeal the English Parliament is to make under the force of a treaty which depends on the law of nations,—a law which cannot be repealed by the Parliament of England.

I rejoice that the people are a party to this treaty, because they are bound to preserve it. There is not a man of forty shillings freehold that is not associated in this our claim of right, and bound to die in its defence; cities, counties, associations, Protestants and Catholics; it seems as if the people had joined in one great national sacrament; a flame has descended from heaven on the intellect of Ireland, plays round her head, and encompasses her understanding with a consecrated glory.

DOCUMENT 34:

From *The Utility of an Union between Great Britain and Ireland,
Considered* (1787)

The Act of Union between Great Britain and Ireland was legally passed in
1800; the idea of a union between the two countries was debated for years
dating to the Act of Union between England and Scotland in 1707. This
pamphlet was published in Dublin in 1787, at a time when most in Ireland did
not support the idea of a union with Great Britain.

e

At present, there is as much delay, difficulty, and opposition to the arrangement of any matter of politics or commerce with Ireland, as in a treaty
with a foreign court: a circumstance that may, if not remedied by the single
possible mode, an Union, whenever a foreign war breaks out, be attended
with fatal consequences to both countries.

Ireland contains about three millions of people. The greater part of these
are Roman Catholics. A people, from the very essence of their religion more
attached to a foreign power, than to their own constitution. Should a war
break out, and the military force be draughted off to distant parts, their
elasticity might act powerfully when the weight that kept it down were
removed. Their attachment to a foreign power, and the idea of a title to the
lands the rebellions of their ancestors legally and in an unconstitutional war
forfeited, might swell and ride to a height that would overflow the narrow
and shallow limits distant war could afford to embank it at home ...

The advantages which would accrue to both countries from an Union,
are many and important. England would acquire an addition of territory
and of people. Her constitution would be more complete, and her commerce more extended, by the partnership. Ireland, on her part, would more
fully participate in the British constitution, trade and police, her peers be
British peers, and her Senators possess a voice in the British Parliament. The
empire would be more compact, and consequently her force greater: every
design to disunite the empire, either by domestic malecontents, or foreign
enemies, wither in the bid: the manners, the morals, and the British spirit
of freedom, become more largely diffused through those ranks of the Irish
to whom they may as yet have omitted to extend their salutary influence;
odious distinctions, and national reflections would be absorbed and lost in
the Union: the inconveniencies arising from divided and too often jarring
councils, be removed; the mode of connection between the two countries
be more honourable. And as the reputation of a country generally bears
a portion to its civilization and culture of the useful arts of life, probably,

multitudes from foreign countries, invited by the mild climate, and fertile soil of Ireland, would pour in, and establish useful manufactures, the riches of which flowing to the heart, and thence returning to the extremities of the empire, would be a circulation nutritious of strength, power, and honour. For most foreigners admire and love the constitution of England: and the advantages that would accrue from that affection, are greatly lost, by the high price of provisions, and a too much reserve and contempt for strangers; very flattering to selfish pride, but injurious to the wealth of the State....

It is reasonable to suppose that a measure so exceedingly extensive in its consequences will meet with some opposition. It is a melancholy trait in the human character, that few as those persons are who know their own interest, the number is still less of those who prefer their country's. Pride, envy, self-interest misunderstood, will throw obstacles in the way of every important measure. Some difficulties certainly may occur in the progress of so weighty an undertaking, but not so many as its enemies wish to persuade the world. We may recollect, that the great **Sir Edward Coke** imagined it would be impracticable ever to accomplish an Union with Scotland: that, at the time it was in agitation, that nation was in a ferment, and opposed it as a subversion of their constitution, an annihilation of their commerce, and pregnant with utter ruin to their country. Notwithstanding this it took effect, by the application of those means which alone can carry any great measure into execution, industry, patience, resolution, and perseverance. How much the opposers of it were mistaken the result has proved. And from this example is it now clear, that the difficulty of such an undertaking, ought not to be considered as an obstacle to its accomplishment....

Sir Edward Coke: An English lawyer and politician, lived from 1552 to 1634.

For the accomplishment of this salutary Union proposed, what period can be so proper as the present, when neither foreign war nor domestic feuds engage the public attention; when the kingdom's finances, resources, and warlike affairs, are in so flourishing a situation, as at this time to bid defiance to the malice or envy of all her natural enemies; when there exist no particular causes or subjects of animosity between the sister countries, and before the enemies of both sow the seeds of dissention, or the well-meaning but misinformed friends of either conceive that their interests can in any case be opposite. How superior is the glory attendant on that minister, who, instead of carrying desolation, rapine, and bloodshed into foreign countries, to encrease an empire of vast extent, employs the influence of power by uniting and consolidating all the parts of the dominions Great Britain yet possesses, to promote the prosperity and augment the happiness of the whole!

DOCUMENT 35:

Theobald Wolfe Tone, et al., *Declaration and Resolutions of the Society of United Irishmen of Belfast* (1791)

Theobald Wolfe Tone (1763–98) was one of the founding members of the United Irishmen, a republican society founded in 1791 that sought to reform the Irish parliament to incorporate the principles of civil, political, and religious liberty. They were inspired by the French Revolution, begun two years earlier in 1789. Wolfe Tone likely wrote the declaration alone, although with the advice and consultation of other members. The group was driven underground after war broke out between France and Great Britain, and became a secret revolutionary society. It organized the revolution of 1798, which failed. Wolfe Tone and other leaders were executed for treason that same year.

In the present great era of reform, when unjust Governments are falling in every quarter of Europe; when religious persecution is compelled to abjure her tyranny over conscience; when the rights of man are ascertained in theory, and that theory substantiated by practice; when antiquity can no longer defend absurd and oppressive forms against the common sense and common interests of mankind; when all Government is acknowledged to originate from the people, and to be so far only obligatory as it protects their rights and promotes their welfare; we think it our duty, as Irishmen, to come forward, and state what we feel to be our heavy grievance, and what we know to be its effectual remedy. We have no national Government—we are ruled by Englishmen, and the servants of Englishmen whose object is the interest of another country, whose instrument is corruption, and whose strength is the weakness of Ireland; and these men have the whole of the power and patronage of the country as means to seduce and subdue the honesty and spirit of her representatives in the legislature.

Such an extreme power, acting with uniform force, in a direction too frequently opposite to the true line of our obvious interests, can be resisted with effect solely by unanimity, decision and spirit in the people—qualities which may be exerted most legally, constitutionally, and efficaciously by that great measure essential to the prosperity, and freedom of Ireland—an equal representation of all the people in Parliament. We do not here mention as grievances the rejection of a place-bill, of a pension bill, of a responsibility-bill, the sale of peerages in one house, the corruption publicly avowed in the other, nor the notorious infamy of borough traffic between both, not that we are insensible to their enormity, but that we consider them as but symptoms of that mortal disease which corrodes the vitals of our constitution, and leaves to the people in their own government but the shadow of a name.

Impressed with these sentiments, we have agreed to form an association to be called "The Society of United Irishmen," and we do pledge ourselves to our country, and mutually to each other, that we will steadily support and endeavour, by all due means, to carry into effect the following resolutions:

FIRST RESOLVED: That the weight of English influence on the Government of this country is so great as to require a cordial union among all the people of Ireland to maintain that balance which is essential to the preservation of our liberties and the extension of our commerce.

SECOND: That the sole constitutional mode by which this influence can be opposed is by a complete and radical reform of the representation of the people in Parliament.

THIRD: That no reform is practicable, efficacious, or just, which shall not include Irishmen of every religious persuasion.

Satisfied, as we are, that the intestine divisions among Irishmen have too often given encouragement and impunity to profligate, audacious and corrupt administrations, in measure which, but for these divisions, they durst not have attempted, we submit our resolutions to the nation as the basis of our political faith. We have gone to what we conceive to be the root of the evil. We have stated what we conceive to be the remedy. With a Parliament thus reformed, everything is easy; without it, nothing can be done. And we do call on, and most earnestly exhort, our countrymen in general to follow our example, and to form similar societies in every quarter of the kingdom for the promotion of constitutional knowledge, the abolition of bigotry in religion and politics, and the equal distribution of the rights of men through all sects and denominations of Irishmen. The people, when thus collected, will feel their own weight, and secure that power which theory has already admitted to be their portion, and to which, if they be not aroused by their present provocation to vindicate it, they deserve to forfeit their pretensions for ever.

DOCUMENT 36:

From Patrick Sheehy, *Union a Plague* (1799)

In the aftermath of the 1798 Rebellion the question of a union between Great Britain and Ireland received renewed attention. Many in Ireland were opposed to a union. The Irish parliament had gained legislative independence in 1782 and they did not wish to lose their legislative independence. Ultimately the Acts of Union were passed in both the parliament of Great Britain and the parliament of Ireland in 1800. This pamphlet is an example of anti-unionist sentiment that circulated in Ireland prior to the passage of the Act.

Let us consider but for a moment, we must clearly see the folly of two independent nations attempting to discuss a treaty, by which one of them surrenders her independence to the other. This should not be called a treaty, it ill deserves the name; call it rather an imposition. If ever the treaty of an Union is carried into effect, believe me both nations will not agree on the terms. The surrendering party will not yield its consent to the loss of its legislature, to the loss of its independence. Depend upon it, something besides the conviction of its utility will urge the adoption of this fatal measure. It may not be unwise to observe, that an Union has been always a favorite object with Great Britain, but a nauseous pill to Ireland, from which she turned aside when even mention was made of it. Whence this disgust, this loathing, this universal detestation of a reprobated measure? From a conviction that it is a measure that will be big with mischief and calamity to Ireland. Why is Great Britain so peculiarly attached to the object of an Union? Has she from time to time immemorial looked with an impartial eye on Ireland, and unceasingly urged every or any measure that might promote the interest of Ireland? Or has she not considered every beneficial measure granted her sister as a diminution of her own capital? Look then with a jealous eye, my countrymen, on this superannuated project of an Union; it is the deformed offspring of British ambition. This decrepit unnatural child has a claim on the British minister, and behold the time when the claim is renewed; in the Memoire it is said "Our dissensions and our calamities have called forth the project of a new, and it is hoped, a final arrangement in the politics of this island"; that is, the old project is revived when we are divided and oppressed with calamity. What a fine time for discussion, for sober temperate discussion, which is recommended by the Author of *Arguments For and Against an Union* considered. When an advantage is thus taken of our distressed situation, in what light shall we view an offer of this kind? In our sober senses we would look on it with horror; we would fly from it as from an hideous monster; and now that we are intoxicated with misery and dissension, we are invited to a sober discussion of this seemingly less monstrous subject.

He must be a great prophet that can say this arrangement will be final as to our dissensions and calamities. Is it not possible that the introduction of this once hateful measure may increase our dissensions and calamities? It is not impossible but this very Union may work a contrary way, and produce a separation, a calamity to be dreaded by Great Britain as well as Ireland. We have sometimes heard of one disorder being banished by another; may not the detestation of an Union banish the rage of political and even religious animosity? Though the latter is not now, thank God, very rancorous, at least universally so, as in the days of ignorance, I am happy enough to see bigotry so weak and feeble as to be obliged sometimes to ride on the backs of police and self-interest. She has lost much of her poisonous vigour, and is in need of other assistance to perpetrate horrid deeds. May she grow weaker day by day, nay, hour by hour, until my fair country will have to rejoice at her death, and be no more torn by religious animosity, or rather besotted ignorance. Expecting to be pardoned this digression, I say one madness may expel another, Catholic and Protestant may lay aside their dissensions, their hellish feuds, and become Irishmen; then the minister would find that he introduced a final arrangement of politics that would not be very pleasing to him....

Though the Union did not strike the gentleman with an assemblage of horrors when he wrote his Memoire, perhaps, though in the abstract, it will now strike him with horror. The conditions of the contract shall not delay my decision; I see the measure is in its nature pernicious, the conditions cannot be salutary; I am obliged to resist the measure **in limine**, and its discussion is at all events inadmissible. If a robber, or any evil disposed person, shall come to my house at an unreasonable hour, and talk to me of a treaty, I shall resist the measure, I shall listen to no conditions; they must be pernicious; the thief shall not pass the threshold; constant experience is my monitor; I see every day such treaties attempted, to rob, and sometimes to murder the inhabitants. What does experience tell us of treaties of union between nations, that the weaker has invariably been robbed, plundered, and enslaved by the stronger. That an Union bears on its front strong features of mischief and injury to Ireland is certain, from the contradictory language brought forward to support it. The gentleman cannot admit a separate legislature to be essential to Ireland, and yet he recommends a treaty for consolidating the parliaments of Great Britain and Ireland. How can the parliament of Ireland be consolidated, if Ireland be supposed not to have a separate legislature? Perhaps by consolidated is meant incorporated; that is, mixing the two bodies into one: if so, one condition of the Union has transpired, from which we may learn the nature of this monstrous incorporation; one

In limine: On the threshold.

hundred out of three of the Irish legislature will be sent to the English house; in other words, a part or member of the Irish body shall be grafted on the English body. No doubt, the Irish member hanging on the English body will cut a fine figure: is this incorporation? Is this mixing body with body? This inconsistency must contribute to prove, that the treaty is inadmissible at all events....

PART 3

Modern Ireland and England before Independence (1800–1921)

DOCUMENT 37:

From An Act for the Union of Great Britain and Ireland (1800)

> Parallel acts were passed in the parliaments of both Great Britain and Ireland in 1800. They came into force on 1 January 1801 and the parliament of Ireland was dissolved. A new parliament of the United Kingdom was created, which contained representatives from Ireland but which met in London.

℮

Preamble.

Whereas in pursuance of his Majesty's most gracious recommendation to the two Houses of Parliament in Great Britain and Ireland respectively, to consider of such measures as might best tend to strengthen and consolidate the connection between the two kingdoms, the two Houses of the Parliament of Great Britain and the two Houses of the Parliament of Ireland have severally agreed and resolved, that, in order to promote and secure the essential interests of Great Britain and Ireland, and to consolidate the strength, power and resources of the British Empire, it will be adviseable to concur in such measures as may best tend to unite the two kingdoms of Great Britain and Ireland into one kingdom, in such manner, and on such terms and conditions, as may be established by the Acts of the respective Parliaments of Great Britain and Ireland:

The Parliaments of England and Ireland have agreed upon the articles following:

And whereas, in furtherance of the said resolution, both Houses of the said two Parliaments respectively have likewise agreed upon certain Articles for effectuating and establishing the said purposes, in the tenor following:

Article First

That Great Britain and Ireland shall upon Jan. 1, 1801, be united into one kingdom; and that the titles appertaining to the crown, &c. shall be such as his Majesty shall be pleased to appoint.

That it be the First Article of the Union of the kingdoms of Great Britain and Ireland, that the said kingdoms of Great Britain and Ireland shall, upon the first day of January which shall be in the year of our Lord one thousand eight hundred and one, and for ever after, be united into one kingdom, by the name of the United Kingdom of Great Britain and Ireland, and that the royal stile and titles appertaining to the imperial crown of the said United Kingdom and its dependencies, and also the ensigns, armorial flags and banners thereof, shall be such as his Majesty, by his royal proclamation under the Great Seal of the United Kingdom, shall be pleased to appoint.

Article Second

That the succession to the crown shall continue limited and settled as at present.

That it be the Second Article of Union, that the succession to the imperial crown of the said United Kingdom, and of the dominions thereunto belonging, shall continue limited and settled in the same manner as the succession to the imperial crown of the said kingdoms of Great Britain and Ireland now stands limited and settled, according to the existing laws and to the terms of union between England and Scotland.

Article Third

That the United Kingdom be represented in one Parliament.

That it be the Third Article of Union, that the said United Kingdom be represented in one and the same Parliament, to be styled the Parliament of the United Kingdom of Great Britain and Ireland....

[...]

Article Sixth

The subjects of Great Britain and Ireland shall be on the same footing in respect of trade and navigation, and in all treaties with foreign powers the subjects of Ireland shall have the same privileges as British subjects.

That it be the Sixth Article of Union, that his Majesty's subjects of Great Britain and Ireland shall from and after the first day of January one thousand eight hundred and one be entitled to the same privileges and be on the same footing, as to encouragements and bounties on the like articles, being the growth, produce or manufacture of either country respectively, and generally in respect of trade and navigation in all ports and places in the United Kingdom and its dependencies; and that in all treaties made by his Majesty his heirs and successors, with any foreign power, his Majesty's subjects of Ireland shall have the same privileges and be on the same footing as his Majesty's subjects of Great Britain.

From January 1, 1801, all prohibitions and bounties on the export of articles the produce or manufacture of either country to the other shall cease.

That from the first day of January one thousand eight hundred and one all prohibitions and bounties on the export of articles, the growth, produce or manufacture of either country, to the other shall cease and determine; and that the said articles shall thenceforth be exported from one country to the other without duty or bounty on such export:

All articles the produce or manufacture of either country, not herein-after enumerated as subject to specific duties, shall be imported into each country from the other, duty free, other than the countervailing duties in the Schedule No. 1. or to such as shall hereafter be imposed by the united Parliament;

That all articles, the Growth, Produce or Manufacture of either Country (not herein-after enumerated as subject to specific duties), shall from thenceforth be imported into each country from the other free from duty other than such countervailing duties ... as shall hereafter be imposed by the Parliament of the United Kingdom, in the manner herein-after provided.

DOCUMENT 38:

From the Catholic Relief Act (1829)

Also known as the Catholic Emancipation Act, this was passed by the parliament of the United Kingdom following a vigorous campaign led by the Irish politician Daniel O'Connell. The act permitted members of the Catholic church, such as O'Connell, to serve in parliament. A compromise to ensure that the controversial bill passed was to simultaneously pass the *Parliamentary Elections (Ireland) Act* of 1829, which disenfranchised small landholders.

ev

AN ACT FOR THE RELIEF OF HIS MAJESTY'S ROMAN CATHOLIC SUBJECTS

Whereas by various Acts of parliament certain restraints and disabilities are imposed on the Roman Catholic subjects of his Majesty, to which other subjects of his Majesty are not liable, and whereas it is expedient that such restraints and disabilities shall be from henceforth discontinued, and whereas by various Acts certain oaths and certain declarations, commonly called the declarations against transubstantiation and the invocation of saints and the sacrifice of the mass, as practised in the Church of Rome, are or may be required to be taken, made, and subscribed by the subjects of his Majesty as qualifications for sitting and voting in parliament and for the enjoyment of certain offices, franchises, and civil rights, be it enacted ... that from and after the commencement of this Act all such parts of the said Acts as require the said declarations, or either of them, to be made or subscribed by any of his Majesty's subjects as a qualification for sitting and voting in parliament or for the exercise or enjoyment of any office, franchise, or civil right, be and the same are (save as hereinafter provided and excepted) hereby repealed.

II. And be it enacted that ... it shall be lawful for any person professing the Roman Catholic religion, being a peer, or who shall after the commencement of this Act be returned as a member of the House of Commons, to sit and vote in either house of parliament respectively, being in all other respects duly qualified to sit and vote therein, upon taking and subscribing the following oath, instead of the oaths of allegiance, supremacy, and abjuration: I, A.B., do sincerely promise and swear that I will be faithful and bear true allegiance to his majesty King **George the Fourth** and will defend him to the utmost of my power against all conspiracies and attempts whatever, which shall be made against his person, crown, or dignity. And I will do my utmost endeavour to disclose and make known to his Majesty, his heirs and

George the Fourth:
George IV (1762–1830, r. 1820–30) was very reluctant to grant royal assent to this act.

successors, all treasons and traitorous conspiracies which may be formed against him or them. And I do faithfully promise to maintain, support, and defend, to the utmost of my power, the succession of the Crown, which succession, by an Act entitled An Act for the further limitation of the Crown and better securing the rights and liberties of the subject, is and stands limited to the **Princess Sophia, electress of Hanover**, and the heirs of her body, being Protestants; hereby utterly renouncing and abjuring any obedience or allegiance unto any other person claiming or pretending a right to the Crown of this realm. And I do further declare that it is not an article of my faith, and that I do renounce, reject, and abjure the opinion that princes excommunicated or deprived by the Pope or any other authority of the see of Rome may be deposed or murdered by their subjects or by any person whatsoever. And I do declare that I do not believe that the Pope of Rome, or any other foreign prince, prelate, person, state, or potentate, hath or ought to have any temporal or civil jurisdiction, power, superiority, or pre-eminence, directly or indirectly, within this realm. I do swear that I will defend to the utmost of my power the settlement of the property within this realm as established by the laws, and I do hereby disclaim, disavow, and solemnly abjure any intention to subvert the present church establishment as settled by law within this realm, and I do solemnly swear that I never will exercise any privilege to which I am or may become entitled, to disturb or weaken the Protestant religion or Protestant government in the United Kingdom. And I do solemnly, in the presence of God, profess, testify, and declare that I do make this declaration and every part thereof in the plain and ordinary sense of the words of this oath, without any evasion, equivocation, or mental reservation whatsoever. So help me God.

> **Princess Sophia, electress of Hanover:** (1630–1714) a protestant heir of James I; the Hanoverian dynasty then on the throne claimed the throne of Great Britain through their descent from her.

V. And be it further enacted that it shall be lawful for persons professing the Roman Catholic religion to vote at elections of members to serve in parliament for England and for Ireland, and also to vote at the elections of representative peers of Scotland and of Ireland, and to be elected such representative peers, being in all other respects duly qualified, upon taking and subscribing the oath hereinbefore appointed and set forth....

X. And be it enacted that it shall be lawful for any of his Majesty's subjects professing the Roman Catholic religion to hold, exercise, and enjoy all civil and military offices and places of trust or profit under his Majesty, his heirs or successors; and to exercise any other franchise or civil right ... upon taking and subscribing ... the oath hereinbefore appointed....

XII. Provided also, and be it further enacted that nothing herein contained shall extend or be construed to extend to enable any person or persons professing the Roman Catholic religion to hold or exercise the office of guardians and justices of the United Kingdom or of regent of the United Kingdom, under whatever name, style, or title such office may be constituted, nor to enable any person, otherwise than as he is now by law enabled, to hold or enjoy the office of lord high chancellor, lord keeper or lord commissioner of the great seal of Great Britain or Ireland, or the office of Lord Lieutenant, or lord deputy, or other chief governor or governors of Ireland, or his Majesty's high commissioner to the General Assembly of the Church of Scotland.

XIV. And be it enacted that it shall be lawful for any of his Majesty's subjects professing the Roman Catholic religion to be a member of any lay body corporate, and to hold any civil office or place of trust or profit therein, and to do any corporate act or vote in any corporate election or other proceeding, upon taking and subscribing the oath hereby appointed and set forth, instead of the oaths of allegiance, supremacy, and abjuration, and upon taking also such other oath or oaths as may now by law be required to be taken by any persons becoming members of such lay body corporate....

XXVI. And be it further enacted, that if any Roman Catholic ecclesiastic, or any member of any of the orders, communities, or societies hereinafter mentioned, shall, after the commencement of this Act, exercise any of the rites or ceremonies of the Roman Catholic religion or wear the habits of his order, save within the usual places of worship of the Roman Catholic religion, or in private houses, such ecclesiastic or other person shall, being thereof convicted by due courses of law, forfeit for every such offence the sum of £50.

XXXIV. And be it further enacted that in case any person shall after the commencement of this Act, within any part of this United Kingdom, be admitted or become a Jesuit, or brother, or member of any other such religious order, community, or society as aforesaid, such person shall be deemed and taken to be guilty of a misdemeanour, and being thereof lawfully convicted, shall be sentenced and ordered to be banished from the United Kingdom for the term of his natural life.

XXXVII. Provided always, and be it enacted that nothing herein contained shall extend or be construed to extend in any manner to affect any religious order, community, or establishment consisting of females bound by religious or monastic vows.

DOCUMENT 39:

British and Irish newspaper cartoons of Daniel O'Connell (1840s)

Daniel O'Connell (1775–1847) was arguably the most significant Irish
politician of the nineteenth century. In Ireland he was hailed as "The
Liberator," while opinion in England was more mixed; he was often seen
as a threatening and revolutionary figure despite his public commitment to
nonviolent political agitation. This can be seen in the two illustrations below,
the first by an Irish nationalist cartoonist William Tell, which was published
in Dublin in 1844 and portrays O'Connell as a liberating figure. The second is
from the satirical English magazine *Punch* in 1843, which portrays O'Connell
as a corrupt figure setting himself up as a king.

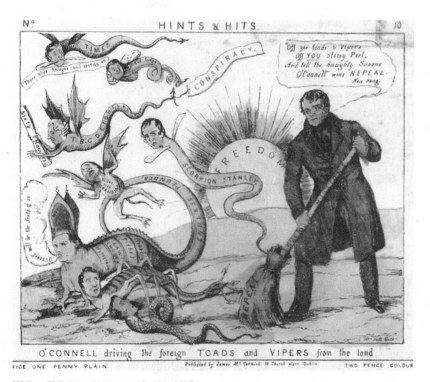

William Tell, *Hints & Hits*, 1844 (held by NLI)

KING O'CONNELL AT TARA.

Punch, 26 August 1843

From Daniel O'Connell, Speeches on Catholic emancipation and the repeal of the Act of Union (1840s)

Daniel O'Connell was born to a wealthy Catholic family in County Kerry. He was educated at Catholic schools in France during the bloodiest years of the French Revolution and developed a lifelong abhorrence of political violence. He rose to prominence in Ireland campaigning for Catholic emancipation and managed to help build a mass movement based around an organization known as the Catholic Association. After achieving Catholic emancipation in 1829 and taking his own seat in parliament, he dedicated the rest of his political career attempting to repeal the Act of Union. O'Connell died in 1847 while on a pilgrimage to Rome.

Letter to the Catholics of Ireland[1]

Fellow-Countrymen—I hope I shall not be deemed presumptuous in addressing you. The part I have taken in Catholic affairs induces me to expect that you will believe me to be actuated by no other motives than those of an honest and an ardent zeal to promote your interests and to attain your freedom.

The period is at length arrived when we may ascertain, and place beyond any doubt, whether it be determined that we are forever to remain a degraded and inferior class in our native land, and so to remain, without any one rational cause, or even any one avowable pretext. We may now reduce the enemies of liberty of conscience to this dilemma: either now to grant us emancipation, or to proclaim to us, and to the world, that as long as the parliament shall be constituted as it is at present, so long all hope of emancipation is to be totally extinguished.

To this dilemma our enemies may be reduced; and it is a precious advantage to be able, for the first time in the history of Catholic affairs, to place them in a situation in which emancipation cannot be refused without an avowal of stern, unrelenting, and inexorable bigotry; or of worse—of disposition to make use of bigotry as an instrument to perpetuate the divisions, dissensions, and consequent degradation and oppression of Ireland.

Our enemies must now be frank and candid. They have not at present—and they will not have, unless we furnish it to them—any, the slightest pretence for resisting emancipation. The pretences which they hitherto used

---

1   John O'Connell, ed., *The Select Speeches of Daniel O'Connell, M.P.* (Dublin: James Duffy, 1862), 63–65.

are all refuted and exploded. Where could the man now be found sufficiently audacious as to resist our claims on the stale pretexts of Catholic illiberality, English hostility, or Irish turbulence?

Catholic illiberality! Why, the man who should use that argument would now be laughed to scorn. He would be told that the first, last, and best examples of religious freedom have been given by Catholic states—Maryland, Hungary, and Bavaria would be triumphantly cited. In short, in every Catholic country in the world, possessing any share of popular government, liberty of conscience is already established.

Even in Spain, the Cortes, of whom two-thirds were priests, proclaimed the liberty of the press, and abolished the Inquisition. We therefore can well afford to make a present to the bigots, of the petticoat-making tyrants of Spain, and of our other worthy ally of Portugal or Brazil; but we can proudly and confidently claim for Catholics the palm of liberality.

No man can now state as a reason for rejecting our claims, the hostility of the people of England. It was a favourite topic with the bigoted part of the present administration. They admitted that emancipation would conciliate Ireland, but then they said that any advantages to be derived from such conciliation would be more than counterbalanced by the irritation and permanent discontent which, they alleged, any concession to the Catholics, would create in England.

Oh, how egregiously they calumniated the intelligent, rational, and honest people of England! What a powerful refutation have the English people given to this calumny? In the voice of assembled myriads they have proclaimed the utter falsehood of the base imputation. Seven centuries of oppression are already forgiven; and the English name, which we seldom pronounced with complacency, begins to sound sweetly in the ears of our children. May their rulers imitate the good sense of the English people, and speak to the heart of the Irish nation a language which she has never yet heard from an imperial legislature! But whether this useful lesson shall be thrown away on the English parliament or not, this much at least is certain—that no apprehension can be entertained of irritating the people of England by conceding to us our rights. It will gratify their generosity as much as it will propitiate our affections and ensure our gratitude.

There remained one other pretext to colour the resistance to our claims—it was Irish turbulence; and where no facts of aggression would be adduced, we were then accused of being turbulent in words. And this was an argument to resist emancipation! Oh, most sapient legislators! Oh, most profound and enlightened statesmen of England! A nation was to continue in slavery because some half dozen of demagogues or agitators, as you were pleased to call us, spoke with bitterness of their oppressions, and taunted with ridicule their oppressors!

But even this poor and paltry pretence is gone by. Not a word, not a breath has escaped us for the last three years which could be found fault with by the most fastidious delicacy; and as to the conduct of the Irish people, it has been and it is exemplary.

In Favour of the Repeal of the Union[2]

I accept with the greatest alacrity the high honor you have done me in calling me to the chair of this majestic meeting. I feel more honored than I ever did in my life, with one single exception, and that related to, if possible, an equally majestic meeting at Tara. But I must say that if a comparison were instituted between them, it would take a more discriminating eye than mine to discover any difference between them. There are the same incalculable numbers; there is the same firmness; there is the same determination; there is the same exhibition of love to old Ireland; there is the same resolution not to violate the peace; not to be guilty of the slightest outrage; not to give the enemy power by committing a crime, but peacefully and manfully to stand together in the open day, to protest before man and in the presence of God against the iniquity of continuing the Union.

At **Tara** I protested against the Union—I repeat the protest at Mullaghmast. I declare solemnly my thorough conviction as a constitutional lawyer, that the Union is totally void in point of principle and of constitutional force. I tell you that no portion of the empire had the power to traffic on the rights and liberties of the Irish people. The Irish people nominated them to make laws, and not legislatures. They were appointed to act under the Constitution, and not annihilate it. Their delegation from the people was confined within the limits of the Constitution, and the moment the Irish Parliament went beyond those limits and destroyed the Constitution, that moment it annihilated its own power, but could not annihilate the immortal spirit of liberty which belongs, as a rightful inheritance, to the people of Ireland. Take it, then, from me that the Union is void....

I want not the support of France; I want not the support of America; I have physical support enough about me to achieve any change; but you know well that it is not my plan—I will not risk the safety of one of you. I could not afford the loss of one of you—I will protect you all, and it is better for you all to be merry and alive, to enjoy the repeal of the Union; but there is not a man of you there that would not, if we were attacked unjustly and illegally, be ready to stand in the open field by my side. Let every man that concurs in that sentiment lift up his hand.

Tara: O'Connell's speech at the Hill of Tara was attended by a crowd of several hundred thousand; this speech at Mullaghmast was apparently almost as big.

---

2   Daniel O'Connell, "In Favor of the Repeal of the Union," in *The World's Famous Orations*, ed. William Jennings Bryan (New York: Funk & Wagnalls, 1906).

The assertion of that sentiment is our sure protection; for no person will attack us, and we will attack nobody. Indeed, it would be the height of absurdity for us to think of making any attack; for there is not one man in his senses, in Europe or America, that does not admit that the repeal of the Union is now inevitable. The English papers taunted us, and their writers laughed us to scorn; but now they admit that it is impossible to resist the application for repeal. More power to you. But that even shows we have power enough to know how to use it. Why, it is only this week that one of the leading London newspapers, called the *Morning Herald,* which had a reporter at the Lismore meeting, published an account of that great and mighty meeting, and in that account the writer expressly says that it will be impossible to refuse so peaceable, so determined, so unanimous a people as the people of Ireland the restoration of their domestic legislature....

O my friends, I will keep you clear of all treachery—there shall be no bargain, no compromise with England—we shall take nothing but repeal, and a Parliament in College Green. You will never, by my advice, confide in any false hopes they hold out to you; never confide in anything coming from them, or cease from your struggle, no matter what promise may be held to you, until you hear me say I am satisfied; and I will tell you where I will say that—near the statue of King William, in College Green. No; we came here to express our determination to die to a man, if necessary, in the cause of old Ireland. We came to take advice of each other, and, above all, I believe you came here to take my advice. I can tell you, I have the game in my hand—I have the triumph secure—I have the repeal certain, if you but obey my advice.

I will go slow—you must allow me to do so—but you will go sure. No man shall find himself imprisoned or persecuted who follows my advice. I have led you thus far in safety; I have swelled the multitude of repealers until they are identified with the entire population, or nearly the entire population, of the land, for seven-eighths of the Irish people are now enrolling themselves repealers. I do not want more power; I have power enough; and all I ask of you is to allow me to use it. I will go on quietly and slowly, but I will go on firmly, and with a certainty of success. I am now arranging a plan for the formation of the Irish House of Commons....

I wish to live long enough to have perfect justice administered to Ireland, and liberty proclaimed throughout the land....

Yes, my friends, the Union was begot in iniquity—it was perpetuated in fraud and cruelty. It was no compact, no bargain, but it was an act of the most decided tyranny and corruption that was ever yet perpetrated. Trial by jury was suspended—the right of personal protection was at an end—courts-martial sat throughout the land—and the County of Kildare, among others, flowed with blood. We shall stand peaceably side by side in the face of every enemy. Oh, how delighted was I in the scenes which I witnessed as I came along here to-day! How my heart throbbed, how my spirit was elevated, how my bosom swelled with delight at the multitude which I beheld, and which I shall behold, of the stalwart and strong men of Kildare! I was delighted at the activity and force that I saw around me, and my old heart grew warm again in admiring the beauty of the dark-eyed maids and matrons of Kildare. Oh, there is a starlight sparkling from the eye of a Kildare beauty that is scarcely equaled, and could not be excelled, all over the world. And remember that you are the sons, the fathers, the brothers, and the husbands of such women, and a traitor or a coward could never be connected with any of them. Yes, I am in a county, remarkable in the history of Ireland for its bravery and its misfortune, for its credulity in the faith of others, for its people judged of the Saxon by the honesty and honor of their own natures. I am in a county celebrated for the sacredness of shrines and **fanes**. I am in a county where the lamp of Kildare's holy shrine burned with its sacred fire, through ages of darkness and storm—that fire which for six centuries burned before the high altar without being extinguished, being fed continuously, without the slightest interruption, and it seemed to me to have been not an inapt representation of the continuous fidelity and religious love of country of the men of Kildare.

Fanes: Temples.

Yes, you have those high qualities—religious fidelity, continuous love of country. Even your enemies admit that the world has never produced any people that exceeded the Irish in activity and strength. The Scottish philosopher has declared, and the French philosopher has confirmed it, that number one in the human race is, blessed be Heaven, the Irishman. In moral virtue, in religion, in perseverance, and in glorious temperance, you excel. Have I any **teetotalers** here? Yes, it is teetotalism that is repealing the Union. I could not afford to bring you together, I would not dare to bring you together, but that I had the teetotalers for my police.

Teetotalers: Someone who never drinks alcohol.

Yes, among the nations of the earth, Ireland stands number one in the physical strength of her sons and in the beauty and purity of her daughters. Ireland, land of my forefathers, how my mind expands, and my spirit walks abroad in something of majesty, when I contemplate the high qualities, inestimable virtues, and true purity and piety and religious fidelity of the inhabitants of your green fields and productive mountains. Oh, what a scene surrounds us! It is not only the countless thousands of brave and active and peaceable and religious men that are here assembled, but Nature herself has written her character with the finest beauty in the verdant plains that surround us.

Let any man run around the horizon with his eye, and tell me if created nature ever produced anything so green and so lovely, so undulating, so teeming with production. The richest harvests that any land can produce are those reaped in Ireland; and then here are the sweetest meadows, the greenest fields, the loftiest mountains, the purest streams, the noblest rivers, the most capacious harbors—and her water power is equal to turn the machinery of the whole world. O my friends, it is a country worth fighting for—it is a country worth dying for; but, above all, it is a country worth being tranquil, determined, submissive, and docile for; disciplined as you are in obedience to those who are breaking the way, and trampling down the barriers between you and your constitutional liberty, I will see every man of you having a vote, and every man protected by the ballot from the agent or landlord. I will see labor protected, and every title to possession recognized, when you are industrious and honest. I will see prosperity again throughout your land—the busy hum of the shuttle and the tinkling of the smithy shall be heard again. We shall see the nailer employed even until the middle of the night, and the carpenter covering himself with his chips. I will see prosperity in all its gradations spreading through a happy, contented, religious land. I will hear the hymn of a happy people go forth at sunrise to God in praise of His mercies—and I will see the evening sun set down among the uplifted hands of a religious and free population. Every blessing that man can bestow and religion can confer upon the faithful heart shall spread throughout the land. Stand by me—join with me—I will say be obedient to me, and Ireland shall be free.

From Benjamin Disraeli, Speech in the House of Commons on the Irish Question (1844)[3]

Benjamin Disraeli (1804–81) was a notable English Conservative politician and twice prime minister of the United Kingdom in 1868 and from 1874 to 1880. The Irish Question was the name given by nineteenth-century British politicians to the debate over how to respond to Irish nationalism. In this excerpt from a House of Commons debate over the state of Ireland in 1844, Disraeli gives his definition of the Irish Question.

... The noble Lord offered a little thing in a great way. That was not what he wished. He wanted to see a public man come forward and say what the Irish question was. One said it was a physical question; another, a spiritual. Now, it was the absence of the aristocracy; then the absence of railroads. It was the Pope one day; potatoes the next. Let them consider Ireland as they would any other country similarly situated, in their closets. Then they would see a teeming population, which with reference to the cultivated soil, was denser to the square mile than that of China; created solely by agriculture, with none of those sources of wealth which are developed with civilization; and sustained consequently upon the lowest conceivable diet, so that in case of failure they had no other means of subsistence upon which they could fall back. That dense population in extreme distress inhabited an island where there was an established church which was not their church; and a territorial aristocracy, the richest of whom lived in distant capitals. Thus they had a starving population, an absentee aristocracy, and an alien Church, and, in addition, the weakest executive in the world. That was the Irish question. Well, then, what would hon. Gentlemen say if they were reading of a country in that position? They would say at once, "The remedy is revolution." But the Irish could not have a revolution; and why? Because Ireland was connected with another and a more powerful country. Then what was the consequence? The connexion with England thus became the cause of the present state of Ireland. If the connexion with England prevented a revolution, and a revolution were the only remedy, England logically was in the odious position of being the cause of all the misery in Ireland. What then, was the duty of an English Minister? To effect by his policy all those changes which a revolution would do by force. That was the Irish question in its integrity. It was quite evident to effect that we must have an executive

3   Hansard: HC Deb 16 February 1844 vol. 72 cc1001–96.

in Ireland which should bear a much nearer relation to the leading classes and characters of the country than it did at present. There must be a much more comprehensive executive, and, then, having produced order, the rest was a question of time. There was no possible way by which the physical condition of the people could be improved by act of Parliament. The moment they had a strong executive, a just administration, and ecclesiastical equality, they would have order in Ireland, and the improvement of the physical condition of the people would follow—not very rapidly, perhaps, and they must not flatter themselves that it would—but what were fifty years even in the history of a nation? But he would say, if these recommendations were adopted, that in fifty years hence the men who should succeed the present generation in Parliament would find the people of Ireland a contented and thriving peasantry.

Thomas Davis, "A Nation Once Again" (1844)[4]

Thomas Davis (1814–45) was an Irish poet and writer. He was also a founding editor of the *Nation*, an Irish nationalist newspaper, and a leader of the Young Ireland movement. Young Ireland was a political and cultural nationalist movement. It split from Daniel O'Connell's Repeal Association in 1847 over the issues of clericalism and the use of physical force in nationalist struggle. Thomas Davis died the year before the split in 1846 from scarlet fever. "A Nation Once Again" is one of his most famous songs/poems, and quickly became a rallying cry for Irish nationalists.

When boyhood's fire was in my blood
I read of ancient freemen,
For Greece and Rome who bravely stood,
Three hundred men and **three men**;
And then I prayed I yet might see
Our fetters rent in twain,
And Ireland, long a province, be
A Nation once again.

And, from that time, through wildest woe,
That hope has shone a far light,
Nor could love's brightest summer glow
Outshine that solemn starlight;
It seemed to watch above my head
In forum, field, and fane,
Its angel voice sang round my bed,
"A Nation once again."

It whisper'd too, that freedom's ark
And service high and holy,
Would be profaned by feelings dark
And passions vain or lowly;
For, Freedom comes from God's right hand,

Three hundred men: A reference to the Battle of Thermopylae where 300 Spartan soldiers held back a much large Persian army.

Three men: A reference to a sixth-century Roman battle where three soldiers defended the Pons Sublicius Bridge while the rest of the Roman army crossed safely.

---

4   Thomas, Davis, *The Poems of Thomas Davis: Now First Collected: with Notes and Historical Illustrations*, Thomas Wallis, ed. (Dublin: J. Duffy, 1846), 73–74.

And needs a Godly train;
And righteous men must make our land
"A Nation once again."

So, as I grew from boy to man,
I bent me to that bidding
My spirit of each selfish plan
And cruel passion ridding;
For, thus I hoped some day to aid,
Oh, can such hope be vain?
When my dear country shall be made
A Nation once again.

DOCUMENT 43:

From Charles Trevelyan, *The Irish Crisis* (1848)

Charles Trevelyan (1807–86) was an English civil servant who served as assistant secretary of the Treasury during the Great Irish Famine (1845–52). In that capacity he oversaw famine relief efforts. Trevelyan was a strong advocate for laissez-faire economics; as director of the famine relief effort he was frequently blamed for the slow and inadequate response of the government to the crisis. *The Irish Crisis* was published in 1848 to respond to those criticisms.

The remedy for this state of things is simply the sale of the encumbered estate, or of a sufficient portion of it to enable the owner to discharge his encumbrances and to place him in a position to do his duty towards the remainder. This is the master-key to unlock the field of industry in Ireland. The seller, in all such cases, is incapable of making a proper use of the land. The purchaser, on the other hand, may safely be assumed to be an improver. It is a natural feeling in which almost all men indulge, and purchases of land are seldom made without a distinct view to further profitable investments in improvements. "To give every prudent facility for the transfer by sale of real property from man to man, by the adoption of a simple, cheap, and secure system of transfer, in lieu of the present barbarous, unsafe, and expensive system, so that real property could be bought and sold in Ireland with as much freedom and security as other property," is, therefore, the object at which we ought to aim, and especially to encourage the investment of small capitals in the land, it being through the instrumentality of small capitalists chiefly that the country can be civilized and improved. "'The purchasers would give extensive and permanent employment to numbers of people around them in carrying out that natural desire of man, the improvement of newly-acquired landed property; they would promote industry everywhere; they would greatly increase the value of land generally. By their number, all property in land would be rendered secure against revolutionary violence. The habits and example of men who had made money by industry, and who might invest their savings in land, would place the social system of Ireland on a solid basis. The best of the Protestants and Roman Catholics, those who had been careful and industrious, would be purchasers of land, and all would have a common interest in peace and order. The surplus population beyond the means of present employment, which now oppresses and embarrasses the country, might gradually be absorbed, and become a source of wealth and strength. Towns would everywhere improve, and new ones might arise by the extension of the railway system, spreading industry and civilization among men now sunk in indolence and almost barbarism.

All the parties concerned in these transfers would be benefitted by them. Lands are comparatively valueless to those who have no capital to improve them, and they are often justly felt to be a burthen and a disgrace, because they entail duties which the nominal owners have no means of performing. The effect on the character and prospects of the whole body of landed proprietors would be as described in the following passage from the author to whom we are already so much indebted: "When men, however young, act under responsibility, they usually proceed with caution; if others will think and act for them, and provide for their wants, and secure them from poverty and danger, their own prudential faculties may become dormant; and a man or any class of men so protected, are likely to exhibit deficiency in the qualities of prudence and good management of their affairs. But owners of land would not evince any such deficiency, if once they felt that they would be ruined, and their families also, if they were not governed by the same rules of prudence which other men must observe, and which necessarily enter into the proper management of all other descriptions of property. The present difficulties of sale of land, and the consequent protection afforded to entailed properties, are the chief reasons why so many persons of the class of proprietors are in difficulties. With more liberty, there would be more prudence and more attention to estates on the part of owners, from which they and the country would be great gainers."

The manner in which the interests of the public at large are affected, is correctly described in the following passage from **the other pamphlet**: "If these premises be correct; if employment with regular wages must be found for the peasantry: if capital be necessary, and the parties holding the land do not possess sufficient for this purpose; it follows, either that Government must continue to supply the capital required, not merely by a loan on an emergency, but as part of its regular system of action; or else that the land must pass into the hands of those who do not possess the means of employing the people—of men who will carry on agriculture as a business, and will bring to their occupation the capital, the habits of business, and the energy and intelligence which have raised the commerce and manufactures of this nation to their present preeminence."

Her Majesty's Government being deeply impressed with the importance of these views, introduced a bill into Parliament in the session of 1847, the object of which was to enable the owners of encumbered estates in Ireland to sell the whole or a portion of them, after the circumstances of each estate had been investigated by a Master in Chancery with a view to secure the due liquidation of every claim upon it. The sale was not to take place without the consent of the first incumbrancer, unless the Court of Chancery

The other pamphlet:
Trevelyan is quoting from an 1847 pamphlet by Jonathan Pim entitled, *Observations on the Evils Resulting to Ireland: From the Insecurity of Title and the Existing Laws of Real Property: with Some Suggestiosn Towards a Remedy.*

should consider the produce sufficient to pay the principal and all arrears of interest, or unless the owner or some subsequent incumbrancer should undertake to pay to the first incumbrancer any deficiency which might exist, and give such security for the performance of his undertaking as the court might direct. This bill passed the House of Lords, but was withdrawn in the Commons, owing to the opposition of some of the Irish proprietors, and to the objections entertained by the great Insurance Companies, who are the principal lenders on Irish mortgages, to having their investments disturbed. The failure of the bill was a national misfortune which cannot be too soon remedied....

It has been a popular argument in Ireland, that as the calamity was an imperial one, the whole amount expended in relieving it ought to be defrayed out of the Public Revenue. There can be no doubt that the deplorable consequences of this great calamity extended to the empire at large, but the disease was strictly local, and the cure was to be obtained only by the application of local remedies. If England and Scotland, and great part of the north and east of Ireland had stood alone, the pressure would have been severe, but there would have been no call for assistance from national funds. The west and south of Ireland was the **peccant** part. The owners and holders of land in those districts had permitted or encouraged the growth of the excessive population which depended upon the precarious potato, and they alone had it in their power to restore society to a safe and healthy state. If all were interested in saving the starving people, they were far more so, because it included their own salvation from the desperate struggles of surrounding multitudes phrenzied with hunger. The economical administration of the relief could only be provided for by making it, in part at least, a local charge....

> **Peccant:** Diseased or causing disease.

A principle of great power has thus been introduced into the social system of Ireland, which must be productive of many important consequences, besides those which directly flow from it. **Mr. Drummond's** apophthegm, that "property has its duties as well as its rights," having now received the sanction of law, it can never hereafter be a matter of indifference to a landed proprietor, what the condition of the people on his estate is. The day has gone by for letting things take their course, and landlords and farmers have the plain alternative placed before them of supporting the people in idleness or in profitable labour. Hitherto the duties of Irish landlords had been, as jurists would say, of imperfect obligation. In other words, their performance depended upon conscience, benevolence, and a more enlightened and far-seeing view of personal interest than belongs to the generality of men; the consequence of which has been a remarkable difference in the conduct of Irish landlords: and while some have made all the sacrifices and exertions which their position required, others have been guilty of that

> **Mr. Drummond:** Thomas Drummond (1797–1840) was a Scottish civil engineer who worked on the Ordnance Survey of Ireland and was later under-secretary for Ireland from 1835 until his death in 1840. He was quite critical of Irish landlords and large estates in Ireland.

entire abandonment of duty which has brought reproach upon their order. For the future this cannot be. The necessity of self-preservation, and the knowledge that rents can be saved from the encroachments of poor-rates, only in proportion as the poor are cared for and profitably employed, will secure a fair average good conduct on the part of landed proprietors, as in England, and more favourable circumstances will induce improved habits. The poor-rate is an absentee tax of the best description; because, besides bringing non-resident proprietors under contribution, it gives them powerful motives either to reside on their estates or to take care that they are managed, in their absence, with a proper regard to the welfare of the poor. Lastly, the performance of duty supposes the enjoyment of equivalent rights. When rich and poor are at one again, the repudiating farmer will find the position of his landlord too strong to allow of his taking his present licence, and it will then be fearlessly asserted that the converse of Mr. Drummond's maxim is also true, and that "Property has its rights as well as its duties." For the first time in the history of Ireland, the poor man has become sensibly alive to the idea that the law is his friend, and the exhortation of the parish priest of Dingle to his flock in September 1847, indicates an epoch in the progress of society in Ireland:—"Heretofore landlords have had agents who collected their rents, and they supported them. The grand jury had agents to collect the county-**cess**, and they supported them. Now, for the first time, the poor man has an agent to collect *his* rent. That agent is the poor-rate collector, and he should be supported by the poor." Time must, however, be allowed for the gradual working of this feeling, before its full effects can be seen.

Cess: A tax.

DOCUMENT 44:

James Mahony, "Condition of Ireland: Illustrations of the New Poor-Law," *Illustrated London News* (22 December 1849)

James Mahony (1810–79) was an artist and engraver living in Cork when he was asked by the *Illustrated London News* to produce a series of illustrations and reports on the Great Irish Famine. Mahony's images of the distress have become iconic representations of the Famine. This story from 1849 is an example of his reporting.

ev

Having last week introduced this important subject to our readers, and given them some of the statistics of **Kilrush**, we shall henceforward allow our Correspondent to speak for himself:—

I assure you (he says) that the objects of which I send you Sketches are not sought after—I do not go out of my way to find them; and other travellers who have gone in the same direction, such as Lord Adair, the Earl of Surrey, and Mr. Horsman, will vouch, I am sure, for the accuracy of my delineations. The Sketch of Moveen, to which I now call your attention, is that of another ruined village in the Union of Kilrush. It is a specimen of the dilapidation I behold all around. There is nothing but devastation, while the soil is of the finest description, capable of yielding as much as any land in the empire. Here, at Tullig, and other places, the ruthless destroyer, as if he delighted in seeing the monuments of his skill, has left the walls of the houses standing, while he has unroofed them and taken away all shelter from the people. They look like the tombs of a departed race, rather than the recent abodes of a yet living people, and I felt actually relieved at seeing one or two half-clad spectres gliding about, as an evidence that I was not in the land of the dead. You may inquire, perhaps, and I am sure your readers will wish to know, why it is that the people have of late been turned out of their houses in such great numbers, and their houses just at this time pulled down, and I will give you my explanation of this fact.

The public records, my own eye, a piercing wall of woe throughout the land—all testify to the vast extent of the evictions at the present time. Sixteen thousand and odd persons unhoused in the Union of Kilrush before the month of June in the present year; seventy-one thousand one hundred and thirty holdings done away in Ireland, and nearly as many houses destroyed, in 1848; two hundred and fifty-four thousand holdings of more than one acre and less than five acres, put an end to between 1841 and 1848: six-tenths, in fact, of the lowest class of tenantry driven from their now roofless or annihilated cabins and houses, makes up the general description of that

Kilrush: A town in County Clare in the west of Ireland. This refers to the much larger Poor Law Union with a workhouse which encompassed 13 electoral districts.

desolation of which Tullig and Moveen are examples. The ruin is great and complete. The blow that effected it was irresistible. It came in the guise of charity and benevolence; it assumed the character of the last and best friend of the peasantry, and it has struck them to the heart. They are prostrate and helpless. The once frolicsome people—even the saucy beggars—have disappeared, and given place to wan and haggard objects, who are so resigned to their doom, that they no longer expect relief. One beholds only shrunken frames scarcely covered with flesh—crawling skeletons, who appear to have risen from their graves, and are ready to be returned frightened to that abode. They have little other covering than that nature has bestowed on the human body—a poor protection against inclement weather; and, now that the only hand from which they expected help is turned against them, even hope is departed, and they are filled with despair. Than the present Earl of Carlisle there is not a more humane nor a kinder-hearted nobleman in the kingdom; he is of high honour and unsullied reputation; yet the Poor-law he was mainly the means of establishing for Ireland, with the best intentions, has been one of the chief causes of the people being at this time turned out of their homes, and forced to burrow in holes, and share, till they are discovered, the ditches and the bogs with otters and snipes.

Poor-law: Refers specifically to the Irish Poor Law Extension Act of 1847 which both made Irish landowners responsible for funding Irish famine relief but also encouraged them to evict many poor tenants.

The instant the **Poor-law** was passed, and property was made responsible for poverty, the whole of the landowners, who had before been careless about the people, and often allowed them to plant themselves on untenanted spots, or divide their tenancies—delighted to get the promise of a little additional rent—immediately became deeply interested in preventing that, and in keeping down the number of the people. Before they had rates to pay, they cared nothing for them; but the law and their self-interest made them care, and made them extirpators. Nothing less than some general desire like that of cupidity falling in with an enactment, and justified by a theory—nothing less than a passion which works silently in all, and safely under the sanction of a law—could have effected such wide-spread destruction. Even humanity was enlisted by the Poor-law on the side of extirpation. As long as there was no legal provision for the poor, a landlord had some repugnance to drive them from every shelter; but the instant the law took them under its protection, and forced the landowner to pay a rate to provide for them, repugnance ceased: they had a legal home, however inefficient, to go to; and eviction began. Even the growth of toleration seems to have worked to the same end. Till the Catholics were emancipated, they were all—rich and poor, priests and peasants—united by a common bond; and Protestant landlords beginning evictions on a great scale would have roused against them the whole Catholic nation. It would have been taken up as a religious question, as well as a question of the poor, prior to 1829. Subsequent to that time—with a Whig administration, with all offices open to Catholics—no religious feelings could mingle with the matter: eviction became a pure question of interest; and while the priests look now perhaps, as much to the Government as to their flocks for support, Catholic landlords are not behind Protestant landlords in clearing their estates. English notions and English habits, without any reference to the causes of English greatness—which are not to be found in a Poor-law and farms of a particular size—impressed law-makers and the landlords of Ireland with a strong desire to enlarge and consolidate farms, and clear them of the squatters and subtenants, who had formerly been permitted, if not encouraged. With a Poor-law, that desire could be safely acted on, and so it supplies a temptation and the means to carry eviction extensively into effect.

The evictions were numerous before the potato rot. It was not that great calamity, therefore, that super induced them, it was the chief cause of the present desolation. The potato harvest and harvests of every kind have been lost many times before 1846, without reducing the people to their present misery. But that calamity threw the people at the mercy of the Government, and the Government used its power directly and indirectly, in accordance with the theory, to clear the land. Out-door relief was established in that season of distress, and relief altogether was coupled with the resignation of the land. The poor were required to give up their heritage, small though it were, for less than a mess of pottage. A law was passed, the 11 and 12 Vic. c. 47,[5] entitled, "An Act for the Protection and Relief of the Destitute Poor Evicted from the Dwellings," which provided a means of evicting them, subjecting the landlords to the necessity of giving notice to Poor-law guardians, and to the share of a common burden. Under such stimuli and such auspices, the clearing process has gone on in an accelerated ratio, and Ireland is now dotted with ruined villages, and filled with a starving population, besieging the doors of crowded workhouses, and creeping into the halls and chambers of the deserted mansions of the nobility and gentry. A gentleman's mansion turned into a poor-house, is a fit emblem of the decay that a mistaken policy has brought on all classes. The system intended to relieve the poor, by making the landlords responsible for their welfare, has at once made it the interest, and therefore the duty, of the landlords to get rid of them. Extirpation is accordingly going forward at a rapid rate; and the evidence of that is now placed before the eyes and the understanding of the readers of the ILLUSTRATED LONDON NEWS.

I will give you, by-and-bye, some notices of driving for rent, of land-owners impoverished by rates, and of bankrupt unions; but at present I

---

5   This act was intended to place some restrictions on evictions; it required seven days notice of eviction to the Poor Law Guardians and the tenant and made the practice of unroofing or demolishing houses set for eviction a misdemeanor.

SCALP OF BRIAN CONNOR, NEAR KILRUSH UNION HOUSE.

must draw attention to some of the other Sketches I send. The Scalp of
Brian Connor (here represented) has been already described; it is another
illustration of the worse than pig-sty habitations of those who did live in
the now roofless cottages.

There is something called a scalp, or hole dug in the earth, some two or
three feet deep. In such a place was the abode of Brian Connor. He has three
in family, and had lived in this hole several months before it was discovered.
It was roofed over with sticks and pieces of turf, laid in the shape of an
inverted saucer. It resembles, though not quite so large, one of the ant-hills
of the African forests.

Another Sketch follows (of Miss Kennedy), which shows that, amidst
this world of wretchedness, all is not misery and guilt. Indeed, it is a part of
our nature that the sufferings of some should be the occasion for the exercise
of virtue in others. Miss Kennedy (about seven years old) is the daughter
of Captain Kennedy, the Poor-law Inspector of the Kilrush Union. She is
represented as engaged in her daily occupation of distributing clothing to
the wretched children brought around her by their more wretched parents.
In the front of the group I noticed one woman crouching like a monkey,
and drawing around her the only rag she had left to conceal her nudity.

MISS KENNEDY DISTRIBUTING CLOTHING AT KILRUSH.

A big tear was rolling down her cheek, with gratitude for the gifts the innocent child was distributing. The effect was heightened by the chilliness and dreariness of a November evening, and by the wet and mire in which the naked feet of the crowd were immersed. On Captain Kennedy being appointed to the Union, his daughter was much affected by the misery of the poor children she saw; and so completely did it occupy her thoughts, that, with the consent of her parents, she gave up her time and her own little means to relieve them. She gave away her own clothes—she was allowed to bestow part of her mother's—and she then purchased coarse materials, and made up clothing for children of her own age; she was encouraged by her father and some philanthropic strangers, from whom she received sums of money, and whose example will no doubt be followed by those who possess property in the neighbourhood; and she devoted herself with all the energy and perseverance of a mature and staid matron to the holy office she has undertaken. The Sketch will, I hope, immortalize the beneficent child, who is filling the place of a saint, and performing the duties of a patriot.

On all sides I hear praises of the amiable child and her excellent father, and this is not without a moral for the landlords. The public officers who are appointed to administer and control the relief of the poor, have it in their power to do much for the people. Mere kindness of manner, though they render no substantial assistance, endears them to the suffering crowd. Captain Kennedy is at once kind, charitable, and judicious. He is at the head of the Union. He fills for the people the most important office in the district. He is the great man of the place. It must be so in other districts. The funds are

BRIDGET O'DONNEL AND CHILDREN.

contributed by the landowners, but they are distributed by public officers. Thus the Poor-law, which disposes of the landowners' property, also deprives them of the pleasure and the burden of distributing it themselves. A public officer is made, in fact, to administer their estates, and he stands between them and their compulsory bounties, securing the respect and confidence which they might and ought to have. The more the subject is examined, the more, I have no doubt, it will be found that the poor-law is as injurious to the landlords as it is to the people.

Searching for Potatoes is one of the occupations of those who cannot obtain out-door relief. It is gleaning in a potato-field—and how few are left after the potatoes are dug, must be known to everyone who has ever seen the field cleared. What the people were digging and hunting for, like dogs after truffles, I could not imagine, till I went into the field, and then I found them patiently turning over the whole ground, in the hopes of finding the few potatoes the owner might have overlooked. Gleaning in a potato-field seems something like shearing hogs, but it is the only means by which the gleaners could hope to get a meal.

The Sketch of a Woman and Children represents Bridget O'Donnel. Her story is briefly this:—"I lived," she said, "on the lands of Gurranenatuoha. My husband held four acres and a half of land, and three acres of bog land; our yearly rent was £7 4s.; we were put out last November; he owed some rent. We got thirty stone of oats from Mr. Marcus Keane, for seed. My husband gave some writing for it: he was paid for it. He paid ten shillings for reaping the corn. As soon as it was stacked, one 'Blake' on the farm, who was put to watch it, took it away to his own haggard and kept it there for a fortnight by Dan Sheedey's orders. They then thrashed it in Frank Lellis's barn. I was at this time lying in fever. Dan Sheedey and five or six men came to tumble my house; they wanted me to give possession. I said that I would not; I had fever, and was within two months of my down-lying (confinement); they commenced knocking down the house, and had half of it knocked down when two neighbours, women, Nell Spellesley and Kate How, carried me out. I had the priest and doctor to attend me shortly after. Father Meehan

SCALPEEN OF TIM DOWNS, AT DUNMORE.

anointed me. I was carried into a cabin, and lay there for eight days, when I had the creature (the child) born dead. I lay for three weeks after that. The whole of my family got the fever, and one boy thirteen years old died with want and with hunger while we were lying sick. Dan Sheedey and Blake took the corn into Kilrush, and sold it. I don't know what they got for it. I had not a bit for my children to eat when they took it from me."

The last Sketch shows the **Scalpeen** of Tim Downs, at Dunmore, in the parish of Kellard, where himself and his ancestors resided on the spot for over a century, with renewal of their lease in 1845. He neither owed rent arrears or taxes up to the present moment, and yet he was pitched out on the roadside, and saw ten other houses, with his own, levelled at one fell swoop on the spot, the ruins of some of which are seen in this Sketch. None of them were mud cabins, but all capital stone-built houses.

I must conclude my present communication with an account of a great catastrophe, which has hurried 37 of the poor wretches that depended on the Union of Kilrush, with four other persons, into eternity. The Union will be relieved by an accident at which humanity mourns:—

"On the evening of Wednesday week intelligence reached the town of Kilrush that a large number of persons, most of whom were paupers, who had been seeking out-door relief at Kilrush, were drowned while crossing the ferry on their return to Moyarta. No less than 33 dead bodies were washed ashore on the northern side of the ferry. They were removed to an adjacent field, and the coroner, Mr. Frank O'Donnell, arriving soon after from Kilkee, an inquest was held on their wretched remains. It appeared upon the inquiry that no less than 43 or 45 persons (for they could not tell the exact number), were allowed to crowd into a crazy and rotten boat, which had been plying on this ferry for the last forty years. The boat moved on as far as the middle of the ferry, when a sea broke over her stern, and filled her at once, the wind blowing strong from the south-west at the time. She upset instantly, and her miserable living freight were immersed in the merciless waters, while four (who were eventually saved) clung to her until a boat from Captain Cox's men came to their assistance. The verdict of the coroner's jury was as usual in such cases, but imputing gross neglect, and attaching censure to the owners of the boat, for admitting such a number of persons into so frail a craft. With the exception of four, the victims were all paupers who had frequently come into the town in vain to seek out-door relief, and were returning that sad evening to their wretched hovels in the parishes of Moyarta and Kilballyowen."

Scalpeen: In a 15 December article Mahony described a scalpeen as: "A Scalpeen is a hole ... It is often erected within the walls when any are left standing, of the unroofed houses, and all that is above the surface is built out of the old materials. It possesses, too, some pieces of furniture, and the Scalpeen is altogether superior to the Scalp."

DOCUMENT 45:

From John Mitchel, *The Last Conquest of Ireland, Perhaps* (1861)

John Mitchel (1815–75) was an Irish nationalist and writer. He was a leader of the Young Ireland Movement, and worked on their newspaper the *Nation*. Convicted of treason in 1848 for his part in a rebellion that year, he was sentenced to transportation but eventually escaped and made his way to the United States. He lived in the American South where he became an advocate for slavery. In 1861 he wrote *The Last Conquest of Ireland, Perhaps* to condemn British policy towards Ireland during the Famine.

e

The Conquest was now consummated—England, great, populous, and wealthy, with all the resources and vast patronage of an existing government in her hands—with a magnificent army and navy—with the established course and current of commerce steadily flowing in the precise direction that suited her interests—with a powerful party on her side in Ireland itself, bound to her by lineage and by interest—and, above all, with her vast brute mass lying between us and the rest of Europe, enabling her to intercept the natural sympathies of other struggling nations, to interpret between us and the rest of mankind, and represent the troublesome sister island, exactly in the light that she wished us to be regarded—England prosperous, potent, and at peace with all the earth besides—had succeeded (to her immortal honour and glory) in anticipating and crushing out of sight the last agonies of resistance in a small, poor, and divided island, which she had herself made poor and divided, carefully disarmed, almost totally defranchised, and totally deprived of the benefits of that very British "law" against which we revolted with such loathing and horror. England had done this; and whatsoever credit and prestige, whatsoever profit and power could be gained by such a feat, she has them all. "Now, for the first time these six hundred years," said the London Times, "England has Ireland at her mercy, and can deal with her as she pleases."

It was an opportunity not to be lost for the interests of British civilization. Parliament met late in January, 1849. The Queen, in her "speech," lamented that "another failure of the potato crop had caused severe distress in Ireland: and thereupon asked Parliament to continue, "for a limited period," the extraordinary power; that is, the power of proclaiming any district under martial law, and of throwing suspected persons into prison, without any charge against them. The Act was passed, of course.

Then, as the famine of 1848 was fully as grievous and destructive as any of the previous famines;—as the rate-payers were impoverished, and in

most of the "unions," could not pay the rates already due—and were thus
rapidly sinking into the condition of paupers; giving up the hopeless effort
to maintain themselves by honest industry, and throwing themselves on
the earnings of others; as the poor-houses were all filled to overflowing,
and the exterminated people were either lying down to die or crowding
into the emigrant-ships;—as, in short, the Poor Law, and the New Poor
Law, and the Improved Poor Law, and the Supplementary Poor Law, had
all manifestly proved a "failure," **Lord John Russell's** next step was to give
Ireland more Poor Law....

Yet Ireland, we are told, is "improving" and "prosperous." Yes; it cannot
be denied that three millions of the people have been slain or driven to seek
safety by flight, the survivors begin to live better for the present. There is a
smaller supply of labour, with the same demand for it—therefore wages are
higher. There is more cattle and grain for export to England, because there
are fewer mouths to be fed; and England (in whose hands are the issues
of life and death for Ireland) can afford to let so many live. Upper classes,
and lower classes, merchants, lawyers, state-officials, civil and military, are
indebted for all that they have, for all that they are or hope for, to the suf-
ferance and forbearance of a foreign and hostile nation. This being the case,
every one must see that the prosperity of Ireland, even such ignominious
prosperity as it is, has no guarantee or security. Whenever Irishmen grow
numerous again (as they surely will), and whenever "that ancient swelling
and desire of liberty," as **Lord Mountjoy** expressed it, shall once more stir
their souls (as once more it certainly will), why, the British Government
can crush them again, with greater ease than ever; for the small farmers are
destroyed; the middle classes are extensively corrupted; and neither stipen-
diary officials nor able-bodied paupers ever make revolutions.

This very dismal and humiliating narrative draws to a close. It is the story
of an ancient nation stricken down by a war more ruthless and sanguinary
than any seven years' war, or thirty years' war, that Europe ever saw. No sack
of Magdeburg, or ravage of the Palatinate, ever approached in horror and
desolation to the slaughters done in Ireland by mere official red tape and
stationery, and the principles of political economy. A few statistics may fitly
conclude this dreary subject....

Now, that million and a half of men, women, and children, were carefully, prudently, and peacefully slain by the English government. They died
of hunger in the midst of abundance, which their own hands created; and
it is quite immaterial to distinguish those who perish in the agonies of
famine itself from those who died of typhus fever, which in Ireland is always
caused by famine.

Further, I have called it an artificial famine: that is to say, it was a famine
which desolated a rich and fertile island, that produced every year abundance

and superabundance to sustain all her people and many more. The English, indeed, call that famine a "dispensation of Providence"; and ascribe it entirely to the blight of the potatoes. But potatoes failed in like manner all over Europe; yet there was no famine save in Ireland. The British account of the matter, then, is first, a fraud—second, a blasphemy. The Almighty, indeed, sent the potato blight, but the English created the famine.

And lastly, I have shown, in the course of this narrative, that the depopulation of the country was not only encouraged by artificial means, namely, the Out-door Relief Act, the Labour-Rate Act, and the emigration schemes, but that extreme care and diligence were used to prevent relief coming to the doomed island from abroad; and that the benevolent contributions of Americans and other foreigners were turned aside from their destined objects—not, let us say, in order that none should be saved alive, but that no interference should be made with the principles of political economy.

The Census Commissioners close their last Report with these words:—

"In conclusion, we feel it will be gratifying to your Excellency, to find, that, although the population has been diminished in so remarkable a manner, by famine, disease, and emigration, and has been since decreasing, the results of the Irish census are, on the whole, satisfactory."

The Commissioners mean that the Census exhibits an increase in sheep and cattle for the English market—and that while men are lean, hogs are fat. "The good of this," said **Dean Swift**—more than a century ago—"the good of this is, that the more sheep we have, the fewer human creatures are left to wear the wool or eat the flesh. Ajax was mad when he mistook a flock of sheep for his enemies; but we shall never be sober until we have the same way of thinking."

Dean Swift: Jonathan Swift, author of Document 29.

The subjection of Ireland is now probably assured until some external shock shall break up that monstrous commercial firm, the British Empire; which, indeed, is a bankrupt firm, and trading on false credit, and embezzling the goods of others, or robbing on the highway, from Pole to Pole, but its doors are not yet shut; its cup of abomination is not yet running over. If any American has read this narrative, however, he will never wonder hereafter when he hears an Irishman in America fervently curse the British Empire. So long as this hatred and horror shall last—so long as our island refuses to become, like Scotland, a contented province of her enemy, Ireland is not finally subdued. The passionate aspiration for Irish nationhood will outlive the British Empire.

DOCUMENT 46:

From J.L. Porter, *The Life and Times of Henry Cooke* (1871)

Henry Cooke (1783–1868) was an Irish Presbyterian minister famous for his opposition to repealing the Act of Union. Cooke was born in County Down in Ulster to a family of English and Scottish descent. His opposition to Daniel O'Connell's Repeal Association helped to organize the Ulster Unionist movement. His biography was written by his son-in-law Josias Porter; this excerpt contains both Porter's account of Cooke's career and an excerpt from a speech given by Cooke opposing repealing the Act of Union.

At an early part of his career, O'Connell saw the rising influence of Cooke in Ulster, and he tried to counteract it. His special aim was to attach to his own party those Presbyterians who held Liberal views in politics. He professed to have the good of the entire nation at heart in his plan of repeal. To convince the Protestants of his good will, he actually toasted the "Immortal Memory" of **William** in a glass of **Boyne water**. He tried to make it appear that his principles did not differ, fundamentally, from those of the Prince of Orange, whose name has been for nearly two centuries the watchword of Irish Protestants. But the task was too great, even for O'Connell. The scheme was too shallow to deceive thoughtful men. Even the most Radical of Protestants refused to participate in the Repeal movement. New tactics were therefore adopted by the Liberator. Advantage was taken of garbled extracts from Dr. Cooke's parliamentary evidence to excite the fanaticism of Roman Catholics. He was denounced as a slanderer and false witness, by a great aggregate meeting in Dublin.

Hitherto the Protestants and Papists of Ulster had lived together in peace. Those feelings of brotherly kindness which Protestantism inculcates, had produced a salutary effect upon all parties. The enterprise of Protestant manufacturers, the industry of Protestant agriculturists, and the capital which they were able to command and willing to invest, gave them the means of offering lucrative employment, and affording relief when needed, which they did without distinction. The vast body of Roman Catholics, therefore, showed no jealousy of Protestant success. The spirit of fanaticism which generally characterises their faith had well-nigh disappeared. They even joined with their Protestant brethren in the celebration of those national jubilees, the observance of which has of late given rise to scenes of strife and bloodshed which bring disgrace upon our country. Under the influence of O'Connell, a system of agitation was inaugurated which changed the whole tone of society in Ulster. A newspaper called *The Vindicator* was

William: King William III, whose victory at the Battle of the Boyne in 1691 secured Protestant rule over Ireland.

Boyne water: Reference to the Boyne River, the site of the Battle of the Boyne.

The Vindicator: A Catholic newspaper in Ulster, founded in 1839.

established in Belfast, whose chief mission was to inflame sectarian passion, and stir up Roman Catholics against their Protestant fellow-countrymen. Unfortunately the Roman Catholic clergy became the tools of O'Connell. Roman Catholics were reminded of their vast numerical preponderance. They were told that they had a right to proportional influence, power, and representation in all government, local as well as Imperial. Protestants were denounced as heretics, usurpers, aliens. It was shown how they had taken Ireland by the sword; how they had driven out or murdered its patriotic native chiefs; how they had enslaved their brave and attached subjects. It was a touching picture, and though utterly false, its effects upon an uneducated and excitable people were lamentable. Most of them believed it to be literally true. They groaned in agony when addressed as "Hereditary Bondsmen." They were inspired with intense hatred of Protestants. They looked upon them as enemies and oppressors. They could not as yet drive them from the country, or appropriate the fruits of their toil and industry; but they could, and they did eventually, stir up a spirit of enmity which has destroyed the peace, and materially retarded the prosperity of Ulster....

Dr. Cooke saw the danger, and resolved to avert it. He determined by a bold stroke to stop the progress of Repeal in the North. He knew the chivalrous nature of the Irish people. He knew how dearly they loved a battle of any kind—physical or intellectual. He knew that through pure love of the conflict they would give a fair field to any combatants, and resist all attempts to withdraw from the gage of battle. He knew that to shrink as a coward, no matter under what pretence, from an open challenge, would largely contribute to shake popular confidence in any man. The merits of Repeal, besides, were disputed in Ulster. Protestants who agreed with O'Connell in his general political principles, differed from him in this. The more enlightened Roman Catholics, though their hearts were with the Liberator, were not quite certain that repeal was possible, or, if even achieved, that it would prove an unmitigated blessing. The question was fairly open to discussion. It needed fresh light. Dr. Cooke, therefore, resolved to challenge O'Connell to a public discussion, in Belfast, on the "Advantages or disadvantages of a Repeal of the Legislative Union."

Cooke's Speech against Repeal

The moment his portentous visit was threatened, my duty became a matter of solemn prayer to Him who can employ the "weak to confound the mighty." ... I did believe that in 1841 I saw the fearful shadow of **1641**. I saw the circumstances merely so far changed that, in 1641, physical force marched in the van of rebellion and massacre; but in 1841 intellect and eloquence, enlisting argument, prejudice and passion, advanced in the front, to mask and cover

1641: In the 1641 rebellion, Irish Catholic rebels killed thousands of Protestant settlers.

the array of physical force that fearfully gathered behind. I judged the spirit of the terrible movement to lie in pretended appeals to reason, interest, and facts. And I said in my heart, Shall we see the sword coming, and will not man give warning, and grapple with it, ere it come too nigh? I did believe, and I do still believe that this mighty conspiracy may, under Providence, be met and averted: therefore did I take one step in advance to meet it....

So sits he [O'Connell] whispering his dreams of Repeal into the ear of the people, and infusing the poison of his Popery into the vitals of the Constitution. But as the spear of **Ithuriel** compelled the foul toad to start into his native Satanic form, so shall the history of the past, and the condition of the present, compel O'Connell to appear in form, what he is in heart—the genius of knavery, the apostle of rebellion....

Look at the town of Belfast. When I was a youth it was almost a village. But what a glorious sight does it now present? The masted grove within our harbour—our mighty warehouses teeming with the wealth of every clime—our giant manufactories lifting themselves on every side—our streets marching on, as it were, with such rapidity, that an absence of a few weeks makes us strangers in the outskirts of our town. And all this we owe to the Union. No, not all—for throned above our fair town, and looking serenely from our mountain's brow, I behold the genii of Protestantism and Liberty, sitting inseparable in their power, while the genius of Industry which nightly reclines at their feet, starts with every morning in renovated might, and puts forth his energies, and showers down his blessings, on the fair and smiling lands of a **Chichester**, a **Conway**, and a **Hill**. Yes, we will guard the Union, as we will guard our liberties, and advance and secure the prosperity of our country.

Ithuriel: In John Milton's *Paradise Lost*, Ithuriel is an angel who finds Satan hiding in the form of a frog and uses his spear to transform him back.

Chichester: An important and wealthy family in Northern Ireland, Arthur Chichester (1563–1625) was a lord deputy of Ireland during the Plantation of Ulster.

Conway: Another important family in Northern Ireland, Sir Fulke Conway and his brother purchased extensive land in Northern Ireland during the Plantation of Ulster.

Hill: Another important family in Northern Ireland, Sir Moyses Hill was granted extensive land in Northern Ireland in 1611.

DOCUMENT 47:

Punch Cartoons on Ireland

Punch, or the London Charivari was a weekly British newspaper known for its humor and satire. Founded in 1841 it was famous for its illustrations and popularized the term 'cartoon' to refer to its political drawings. Below are a few examples of how Punch portrayed Ireland or Irish politics during its height in the nineteenth century. Each of these images is attributed to Sir John Tenniel (1820–1914) an English illustrator and political cartoonist, most known for his work for *Punch* and his illustrations for *Alice's Adventures in Wonderland.*

The Fenian-Pest
Hibernia. "O my dear Sister, what ARE we to do with these troublesome people?"
Britannia. "Try isolation first, my dear, and then—"
3 March 1866

Fenian: The Fenian Brotherhood was a nineteenth-century Irish revolutionary nationalist organization. The term Fenian came to be a derogatory umbrella term for all Irish nationalists.

Hibernia: The Latin name for Ireland, also frequently used in cartoon as a national personification for Ireland. In the nineteenth-century Hibernia is frequently drawn as young, attractive, and vulnerable, a younger sister to Britannia.

Britannia: The Latin name for the island of Great Britain, also the national personification for Great Britain.

3 March 1866: In March 1866, a bill to suspend Habeas Corpus in Ireland was passed in response to nationalist activity.

TWO FORCES.

29 October 1881

GUNPOWL

THE FENIAN GUY FAWKES.

The Fenian Guy Fawkes
28 December 1867

Guy Fawkes: A member of the 1605 English Catholic plot to blow up the Houses of Parliament.

28 December 1867: In December 1867, Irish Nationalists attempted to blow a wall in the Clerkenwell House of Detention to rescue two Irish Nationalist prisoners held there. Twelve people died and 120 were wounded in the explosion.

Charles Stewart Parnell, *Speech at Cork* (1885)[6]

Charles Stewart Parnell (1846–91) was an Irish nationalist politician and a leader of the Irish Home Rule movement. He was a member of parliament from 1875 to his death in 1891. As head of the Irish Parliamentary Party he sought to have the Act of Union repealed. He rose to prominence as a leader of the Irish National Land League, a political organization that sought to aid Irish tenant farmers. Parnell lost influence in 1890 upon the public revelation of his involvement in an adulterous relationship with Katherine O'Shea, whom he married in 1891.

❧

At Cork—January 21st, 1885

I hold that it is better even to encourage you to do what is beyond your strength, even should you fail sometimes in the attempt, than to teach you to be subservient and unreliant…. We consider that whatever class tries to obstruct the labourer in the possession of those fair and just rights to which he is entitled that class shall be put down—and coerced if you will—into doing justice to the labourer…. It is given to none of us to forecast the future, and just as it is impossible for us to say in what way or by what means the National question may be settled—in what way full justice may be done to Ireland—so it is impossible for us to say to what extent that justice should be done. We cannot ask for less than the restitution of **Grattan's Parliament**, with its important privileges, and wide and far-reaching constitution. We cannot, under the British Constitution, ask for more than the restitution of Grattan's Parliament, but no man has a right to fix the boundary of a march of a nation. No man has a right to say "Thus far shalt thou go, and no further"; and we have never attempted to fix the *ne plus ultra* to the progress of Ireland's nationhood, and we never shall. But, gentlemen, while we leave these things to time, circumstances, and the future, we must each one of us resolve in our own hearts that we shall at all times do everything that within us lies to obtain for Ireland the fullest measure of her rights. In this way we shall avoid difficulties and contentions amongst each other. In this way we shall not give up anything which the future may put in favour of our country: and while we struggle to-day for that which may

Grattan's Parliament:
Henry Grattan, author of Document 33.

---

6   Charles Stewart Parnell, *Words of the Dead Chief: Being Extracts from the Public Speeches and Other Pronouncements of Charles Stewart Parnell*, ed. Jennie Wyse-Power (Dublin: Sealy, Bryers & Walker, 1892), 96–97.

seem possible for us without combination, we must struggle for it with the proud consciousness that we shall not do anything to hinder or prevent better men who may come after us from gaining better things than those for which we now contend.

DOCUMENT 49:

From A. V. Dicey, *England's Case against Home Rule* (1887)

Albert Venn Dicey (1835–1922) was a British jurist and constitutional theorist. He was a professor of law at Oxford University and one of the most respected constitutional scholars of his time. Around 1886, at the time that the First Home Rule Bill for Ireland was introduced in parliament, Dicey became a vocal opponent of Home Rule. He argued that Ireland was an integral part of the United Kingdom and that no concession ought to be made to Irish nationalism.

ev

An author who publishes a book having any reference to Irish affairs may, not unnaturally, be supposed either to possess some special knowledge of Ireland, or else to be advocate of some new specific cure of Irish discontent. Of neither of these suppositions can I claim the benefit. My knowledge of Ireland is merely the knowledge—perhaps it were better to say ignorance—of an educated Englishman. It is derived from conversation with better informed friends, from careful attention, and from books accessible to ordinary readers. If I can claim no special acquaintance with Ireland, still less have I the presumption or the folly to come forward as the inventor of any political nostrum. My justification for publishing my thoughts on Home Rule is that the movement in favour of the Parliamentary independence of Ireland constitutes, whether its advocates recognize the fact or not, a demand for fundamental alterations in the whole Constitution of the United Kingdom; and while I may without presumption consider myself moderately acquainted with the principles of Constitutional law, I entertain the firmest conviction that any scheme for Home Rule in Ireland involves dangerous if not fatal innovations on the Constitution of Great Britain....

Home Rule is no doubt primarily a scheme for the government of Ireland, but it is also much more than this: it is a plan for revolutionising the constitution of the whole United Kingdom. There is no unfairness, therefore, in insisting that the proposed change must not take place if it be adverse to the interests of Great Britain. This is merely to assert that the welfare of thirty millions of citizens must, if a conflict of interest arise, be preferred to the interest of five millions of citizens. Home Rulers, it must again and again be repeated, demand not the national independence of Ireland, but the maintenance of the connection between England and Ireland on terms different from the conditions contained in the Act of Union. To keep one's mind clear on this point is of importance, because the result follows that, as already intimated, a whole series of arguments or claims which may fairly be put forward by a Nationalist are not available to a Home Ruler. A Nationalist, for example, may urge that the will of the Irish people to independent is decisive of their moral right to independence, and that the perils which a free Ireland may bring upon England need not in any way concern him or his country.... What, however, is here insisted upon is not that the principle of nationality is unsound, but that this principle does not cover the demand for Home Rule. A Home Ruler asks not for the political separation, but for the political partnership of England and Ireland. He wishes not that the firm should be dissolved, but that the Articles of Association should be revised. There is not then the least unfairness in the answer that no modification can be allowed which in the judgement of his associates is fatal to the prosperity of the concern. To crowds excited by pictures of past generations or of past struggles, by the hope of future prosperity to be brought about by miracles wrought by substituting the rule of love for the rule of law, there may appear to be something prosaic, not to say repulsive, in comparison of the relation between Great Britain and Ireland to the relation between shareholders in a trading company. But at a period when a fundamental change in the constitution is advocated on grounds of faith, benevolence, or generosity, a good deal is to be gained by bringing into relief the business aspect of constitutional reforms.... It is at moments of revolutionary fervour, when men measure proposed policies rather by their wishes than by their experience, that every citizen needs to have impressed upon his mind that government and legislation are matters of reason and judgement, and not of inclination. Nor let any one imagine that the expression of the belief constantly avowed or implied throughout these pages, that Home Rule would be as great an evil to England as Irish independence, shows a reckless and most unbusinesslike indifference to the perils and losses of separation. My conviction is unalterable that separation would be to England, as also to Ireland, a gigantic evil.

DOCUMENT 50:

Douglas Hyde, *The Necessity of De-Anglicizing Ireland* (1892)[7]

Douglas Hyde (1860–1949) was an Irish academic and linguist. He also went on to serve as the first president (uachtaran) of Ireland from 1938 to 1945. Hyde was a leading figure in the Gaelic Revival and the first president of the Gaelic League, one of the most influential cultural organizations in Irish history. The Gaelic League sought to promote the use of the Irish language, then dying out, in Ireland and around the world. This speech was delivered before the Irish National Literary Society in Dublin on 25 November 1892.

&

When we speak of "The Necessity for De-Anglicising the Irish Nation," we mean it, not as a protest against imitating what is best in the English people, for that would be absurd, but rather to show the folly of neglecting what is Irish, and hastening to adopt, pell-mell, and indiscriminately, everything that is English, simply because it is English.

This is a question which most Irishmen will naturally look at from a National point of view, but it is one which ought also to claim the sympathies of every intelligent Unionist, and which, as I know, does claim the sympathy of many.

If we take a bird's eye view of our island today, and compare it with what it used to be, we must be struck by the extraordinary fact that the nation which was once, as every one admits, one of the most classically learned and cultured nations in Europe, is now one of the least so; how one of the most reading and literary peoples has become one of the least studious and most un-literary, and how the present art products of one of the quickest, most sensitive, and most artistic races on earth are now only distinguished for their hideousness.

I shall endeavour to show that this failure of the Irish people in recent times has been largely brought about by the race diverging during this century from the right path, and ceasing to be Irish without becoming English. I shall attempt to show that with the bulk of the people this change took place quite recently, much more recently than most people imagine, and is, in fact, still going on. I should also like to call attention to the illogical position of men who drop their own language to speak English, of men who translate their euphonious Irish names into English monosyllables, of men who read English books, and know nothing about Gaelic literature,

---

7   Douglas Hyde, *Necessity of De-Anglicising Ireland*, http://www.gaeilge.org/deanglicising.html.

nevertheless protesting as a matter of sentiment that they hate the country which at every hand's turn they rush to imitate.

I wish to show you that in Anglicising ourselves wholesale we have thrown away with a light heart the best claim which we have upon the world's recognition of us as a separate nationality. What did **Mazzini** say? What is **Goldwin Smith** never tired of declaiming? What do the Spectator and Saturday Review harp on? That we ought to be content as an integral part of the United Kingdom because we have lost the notes of nationality, our language and customs.

It has always been very curious to me how Irish sentiment sticks in this half-way house—how it continues to apparently hate the English, and at the same time continues to imitate them; how it continues to clamour for recognition as a distinct nationality, and at the same time throws away with both hands what would make it so. If Irishmen only went a little farther they would become good Englishmen in sentiment also. But—illogical as it appears—there seems not the slightest sign or probability of their taking that step. It is the curious certainty that come what may Irishmen will continue to resist English rule, even though it should be for their good, which prevents many of our nation from becoming Unionists upon the spot. It is a fact, and we must face it as a fact, that although they adopt English habits and copy England in every way, the great bulk of Irishmen and Irishwomen over the whole world are known to be filled with a dull, ever-abiding animosity against her, and right or wrong—to grieve when she prospers, and joy when she is hurt. Such movements as Young Irelandism, Fenianism, Land Leagueism, and Parliamentary obstruction seem always to gain their sympathy and support. It is just because there appears no earthly chance of their becoming good members of the Empire that I urge that they should not remain in the anomalous position they are in, but since they absolutely refuse to become the one thing, that they become the other; cultivate what they have rejected, and build up an Irish nation on Irish lines.

But you ask, why should we wish to make Ireland more Celtic than it is—why should we de-Anglicise it at all?

I answer because the Irish race is at present in a most anomalous position, imitating England and yet apparently hating it. How can it produce anything good in literature, art, or institutions as long as it is actuated by motives so contradictory? Besides, I believe it is our Gaelic past which, though the Irish race does not recognise it just at present, is really at the bottom of the Irish heart, and prevents us becoming citizens of the Empire, as, I think, can be easily proved.

To say that Ireland has not prospered under English rule is simply a truism; all the world admits it, England does not deny it. But the English retort is ready. You have not prospered, they say, because you would not settle down

Giuseppe Mazzini: Mazzini (1805–72) was an Italian nationalist politician and leader of the Young Italy movement.

Goldwin Smith: Smith (1823–1910) was a British historian and journalist and was opposed to Irish Home Rule.

contentedly, like the Scotch, and form part of the Empire. "Twenty years of good, resolute, grandfatherly government," said a well-known Englishman, will solve the Irish question. He possibly made the period too short, but let us suppose this. Let us suppose for a moment—which is impossible—that there were to arise a series of Cromwells in England for the space of one hundred years, able administrators of the Empire, careful rulers of Ireland, developing to the utmost our national resources, whilst they unremittingly stamped out every spark of national feeling, making Ireland a land of wealth and factories, whilst they extinguished every thought and every idea that was Irish, and left us, at last, after a hundred years of good government, fat, wealthy, and populous, but with all our characteristics gone, with every external that at present differentiates us from the English lost or dropped; all our Irish names of places and people turned into English names; the Irish language completely extinct; the O's and the Macs dropped; our Irish into-nation changed, as far as possible by English schoolmasters into something English; our history no longer remembered or taught; the names of our rebels and martyrs blotted out; our battlefields and traditions forgotten; the fact that we were not of Saxon origin dropped out of sight and memory, and let me now put the question—How many Irishmen are there who would purchase material prosperity at such a price? It is exactly such a question as this and the answer to it that shows the difference between the English and Irish race. Nine Englishmen out of ten would jump to make the exchange, and I as firmly believe that nine Irishmen out of ten would indignantly refuse it.

And yet this awful idea of complete Anglicisation, which I have here put before you in all its crudity is, and has been, making silent inroads upon us for nearly a century.

Its inroads have been silent, because, had the Gaelic race perceived what was being done, or had they been once warned of what was taking place in their own midst, they would, I think, never have allowed it. When the picture of complete Anglicisation is drawn for them in all its nakedness Irish sentimentality becomes suddenly a power and refuses to surrender its birthright....

So much for the greatest stroke of all in our Anglicisation, the loss of our language. I have often heard people thank God that if the English gave us nothing else they gave us at least their language. In this way they put a bold face upon the matter, and pretend that the Irish language is not worth knowing, and has no literature. But the Irish language is worth knowing, or why would the greatest philologists of Germany, France, and Italy be emulously studying it, and it does possess a literature, or why would a German savant have made the calculation that the books written in Irish between the eleventh and seventeenth centuries, and still extant, would fill a thousand octavo volumes.

I have no hesitation at all in saying that every Irish-feeling Irishman, who hates the reproach of **West-Britonism**, should set himself to encourage the efforts, which are being made to keep alive our once great national tongue. The losing of it is our greatest blow, and the sorest stroke that the rapid Anglicisation of Ireland has inflicted upon us. In order to de-Anglicise ourselves we must at once arrest the decay of the language. We must bring pressure upon our politicians not to snuff it out by their tacit discouragement merely because they do not happen themselves to understand it. We must arouse some spark of patriotic inspiration among the peasantry who still use the language, and put an end to the shameful state of feeling—a thousand-tongued reproach to our leaders and statesmen—which makes young men and women blush and hang their heads when overheard speaking their own language. **Maynooth** has at last come splendidly to the front, and it is now incumbent upon every clerical student to attend lectures in the Irish language and history during the first three years of his course. But in order to keep the Irish language alive where it is still spoken—which is the utmost we can at present aspire to—nothing less than a house-to-house visitation and exhortation of the people themselves will do, something—though with a very different purpose—analogous to the procedure that **James Stephens** adopted throughout Ireland when he found her like a corpse on the dissecting table. This and some system of giving medals or badges of honour to every family who will guarantee that they have always spoken Irish amongst themselves during the year. But unfortunately, distracted as we are and torn by contending factions, it is impossible to find either men or money to carry out this simple remedy, although to a dispassionate foreigner—to a **Zeuss, Jubainville, Zimmer, Kuno Meyer, Windisch, or Ascoli,** and the rest—this is of greater importance than whether **Mr. Redmond** or **Mr. MacCarthy** lead the largest wing of the Irish party for the moment, or Mr. So-and-So succeed with his election petition. To a person taking a bird's eye view of the situation a hundred or five hundred years hence, believe me, it will also appear of greater importance than any mere temporary wrangle, but, unhappily, our countrymen cannot be brought to see this.

We can, however, insist, and we shall insist if Home Rule be carried, that the Irish language, which so many foreign scholars of the first calibre find so worthy of study, shall be placed on a par with—or even above—Greek, Latin, and modern languages, in all examinations held under the Irish Government. We can also insist, and we shall insist, that in those baronies where the children speak Irish, Irish shall be taught, and that Irish-speaking schoolmasters, petty sessions clerks, and even magistrates be appointed in Irish-speaking districts. If all this were done, it should not be very difficult, with the aid of the foremost foreign scholars, to bring about a tone of thought which would make it disgraceful for an educated Irishman especially of the old Celtic

West-Britonism: West Britain is a description of Ireland that emphasizes it as under British influence. West Briton is usually a derogatory term for an Irish person who is too much of an Anglophile.

Maynooth: Site of one of the constituent colleges of the Catholic University of Ireland.

James Stephens: An Irish Republican (1825–1901) and a founding member of the Irish Republican Brotherhood.

Zeuss, Jubainville, Zimmer, Kuno Meyer, Windisch, or Ascoli: Continental European scholars in the field of Celtic languages.

Mr. Redmond: John Redmond (1856–1918) was the leader of the Irish Parliamentary Party, the leading political force for Irish Home Rule, from 1900 to 1918.

Mr. MacCarthy: Justin McCarthy (1830–1912) was an Irish Nationalist politician and member of the Irish Parliamentary Party.

race, MacDermotts, O'Conors, O'Sullivans, MacCarthys, O'Neills—to be ignorant of his own language—would make it at least as disgraceful as for an educated Jew to be quite ignorant of Hebrew....

I have now mentioned a few of the principal points on which it would be desirable for us to move, with a view to de-Anglicising ourselves; but perhaps the principal point of all I have taken for granted. That is the necessity for encouraging the use of Anglo-Irish literature instead of English books, especially instead of English periodicals. We must set our face sternly against penny dreadfuls, shilling shockers, and still more, the garbage of vulgar English weeklies like Bow Bells and the Police Intelligence. Every house should have a copy of **Moore** and **Davis**. In a word, we must strive to cultivate everything that is most racial, most smacking of the soil, most Gaelic, most Irish, because in spite of the little admixture of Saxon blood in the north-east corner, this island is and will ever remain Celtic at the core, far more Celtic than most people imagine, because, as I have shown you, the names of our people are no criterion of their race. On racial lines, then, we shall best develop, following the bent of our own natures; and, in order to do this, we must create a strong feeling against West-Britonism, for it—if we give it the least chance, or show it the smallest quarter—will overwhelm us like a flood, and we shall find ourselves toiling painfully behind the English at each step following the same fashions, only six months behind the English ones; reading the same books, only months behind them; taking up the same fads, after they have become stale there, following them in our dress, literature, music, games, and ideas, only a long time after them and a vast way behind. We will become, what, I fear, we are largely at present, a nation of imitators, the **Japanese of Western Europe**, lost to the power of native initiative and alive only to second-hand assimilation. I do not think I am overrating this danger. We are probably at once the most assimilative and the most sensitive nation in Europe. A lady in Boston said to me that the Irish immigrants had become Americanised on the journey out before ever they landed at Castle Gardens. And when I ventured to regret it, she said, shrewdly, "If they did not at once become Americanised they would not be Irish." I knew fifteen Irish workmen who were working in a **haggard** in England give up talking Irish amongst themselves because the English farmer laughed at them. And yet O'Connell used to call us the "finest peasantry in Europe." Unfortunately, he took little care that we should remain so. We must teach ourselves to be less sensitive, we must teach ourselves not to be ashamed of ourselves, because the Gaelic people can never produce its best before the world as long as it remains tied to the apron-strings of another race and another island, waiting for it to move before it will venture to take any step itself.

Thomas Moore: An Irish writer and poet (1779–1852).

Thomas Davis: Author of Document 42.

Japanese of Western Europe: A reference to the Meiji Restoration, a political movement in late nineteenth-century Japan that saw the nation rapidly industrialize and adopt many Western ideas and influences.

Haggard: A farmyard.

In conclusion, I would earnestly appeal to every one, whether Unionist or Nationalist, who wishes to see the Irish nation produce its best—surely whatever our politics are we all wish that—to set his face against this constant running to England for our books, literature, music, games, fashions, and ideas. I appeal to every one whatever his politics—for this is no political matter—to do his best to help the Irish race to develop in future upon Irish lines, even at the risk of encouraging national aspirations, because upon Irish lines alone can the Irish race once more become what it was of yore—one of the most original, artistic, literary, and charming peoples of Europe.

DOCUMENT 51:

From George Bernard Shaw, *John Bull's Other Island* (1904)[8]

George Bernard Shaw (1856–1950) was an Anglo-Irish playwright. Shaw tended to support Irish Home Rule but was deeply critical of militant Irish nationalism. This is one of only two plays he wrote set in Ireland. The play focuses on two characters, an Irishman, Larry Doyle, who has become Anglicized, and an Englishman, Tom Broadbent, who has a romanticized view of Ireland. In the preface to the play Shaw discusses the origins of the play and details his own views on Irish nationalism.

℮

Preface for Politicians

Mr William Butler Yeats:
The poet W.B. Yeats, author of Document 56.

Neo-Gaelic Movement:
A reference to the Gaelic Revival.

John Bull's Other Island was written in 1904 at the request of **Mr William Butler Yeats**, as a patriotic contribution to the repertory of the Irish Literary Theatre. Like most people who have asked me to write plays, Mr Yeats got rather more than he bargained for.... There was another reason for changing the destination of John Bull's Other Island. It was uncongenial to the whole spirit of the **neo-Gaelic movement**, which is bent on creating a new Ireland after its own ideal, whereas my play is a very uncompromising presentment of the real old Ireland....

Now I have a good deal more to say about the relations between the Irish and the English than will be found in my play. Writing the play for an Irish audience, I thought it would be good for them to be shewn very clearly that the loudest laugh they could raise at the expense of the absurdest Englishman was not really a laugh on their side; that he would succeed where they would fail; that he could inspire strong affection and loyalty in an Irishman who knew the world and was moved only to dislike, mistrust, impatience and even exasperation by his own countrymen; that his power of taking himself seriously, and his insensibility to anything funny in danger and destruction, was the first condition of economy and concentration of force, sustained purpose, and rational conduct....

But it is not the spoils that matter. It is the waste, the sterilization, the perversion of fruitful brain power into flatulent protest against unnecessary evil, the use of our very entrails to tie our own hands and seal our own lips in the name of our honor and patriotism. As far as money or comfort is concerned, the average Irishman has a more tolerable life—especially now that the population is so scanty—than the average Englishman. It is true

---

8   George Bernard Shaw, *John Bull's Other Island and Major Barbara* (New York: Brentano's, 1907).

that in Ireland the poor man is robbed and starved and oppressed under judicial forms which confer the imposing title of justice on a crude system of bludgeoning and perjury. But so is the Englishman. The Englishman, more docile, less dangerous, too lazy intellectually to use such political and legal power as lies within his reach, suffers more and makes less fuss about it than the Irishman. But as least he has nobody to blame but himself and his fellow countrymen. He does not doubt that if an effective majority of the English people made up their minds to alter the Constitution, as the majority of the Irish people have made up their minds to obtain Home Rule, they could alter it without having to fight an overwhelmingly powerful and rich neighboring nation, and fight too, with ropes around their necks. He can attack any institution in his country without betraying it to foreign vengeance and foreign oppression. True, his landlord may turn him out of his cottage if he goes to a Methodist chapel instead of to the parish church. His customers may stop their orders if he votes Liberal instead of Conservative. English ladies and gentlemen who would perish sooner than shoot a fox do these things without the smallest scent of indecency and dishonor. But they cannot muzzle his intellectual leaders. The English philosopher, the English author, the English orator can attack every abuse and expose every superstition without strengthening the hands of any common enemy. In Ireland every such attack, every such exposure, is a service to England and stab to Ireland. If you expose the tyranny and rapacity of the Church, it is an argument in favor of Protestant ascendancy. If you denounce the nepotism and jobbery of the new local authorities, you are demonstrating the unfitness of the Irish to govern themselves, and the superiority of the old oligarchical grand juries.

And there is the same pressure on the other side. The Protestant must stand by the garrison at all costs: the Unionist must wink at every bureaucratic abuse, connive at every tyranny, magnify every official blockhead, because their exposure would be a victory for the Nationalist enemy. Every Irishman is in Lancelot's position: his honor rooted in dishonor stands; and faith unfaithful keeps him falsely true....

It is hardly possible for an Englishman to understand all that this implies. A conquered nation is like a man with cancer: he can think of nothing else, and is forced to place himself, to the exclusion of all better company, in the hands of quacks who profess to treat or cure cancer.... A healthy nation is as unconscious of its nationality as a healthy man of his bones. But if you break a nation's nationality it will think of nothing else but getting it set again. It will listen to no reformer, to no philosopher, to no preacher, until the demand of the Nationalist is granted. It will attend to no business, however vital, except the business of unification and liberation....

Finally, some words of warning to both nations. Ireland has been deliberately ruined again and again by England. Unable to compete with us industrially, she has destroyed our industries by the brute force of prohibitive taxation. She was perfectly right. That brute force was a more honorable weapon than the poverty which we used to undersell her. We lived with and as our pigs, and let loose our wares in the Englishman's market at prices which he could compete with only by living like a pig himself. Having the alternative of stopping our industry altogether, he very naturally and properly availed himself of it. We should have done the same in his place. To bear malice against him on that score is to poison our blood and weaken our constitution with unintelligent rancor. In wrecking all the industries that were based on the poverty of our people England did us an enormous service. In omitting to do the same on her own soil, she did herself a wrong that has rotted her almost to the marrow. I hope that when Home Rule is at last achieved, one of our first legislative acts will be to fortify the subsistence of our people behind the bulwark of a standard wage, and impose crushing import duties on every English trade that flourishes in the slum and fattens on the starvation of our unfortunate neighbors....

Now for England's share of warning. Let her look to her Empire; for unless she makes it such a Federation for civil strength and defense that all free peoples will cling to it voluntarily, it will inevitably become a military tyranny to prevent them from abandoning it; and such a tyranny will drain the English taxpayer of his money more effectually than its worst cruelties can ever drain its victims of their liberty....

DOCUMENT 52:

The Solemn League and Covenant (1912)

The Solemn League and Covenant or the Ulster Covenant was signed
by nearly half a million Northern Irish unionists in 1912 to express their
opposition to the Third Home Rule Bill for Ireland, which was introduced in
parliament that year. There was a separate declaration signed by women.

Being convinced in our consciences that Home Rule would be disastrous to
the material well being of Ulster as well as of the whole of Ireland, subversive
of our civil and religious freedom, destructive of our citizenship, and perilous
to the unity of the Empire, we, whose names are underwritten, men of Ulster,
loyal subjects of His Gracious Majesty King George V, humbly relying on
the God whom our fathers in days of stress and trial confidently trusted,
do hereby pledge ourselves in solemn Covenant, throughout this our time
of threatened calamity, to stand by one another in defending, for ourselves
and our children, our cherished position of equal citizenship in the United
Kingdom, and in using all means which may be found necessary to defeat
the present conspiracy to set up a Home Rule Parliament in Ireland. And
in the event of such a Parliament being forced upon us, we further solemnly
and mutually pledge ourselves to refuse to recognise its authority.

In sure confidence that God will defend the right, we hereto subscribe our
names.

The Declaration (for women)

We, whose names are underwritten, women of Ulster, and loyal subjects of
our gracious King, being firmly persuaded that Home Rule would be disastrous to our Country, desire to associate ourselves with the men of Ulster
in their uncompromising opposition to the Home Rule Bill now before
Parliament, whereby it is proposed to drive Ulster out of her cherished
place in the Constitution of the United Kingdom, and to place her under
the domination and control of a Parliament in Ireland.

Praying that from this calamity God will save Ireland, we hereto subscribe
our names.

DOCUMENT 53:

Gaelic League Poster (1913)

Conradh na Gaeilge or the Gaelic League was leading organization promoting the Gaelic Revival. The organization, founded by Douglas Hyde (Document 50), sought to promote the Irish language both within Ireland and around the world. Posters like this one from 1913 were used to raise money for the organization.

John Redmond, Woodenbridge Speech (20 September 1914)[9]

John Redmond (1856–1918) was an Irish Nationalist politician and leader of
the Irish Parliamentary Party. He was the leading politician advocating for
Irish Home Rule. The Third Home Rule Bill, which would have granted
this, was given royal assent in September 1914, just after the beginning of
World War I, but the decision was made to delay implementation until
the war ended. In this speech given to the Irish Volunteers, a paramilitary
organization founded to defend Home Rule against Unionist opposition,
Redmond urged the Volunteers to enlist in the war effort.

❧

Fellow countrymen, it was indeed fortunate chance that enabled me to be
present here today. I was motoring past, and I did not know until I arrived
here that this gathering of the Volunteers was to take place at Woodenbridge.
I could not deny myself the pleasure and honour of waiting to meet you, to
meet so many of those whom I have personally known for many long years,
and to see them fulfilling a high duty to their country. I have no intention of
making a speech. All I desire to say to you is that I congratulate you upon
the favourable beginning of the work you have made.

You have only barely made a beginning. You will yet have hard work
before you can call yourselves efficient soldiers, and you will have to have in
your hand—every man—as efficient weapons as I am glad to see in hands of
some, at any rate, of your numbers. Looking back as I naturally do, upon the
history of Wicklow I know that you will make efficient soldiers. Efficient
soldiers for what?

Wicklow Volunteers, in spite of the peaceful happiness and beauty of the
scene in which we stand, remember this country at this moment is in a state
of war, and your duty is a twofold Duty. The duty of the manhood of Ireland
is twofold. Its duty is, at all costs, to defend the shores of Ireland against
foreign invasion. It is a duty more than that of taking care that Irish valour
proves itself: on the field of war it has always proved itself in the past. The
interests of Ireland—of the whole of Ireland—are at stake in this war. This
war is undertaken in the defence of the highest principles of religion and
morality and right, and it would be a disgrace for ever to our country and a
reproach to her manhood and a denial of the lessons of her history if young
Ireland confined their efforts to remaining at home to defend the shores of
Ireland from an unlikely invasion, and to shrinking from the duty of proving

---

9   *Irish Independent*, 21 September 1914.

on the field of battle that gallantry and courage which has distinguished our race all through its history. I say to you therefore, your duty is twofold. I am glad to see such magnificent material for soldiers around me, and I say to you—Go on drilling and make yourself efficient for the Work, and then account yourselves as men, not only for Ireland itself, but wherever the fighting line extends, in defence of right, of freedom and religion in this war.

The Easter Rising Proclamation (1916)

The Proclamation of the Irish Republic was made on 24 April 1916. It was read aloud outside the General Post Office on the first day of the Easter Rising after rebel forces had occupied the building. The Rising was an armed insurrection of several nationalist organizations, organized by the Military Council of the Irish Republican Brotherhood. After six days the rebel forces were defeated by the British Army and the signatories of this proclamation were all court martialed and executed.

e

POBLACHT NA h-EIREANN
THE PROVISIONAL GOVERNMENT OF THE
IRISH REPUBLIC
TO THE PEOPLE OF IRELAND

IRISHMEN AND IRISHWOMEN: In the name of God and of the dead generations from which she receives her old tradition of nationhood, Ireland, through us, summons her children to her flag and strikes for her freedom.

Having organized and trained her manhood through her secret revolutionary organization, the Irish Republican Brotherhood, and through her open military organizations, the Irish Volunteers and the Irish Citizen Army, having patiently perfected her discipline, having resolutely waited for the right moment to reveal itself, she now seizes that moment, and, supported by her exiled children in America and by gallant allies in Europe, but relying in the first on her own strength, she strikes in full confidence of victory.

We declare the right of the people of Ireland to the ownership of Ireland, and to the unfettered control of Irish destinies, to be sovereign and indefeasible. The long usurpation of that right by a foreign people and government has not extinguished the right, nor can it ever be extinguished except by the destruction of the Irish people. In every generation the Irish people have asserted their right to national freedom and sovereignty; six times during the past three hundred years they have asserted it in arms. Standing on that fundamental right and again asserting it in arms in the face of the world, we hereby proclaim the Irish Republic as a Sovereign Independent State. And we pledge our lives and the lives of our comrades-in-arms to the cause of its freedom, of its welfare, and of its exaltation among the nations.

The Irish Republic is entitled to, and hereby claims, the allegiance of every Irishman and Irish woman. The Republic guarantees religious and civil liberty, equal rights and equal opportunities of all its citizens, and declares its resolve to pursue the happiness and prosperity of the whole nation and of all its parts, cherishing all the children of the nation equally, and oblivious of the differences carefully fostered by an alien government, which have divided a minority in the past.

Until our arms have brought the opportune moment for the establishment of a permanent National Government, representative of the whole people of Ireland and elected by the suffrages of all her men and women, the Provisional Government, hereby constituted, will administer the civil and military affairs of the Republic in trust for the people.

We place the cause of the Irish Republic under the protection of the Most High God, Whose blessing we invoke upon our arms, and we pray that no one who serves that cause will dishonour it by cowardice, inhumanity, or rapine. In this supreme hour the Irish nation must, by its valour and discipline and by the readiness of its children to sacrifice themselves for the common good, prove itself worthy of the august destiny to which it is called. Signed on behalf of the Provisional Government,

THOMAS J. CLARKE
SEAN MAC DIERMADA
THOMAS MACDONAGH
P.H.PEARSE
EAMONN CEANNT
JAMES CONNOLLY
JOSEPH PLUNKETT

W.B. Yeats, "Easter 1916" (1920)

William Butler Yeats (1865–1939) was an Irish poet and playwright. He was one of the leaders of the Irish Literary Revival and helped to found the Abbey Theatre in Dublin. Yeats wrote this poem between May and September 1916 to describe his feelings about the Easter Rising. It did not appear in print until 1920. Yeats was a committed nationalist but he also rejected the use of violence. Like many in Ireland he was shocked by the abrupt executions of the leaders of the revolution.

I have met them at close of day
Coming with vivid faces
From counter or desk among grey
Eighteenth-century houses.
I have passed with a nod of the head
Or polite meaningless words,
Or have lingered awhile and said
Polite meaningless words,
And thought before I had done
Of a mocking tale or a gibe
To please a companion
Around the fire at the club,
Being certain that they and I
But lived where motley is worn:
All changed, changed utterly:
A terrible beauty is born.

That woman's days were spent
In ignorant good-will,
Her nights in argument
Until her voice grew shrill.
What voice more sweet than hers
When, young and beautiful,
She rode to harriers?
This man had kept a school
And rode our wingèd horse;
This other his helper and friend
Was coming into his force;
He might have won fame in the end,

So sensitive his nature seemed,
So daring and sweet his thought.
This other man I had dreamed
A drunken, vainglorious lout.
He had done most bitter wrong
To some who are near my heart,
Yet I number him in the song;
He, too, has resigned his part
In the casual comedy;
He, too, has been changed in his turn,
Transformed utterly:
A terrible beauty is born.

Hearts with one purpose alone
Through summer and winter seem
Enchanted to a stone
To trouble the living stream.
The horse that comes from the road,
The rider, the birds that range
From cloud to tumbling cloud,
Minute by minute they change;
A shadow of cloud on the stream
Changes minute by minute;
A horse-hoof slides on the brim,
And a horse plashes within it;
The long-legged moor-hens dive,
And hens to moor-cocks call;
Minute by minute they live:
The stone's in the midst of all.

Too long a sacrifice
Can make a stone of the heart.
O when may it suffice?
That is Heaven's part, our part
To murmur name upon name,
As a mother names her child
When sleep at last has come
On limbs that had run wild.
What is it but nightfall?
No, no, not night but death;
Was it needless death after all?
For England may keep faith

For all that is done and said.
We know their dream; enough
To know they dreamed and are dead;
And what if excess of love
Bewildered them till they died?
I write it out in a verse—
MacDonagh and **MacBride**
And **Connolly** and **Pearse**
Now and in time to be,
Wherever green is worn,
Are changed, changed utterly:
A terrible beauty is born.

Thomas MacDonagh:
MacDonagh (1878–1916)
was a leader of the Easter
Rising, executed 3 May 1916.

John MacBride: MacBride
(1868–1916) was a leader of
the Easter Rising, executed
5 May 1916. MacBride was
also the estranged husband
of Maud Gonne, with whom
Yeats was in love.

James Connolly: Connolly
(1868–1916) was a socialist,
trade union leader, and leader
of the Easter Rising. He was
executed on 12 May 1916.

Patrick Pearse: Pearse
(1879–1916) was a leader of
the Easter Rising, executed 3
May 1916.

DOCUMENT 57:

From The Anglo-Irish Treaty (1921)

The Anglo-Irish Treaty officially concluded the Irish War of Independence (1919–21). Deep division over the treaty within Ireland led to the Irish Civil War (1922–24), which was fought between pro-treaty and anti-treaty forces, and eventually won by pro-treaty forces. The Treaty granted Ireland status as a self-governing dominion within the British Empire, but did not grant the full independence that Irish Republicans sought.

e∂

Final text of the Articles of Agreement for a Treaty between
Great Britain and Ireland as signed.

London, 6 December 1921

1. Ireland shall have the same constitutional status in the Community of Nations known as the British Empire as the Dominion of Canada, the Commonwealth of Australia, the Dominion of New Zealand, and the Union of South Africa with a Parliament having powers to make laws for the peace, order and good government of Ireland and an Executive responsible to that Parliament, and shall be styled and known as the Irish Free State.

2. Subject to the provisions hereinafter set out the position of the Irish Free State in relation to the Imperial Parliament and Government and otherwise shall be that of the Dominion of Canada, and the law, practice and constitutional usage governing the relationship of the Crown or the representative of the Crown and of the Imperial Parliament to the Dominion of Canada shall govern their relationship to the Irish Free State.

3. The representative of the Crown in Ireland shall be appointed in like manner as the Governor-General of Canada and in accordance with the practice observed in the making of such appointments.

4. The oath to be taken by Members of the Parliament of the Irish Free State shall be in the following form:—I do solemnly swear true faith and allegiance to the Constitution of the Irish Free State as by law established and that I will be faithful to H.M. King George V., his heirs and successors by law, in virtue of the common citizenship of Ireland with Great Britain and her adherence to and membership of the group of nations forming the British Commonwealth of Nations.

5. The Irish Free State shall assume liability for the service of the Public Debt of the United Kingdom as existing at the date hereof and towards the payment of War Pensions as existing at that date in such proportion as may be fair and equitable, having regard to any just claim on the part of Ireland by way of set-off or counter-claim, the amount of such sums being determined in default of agreement by the arbitration of one or more independent persons being citizens of the British Empire

6. Until an arrangement has been made between the British and Irish Governments whereby the Irish Free State undertakes her own coastal defence, the defence by sea of Great Britain and Ireland shall be undertaken by His Majesty's Imperial Forces, but this shall not prevent the construction or maintenance by the Government of the Irish Free State of such vessels as are necessary for the protection of the Revenue or the Fisheries. The foregoing provisions of this article shall be reviewed at a conference of Representatives of the British and Irish governments, to be held at the expiration of five years from the date hereof with a view to the undertaking by Ireland of a share in her own coastal defence.

7. The Government of the Irish Free State shall afford to His Majesty's Imperial Forces
(a) In time of peace such harbour and other facilities as are indicated in the Annex hereto, or such other facilities as may from time to time be agreed between the British Government and the Government of the Irish Free State; and
(b) In time of war or of strained relations with a Foreign Power such harbour and other facilities as the British Government may require for the purposes of such defence as aforesaid.

8. With a view to securing the observance of the principle of international limitation of armaments, if the Government of the Irish Free State establishes and maintains a military defence force, the establishments thereof shall not exceed in size such proportion of the military establishments maintained in Great Britain as that which the population of Ireland bears to the population of Great Britain.

9. The ports of Great Britain and the Irish Free State shall be freely open to the ships of the other country on payment of the customary port and other dues.

10. The Government of the Irish Free State agrees to pay fair compensation on terms not less favourable than those accorded by the Act of 1920 to

judges, officials, members of Police Forces and other Public Servants who are discharged by it or who retire in consequence of the change of government effected in pursuance hereof. Provided that this agreement shall not apply to members of the Auxiliary Police Force or to persons recruited in Great Britain for the Royal Irish Constabulary during the two years next preceding the date hereof. The British Government will assume responsibility for such compensation or pensions as may be payable to any of these excepted persons.

11. Until the expiration of one month from the passing of the Act of Parliament for the ratification of this instrument, the powers of the Parliament and the Government of the Irish Free State shall not be exercisable as respects Northern Ireland, and the provisions of the Government of Ireland Act 1920, shall, so far as they relate to Northern Ireland, remain of full force and effect, and no election shall be held for the return of members to serve in the Parliament of the Irish Free State for constituencies in Northern Ireland, unless a resolution is passed by both Houses of the Parliament of Northern Ireland in favour of the holding of such elections before the end of the said month.

12. If before the expiration of the said month, an address is presented to His Majesty by both Houses of the Parliament of Northern Ireland to that effect, the powers of the Parliament and the Government of the Irish Free State shall no longer extend to Northern Ireland, and the provisions of the Government of Ireland Act, 1920, (including those relating to the Council of Ireland) shall so far as they relate to Northern Ireland, continue to be of full force and effect, and this instrument shall have effect subject to the necessary modifications. Provided that if such an address is so presented a Commission consisting of three persons, one to be appointed by the Government of the Irish Free State, one to be appointed by the Government of Northern Ireland, and one who shall be Chairman to be appointed by the British Government shall determine in accordance with the wishes of the inhabitants, so far as may be compatible with economic and geographic conditions, the boundaries between Northern Ireland and the rest of Ireland, and for the purposes of the Government of Ireland Act, 1920, and of this instrument, the boundary of Northern Ireland shall be such as may be determined by such Commission.

13. For the purpose of the last foregoing article, the powers of the Parliament of Southern Ireland under the Government of Ireland Act, 1920, to elect members of the Council of Ireland shall after the Parliament of the Irish Free State is constituted be exercised by that Parliament.

14. After the expiration of the said month, if no such address as is mentioned in Article 12 hereof is presented, the Parliament and Government of Northern Ireland shall continue to exercise as respects Northern Ireland the powers conferred on them by the Government of Ireland Act, 1920, but the Parliament and Government of the Irish Free State shall in Northern Ireland have in relation to matters in respect of which the Parliament of Northern Ireland has not power to make laws under the Act (including matters which under the said Act are within the jurisdiction of the Council of Ireland) the same powers as in the rest of Ireland, subject to such other provisions as may be agreed in manner hereinafter appearing.

15. At any time after the date hereof the Government of Northern Ireland and the provisional Government of Southern Ireland hereinafter constituted may meet for the purpose of discussing the provisions subject to which the last foregoing Article is to operate in the event of no such address as is therein mentioned being presented and those provisions may include:—
(a) Safeguards with regard to patronage in Northern Ireland.
(b) Safeguards with regard to the collection of revenue in Northern Ireland.
(c) Safeguards with regard to import and export duties affecting the trade or industry of Northern Ireland.
(d) Safeguards for minorities in Northern Ireland.
(e) The settlement of the financial relations between Northern Ireland and the Irish Free State.
(f) The establishment and powers of a local militia in Northern Ireland and the relation of the Defence Forces of the Irish Free State and of Northern Ireland respectively, and if at any such meeting provisions are agreed to, the same shall have effect as if they were included amongst the provisions subject to which the powers of the Parliament and the Government of the Irish Free State are to be exercisable in Northern Ireland under Article 14 hereof.

16. Neither the Parliament of the Irish Free State nor the Parliament of Northern Ireland shall make any law so as either directly or indirectly to endow any religion or prohibit or restrict the free exercise thereof or give any preference or impose any disability on account of religious belief or religious status or affect prejudicially the right of any child to attend a school receiving public money without attending the religious instruction at the school or make any discrimination as respects State aid between schools under the management of different religious denominations or divert from any religious denomination or any educational institution any of its property except for public utility purposes and on payment of compensation.

17. By way of provisional arrangement for the administration of Southern Ireland during the interval which must elapse between the date hereof and the constitution of a Parliament and Government of the Irish Free State in accordance therewith, steps shall be taken forthwith for summoning a meeting of members of Parliament elected for constituencies in Southern Ireland since the passing of the Government of Ireland Act, 1920, and for constituting a provisional Government, and the British Government shall take the steps necessary to transfer to such provisional Government the powers and machinery requisite for the discharge of its duties, provided that every member of such provisional Government shall have signified in writing his or her acceptance of this instrument. But this arrangement shall not continue in force beyond the expiration of twelve months from the date hereof.

18. This instrument shall be submitted forthwith by His Majesty's Government for the approval of Parliament and by the Irish signatories to a meeting summoned for the purpose of the members elected to sit in the House of Commons of Southern Ireland and if approved shall be ratified by the necessary legislation.

PART 4

Ireland and England Post-Independence (1921–present)

DOCUMENT 58:

From Coal-Cattle Pact Debates in the Dáil Éireann (13 June 1935)[1]

The Coal Cattle Pact concluded the Anglo-Irish trade war. This was a retaliatory trade war begun in 1932, when an Irish government led by Éamon de Valera refused to continue reimbursing Britain for land annuities and other loans as agreed to in the Anglo-Irish Treaty. Britain responded by placing a heavy tariff on Irish agricultural products; Ireland in turn placed a heavy tariff on British coal. As Ireland was far more dependent on exporting to Britain than Britain was, the impact of the trade war was worse in Ireland. Eventually both parties agreed to relax tariffs with the Coal-Cattle Pact of 1935.

᷾᷾

Mr. Minch: ... I believe that this Party hesitated to come out on public platforms to denounce this pact. They felt that it was a step in the right direction, bad as it was, that later on a more reciprocal arrangement would develop, and that as time went on the business relationship between Great Britain and the Irish Free State would gradually work its way into normality. Time, however, showed that this pact, which seemed to be a beginning, was also the end. As such, it is only fair to say that all the gain seems to be on the one side. The producer here pays on the cattle and the consumer pays on the coal. If this Party some time ago had suggested an arrangement of that description on any platform, we would be howled down. We would be warned that we were bending the knee to Great Britain. We would be told that we were advocating abject and complete surrender, that we were encouraging the economic war from the British shore, that we were advocating all that sort of defeatism which had been the curse of this country in the past, that when a national issue was at stake we were the first to try to break the ranks. Yet, we find that when this coal-cattle pact is ultimately arranged by the present Government it is all right, that there is nothing wrong in it, that it is perfectly good business and perfectly genuine national politics....

Mr. Minch: Sydney Minch (1893–1970), a member of the opposition Fine Gael political party.

---

1   "Control of Imports Orders: Motions of Approval," available at https://www.oireachtas.ie.

Mr. J.M. Burke: James Burke (d. 1964), a farmer and Fine Gael politician.

Mr. J.M. Burke: I do not intend to heap any more coals of fire on those which have already been thrown at the head of the Minister for Industry and Commerce in connection with this secret agreement which has been designated a gentlemen's pact. When the vast majority of the Irish people were almost crushed out of existence by the Penal Laws, a member of the Protestant Ascendancy Party, and a very narrow-minded one at that, arose and sent forth this slogan: "Burn everything that comes from England except her coal." That cry became as it were the battle cry of a resurgent people. Now when we are in a position to negotiate on equal terms with "the hereditary foe, the base, bloody and brutal Saxon," there has gone forth a decree from Cæsar Augustus, otherwise the present Government, that the Irish people must burn nothing but English coal. Has there ever been such a complete volte face on the part of the Government? I welcome pacts because they foster international friendship, provided these pacts are founded on sound financial principles, but I ask the Minister when this particular tax is considered in its entirety, what political or what money advantages has it brought to the Free State? It is true that, to a certain extent, it has given relief to the farmers, who, owing to the economic policy of the Government, were overstocked. But at what a price? The farmers of Ireland are being permitted to export into England 150,000 extra cattle. These cattle carry a duty of £5 or £6 a head, payable to the British Government. In addition to that, they can only find their way into a competitive market, a market where they have to compete with cattle from almost every part of the world; whereas, on the other hand, British coal comes in here and gets a monopoly of the market. It has no competitor in the Free State. For that coal every consumer in Ireland has to pay a duty of 5/–a ton.

I cannot honestly say from a financial or from a national point of view that this pact is a good one. Deputy Maguire, a few moments ago, admitted that it was a poor bargain. I listened very attentively to what Deputy Norton said, and he put up a strong case against this particular pact which is going to inflict great hardships on a very large number of poor people, whereas the corresponding advantages are by no means proportionate to the hardships which it will impose on the people who are least able to bear the extra burden. I should like an explanation from the Minister why a tax which was avowedly put on coal as a war measure should be now retained for mere revenue purposes? I am sure the Minister will not deny and cannot deny that that tax was first put on as a war measure. It seems to me that it was a rather slippery, slim and slick way of doing things. In view of the coming coal-cattle pact which must have been in contemplation at the time, it was put on for the purpose of vindicating our determination to fight England in the so-called economic war, and then, when it was on, it has been left on and, as things now stand and in the present straits of the Government, will probably remain for this generation. For these reasons I cannot support the coal-cattle pact....

Mr. Lemass: At all times the British regarded this market as part of their internal market, and when they raised the prices to their own consumers in order to subsidise their exports of coal, they raised the prices to us. At no time during the whole of that ten years from 1922 to 1932 was this country regarded by the British coal exporters as an export market, and at no time during that period was the export price made available to us....

Mr. Lemass: I do not think that that is a satisfactory position. For the first time, our people have learned that they can get better and cheaper coal outside Britain, and if at the present time there was a free market for coal, our people would buy German and Polish coal in preference to British coal....

Mr. Lemass: Sean Lemass (1899–1971) was a Fianna Fáil (leading party) politician and the minister for industry and commerce from 1932 to 1939. He would go on to become Taoiseach (prime minister) from 1959 to 1966.

From Bunreacht Na hÉireann (Constitution of Ireland) (1937)

The Constitution of 1937 replaced the Constitution of the Irish Free State written in 1922. This constitution was assembled by then head of state Éamon de Valera; it was approved by a nationwide plebiscite on 1 July 1937.

PREAMBLE

In the name of the Most Holy Trinity, from Whom is all authority and to Whom, as our final end, all actions both of men and States must be referred,

We, the people of Éire,

Humbly acknowledging all our obligations to our Divine Lord, Jesus Christ, Who sustained our fathers through centuries of trial,

Gratefully remembering their heroic and unremitting struggle to regain the rightful independence of our Nation,

And seeking to promote the common good, with due observance of Prudence, Justice and Charity, so that the dignity and freedom of the individual may be assured, true social order attained, the unity of our country restored, and concord established with other nations,

Do hereby adopt, enact, and give to ourselves this Constitution.

THE NATION

Article 1.

The Irish nation hereby affirms its inalienable, indefeasible, and sovereign right to choose its own form of Government, to determine its relations with other nations, and to develop its life, political, economic and cultural, in accordance with its own genius and traditions.

Article 2.

The national territory consists of the whole island of Ireland, its islands and the territorial seas.

Article 3.

Pending the re-integration of the national territory, and without prejudice to the right of the Parliament and Government established by this Constitution to exercise jurisdiction over the whole of that territory, the laws enacted by that Parliament shall have the like area and extent of application as the laws of Saorstát Éireann and the like extra-territorial effect.

THE STATE

Article 4.

The name of the State is Éire, or in the English language, Ireland.

Article 5.

Ireland is a sovereign, independent, democratic state.

Article 6.

1. All powers of government, legislative, executive and judicial, derive, under God, from the people, whose right it is to designate the rulers of the State and, in final appeal, to decide all questions of national policy, according to the requirements of the common good.
2. These powers of government are exercisable only by or on the authority of the organs of State established by this Constitution.

Article 7.

The national flag is the tricolour of green, white and orange.

Article 8.

1. The Irish language as the national language is the first official language.
2. The English language is recognized as a second official language.
3. Provision may, however, be made by law for the exclusive use of either of the said languages for any one or more official purposes, either throughout the State or in any part thereof....

THE PRESIDENT

Article 12.

1. There shall be a President of Ireland (Uachtarán na hÉireann), hereinafter called the President, who shall take precedence over all other persons in the State and who shall exercise and perform the powers and functions conferred on the President by this Constitution and by law.
2. The President shall be elected by direct vote of the people....

THE NATIONAL PARLIAMENT

Constitution and Powers

Article 15.

1. The National Parliament shall be called and known, and is in this Constitution generally referred to, as the Oireachtas.
2. The Oireachtas shall consist of the President and two Houses, viz.: a House of Representatives to be called Dáil Éireann and a Senate to be called Seanad Éireann.
3. The Houses of the Oireachtas shall sit in or near the City of Dublin or in such other place as they may from time to time determine.
4. The sole and exclusive power of making laws for the State is hereby vested in the Oireachtas: no other legislative authority has power to make laws for the State.
5. Provision may however be made by law for the creation or recognition of subordinate legislatures and for the powers and functions of these legislatures....

INTERNATIONAL RELATIONS

Article 29.

1. Ireland affirms its devotion to the ideal of peace and friendly co-operation amongst nations founded on international justice and morality.
2. Ireland affirms its adherence to the principle of the pacific settlement of international disputes by international arbitration or judicial determination.
3. Ireland accepts the generally recognised principles of international law as its rule of conduct in its relations with other States....

FUNDAMENTAL RIGHTS

Personal Rights.

Article 40.

1. All citizens shall, as human persons, be held equal before the law. This shall not be held to mean that the State shall not in its enactments have due regard to differences of capacity, physical and moral, and of social function.
2. Titles of nobility shall not be conferred by the State.
3. No title of nobility or of honour may be accepted by any citizen except with the prior approval of the Government.
4. The State guarantees in its laws to respect, and, as far as practicable, by its laws to defend and vindicate the personal rights of the citizen....

Religion.

Article 44.

1. The State acknowledges that the homage of public worship is due to Almighty God. It shall hold His Name in reverence, and shall respect and honour religion.
2. Freedom of conscience and the free profession and practice of religion are, subject to public order and morality, guaranteed to every citizen.
3. The State guarantees not to endow any religion.
4. The State shall not impose any disabilities or make any discrimination on the ground of religious profession, belief or status.
5. Legislation providing State aid for schools shall not discriminate between schools under the management of different religious denominations, nor be such as to affect prejudicially the right of any child to attend a school receiving public money without attending religious instruction at that school.
6. Every religious denomination shall have the right to manage its own affairs, own, acquire and administer property, movable and immovable, and maintain institutions for religious or charitable purposes.
7. The property of any religious denomination or any educational institution shall not be diverted save for necessary works of public utility and on payment of compensation.

Winston Churchill, Telegram to Éamon de Valera, 9 December 1941, and extract from Speech on V-E Day (1941 & 1945)

Winston Churchill was appointed prime minister of the United Kingdom on 10 May 1940 shortly after the outbreak of World War II. Ireland declared itself neutral during the war. The telegram Churchill sent to de Valera in 1941 is often interpreted as a promise to support Irish unification if Ireland joined the war effort. In the speech delivered on 13 May 1945 Churchill was very critical of Ireland's policy of official neutrality.

Telegram from Winston Churchill to Éamon de Valera (Dublin)[2]
(No. 120) (Most Immediate)
Received, DUBLIN, 00.30 8 December 1941

Following from Prime Minister for Mr. de Valera. Personal, private and secret. Begins.

Now is your chance. Now or never. "A Nation once again." Am very ready to meet you at any time. Ends.

Speech 13 May 1945[3]

It was five years ago on Thursday last that His Majesty the King commissioned me to form a National Government of all parties to carry on our affairs. Five years is a long time in human life, especially when there is no remission for good conduct. However, this National Government was sustained by Parliament and by the entire British nation at home and by all our fighting men abroad, and by the unswerving co-operation of the Dominions far across the oceans and of our Empire in every quarter of the globe. After various episodes had occurred it became clear last week that so far things have worked out pretty well, and that the British Commonwealth and Empire stands more united and more effectively powerful than at any time in its long romantic history. Certainly we are—this is what may well, I think, be admitted by any fair-minded person—in a far better state to cope with the problems and perils of the future than we were five years ago.

---

2   Telegram from Winston Churchill to Éamon de Valera, available at Documents on Irish Foreign Policy, www.difp.ie.

3   "Churchill's War Time Speeches," Churchill Society.

For a while our prime enemy, our mighty enemy, Germany, overran almost all Europe. France, who bore such a frightful strain in the last great war, was beaten to the ground and took some time to recover. The Low Countries, fighting to the best of their strength, were subjugated. Norway was overrun. Mussolini's Italy stabbed us in the back when we were, as he thought, at our last gasp. But for ourselves—our lot, I mean—the British Commonwealth and Empire, we were absolutely alone. In July, August and September 1940, forty or fifty squadrons of British fighter aircraft in the Battle of Britain broke the teeth of the German air fleet at odds of seven or eight to one. May I repeat again the words I used at that momentous hour: 'Never in the field of human conflict was so much owed by so many to so few.' The name of Air Chief Marshal Lord Dowding will always be linked with this splendid event. But conjoined with the Royal Air Force lay the Royal Navy, ever ready to tear to pieces the barges, gathered from the canals of Holland and Belgium, in which a German invading army could alone have been transported. I was never one to believe that the invasion of Britain, with the tackle that the enemy had at that time, was a very easy task to accomplish. With the autumn storms, the immediate danger of invasion in 1940 passed.

Then began the blitz, when Hitler said he would "rub out our cities." That's what he said: "rub out our cities." This blitz was borne without a word of complaint or the slightest sign of flinching, while a very large number of people—honour to them all—proved that London could take it, and so could our other ravaged centres. But the dawn of 1941 revealed us still in jeopardy. The hostile aircraft could fly across the approaches to our Island, where forty-six millions of people had to import half their daily bread and all the materials they needed for peace or war: these hostile aircraft could fly across the approaches from Brest to Norway and back again in a single flight. They could observe all the movements of our shipping in and out of the Clyde and Mersey, and could direct upon our convoys the large and increasing numbers of U-boats with which the enemy be-spattered the Atlantic—the survivors or successors of which U-boats are now being collected in British harbours.

The sense of envelopment, which might at any moment turn to strangulation, lay heavy upon us. We had only the Northwestern approach between Ulster and Scotland through which to bring in the means of life and to send out the forces of war. Owing to the action of Mr de Valery, so much at variance with the temper and instinct of thousands of Southern Irishmen who hastened to the battle-front to prove their ancient valour, the approaches which the Southern Irish ports and airfields could so easily have guarded were closed by the hostile aircraft and U-boats. This was indeed a deadly moment in our life, and if it had not been for the loyalty and friendship of

Northern Ireland we should have been forced to come to close quarters with Mr de Valery or perish for ever from the earth. However, with a restraint and poise to which, I say, history will find few parallels, His Majesty's Government never laid a violent hand upon them though at times it would have been quite easy and quite natural, and we left the de Valery Government to frolic with the Germans and later with the Japanese representatives to their hearts content.

When I think of these days I think also of other episodes and personalities. I think of **Lieutenant-Commander Esmonde, VC, or Lance-Corporal Connally, VC, and Captain Fegen, VC,** and other Irish heroes that I could easily recite, and then I must confess that bitterness by Britain against the Irish race dies in my heart. I can only pray that in years which I shall not see the shame will be forgotten and the glories will endure, and that the peoples of the British Isles as of the British Commonwealth of Nations will walk together in mutual comprehension and forgiveness....

Lieutenant-Commander Esmonde, VC, or Lance-Corporal Connally, VC, and Captain Fegen, VC: Winners of the Victoria Cross, the highest award for valor in the British Armed Forces, who were from Ireland or of Irish descent.

Éamon de Valera, Response to Churchill (1945)[4]

Éamon de Valera (1882–1975) was an Irish nationalist politician. He took
part in the Easter Rising but escaped execution because he was born in the
United States. He opposed the Anglo-Irish Treaty but eventually returned to
Irish politics in the Free State and formed the political party Fianna Fáil in
1926. He became the head of government in the Irish Free State in 1932 and
remained as Taoiseach (prime minister) until 1948, serving again from 1951
to 1954 and from 1957 to 1959. He was then Uachtaran (president) from 1959
to 1973. In this speech he responds to Winston Churchill's criticism of Irish
neutrality in World War II (see Document 60).

℘

I have here before me the pencilled notes from which I broadcast to you
on 3 September 1939. I had so many other things to do on that day that
I could not find time to piece them together into a connected statement.
From these notes I see that I said that noting the march of events your
Government had decided its policy the previous spring, and had announced
its decision to the world.

The aim of our policy, I said, would be to keep our people out of the war.
I reminded you of what I had said in the Dail that in our circumstances,
with our history and our experience after the last war and with a part of our
country still unjustly severed from us; no other policy was possible.

Certain newspapers have been very persistent in looking for my answer
to Mr. Churchill's recent broadcast. I know the kind of answer I am expected
to make. I know the answer that first springs to the lips of every man of
Irish blood who heard or read that speech, no matter in what circumstances
or in what part of the world he found himself.

I know the reply I would have given a quarter of a century ago. But I
have deliberately decided that that is not the reply I shall make tonight. I
shall strive not to be guilty of adding any fuel to the flames of hatred and
passion which, if continued to be fed, promise to burn up whatever is left
by the war of decent human feeling in Europe.

Allowances can be made for Mr. Churchill's statement, however unworthy,
in the first flush of his victory. No such excuse could be found for me in
this quieter atmosphere. There are, however some things which it is my
duty to say, some things which it is essential to say. I shall try to say them
as dispassionately as I can.

---

4   "Taoiseach's Broadcast to the Nation," *Irish Press*, 17 May 1945.

Mr. Churchill makes it clear that, in certain circumstances, he would have violated our neutrality and that he would justify his action by Britain's necessity. It seems strange to me that Mr. Churchill does not see that this, if accepted, would mean Britain's necessity would become a moral code and that when this necessity became sufficiently great, other people's rights were not to count.

It is quite true that other great Powers believe in this same code—in their own regard—and have behaved in accordance with it. That is precisely why we have the disastrous succession of wars—World War No. 1 and World War No. 2—and shall it be World War No. 3?

Surely Mr. Churchill must see that if his contention be admitted in our regard, a like justification can be framed for similar acts of aggression elsewhere and no small nation adjoining a great Power could ever hope to be permitted to go its own way in peace.

It is indeed fortunate that Britain's necessity did not reach the point when Mr. Churchill would have acted. All credit to him that he successfully resisted the temptation which, I have no doubt, many times assailed him in his difficulties and to which I freely admit many leaders might have easily succumbed. It is indeed hard for the strong to be just to the weak, but acting justly always has its rewards.

By resisting his temptation in this instance, Mr. Churchill, instead of adding another horrid chapter to the already bloodstained record of the relations between England and this country, has advanced the cause of international morality an important step—one of the most important, indeed, that can be taken on the road to the establishment of any sure basis for peace.

As far as the peoples of these two islands are concerned, it may, perhaps, mark a fresh beginning towards the realisation of that mutual comprehension to which Mr. Churchill has referred for which, I hope, he will not merely pray but work also, as did **his predecessor** who will yet, I believe, find the honoured place in British history which is due to him, as certainly he will find it in any fair record of the relations between Britain and ourselves.

That Mr. Churchill should be irritated when our neutrality stood in the way of what he thought he vitally needed, I understand, but that he or any thinking person in Britain or elsewhere should fail to see the reason for our neutrality, I find it hard to conceive.

I would like to put a hypothetical question—it is a question I have put to many Englishmen since the last war. Suppose Germany had won the war, had invaded and occupied England, and that after a long lapse of time and many bitter struggles, she was finally brought to acquiesce in admitting England's right to freedom, and let England go, but not the whole of England, all but, let us say, the six southern counties.

His predecessor:
Churchill's predecessor as Prime Minister was Neville Chamberlain, most famous for his policy of appeasement towards Nazi Germany; de Valera had been able to successfully negotiate an end to the Anglo-Irish Trade War with Chamberlain in 1938.

These six southern counties, those, let us suppose, commanding the entrance to the narrow seas, Germany had singled out and insisted on holding herself with a view to weakening England as a whole, and maintaining the securing of her own communications through the Straits of Dover.

Let us suppose further, that after all this had happened, Germany was engaged in a great war in which she could show that she was on the side of freedom of a number of small nations, would Mr. Churchill as an Englishman who believed that his own nation had as good a right to freedom as any other, not freedom for a part merely, but freedom for the whole— would he, whilst Germany still maintained the partition of his country and occupied six counties of it, would he lead this partitioned England to join with Germany in a crusade? I do not think Mr. Churchill would.

Would he think the people of partitioned England an object of shame if they stood neutral in such circumstances? I do not think Mr. Churchill would.

Mr. Churchill is proud of Britain's stand alone, after France had fallen and before America entered the War.

Could he not find in his heart the generosity to acknowledge that there is a small nation that stood alone not for one year or two, but for several hundred years against aggression; that endured spoliations, famines, massacres in endless succession; that was clubbed many times into insensibility, but that each time on returning consciousness took up the fight anew; a small nation that could never be got to accept defeat and has never surrendered her soul?

Mr. Churchill is justly proud of his nation's perseverance against heavy odds. But we in this island are still prouder of our people's perseverance for freedom through all the centuries. We, of our time, have played our part in the perseverance, and we have pledged our selves to the dead generations who have preserved intact for us this glorious heritage, that we, too, will strive to be faithful to the end, and pass on this tradition unblemished.

Many a time in the past there appeared little hope except that hope to which Mr. Churchill referred, that by standing fast a time would come when, to quote his own words: "… the tyrant would make some ghastly mistake which would alter the whole balance of the struggle."

I sincerely trust, however, that it is not thus our ultimate unity and freedom will be achieved, though as a younger man I confess I prayed even for that, and indeed at times saw no other.

In latter years, I have had a vision of a nobler and better ending, better for both our people and for the future of mankind. For that I have now been long working. I regret that it is not to this nobler purpose that Mr. Churchill is lending his hand rather than, by the abuse of a people who have done him no wrong, trying to find in a crisis like the present excuse for continuing the injustice of the mutilation of our country.

I sincerely hope that Mr. Churchill has not deliberately chosen the latter course but, if he has, however regretfully we may say it, we can only say, be it so.

Meanwhile, even as a partitioned small nation, we shall go on and strive to play our part in the world continuing unswervingly to work for the cause of true freedom and for peace and understanding between all nations.

The Republic of Ireland Act (1948)[5]

Ireland had remained a dominion of the British Empire since the Anglo-Irish Treaty. This act passed in Ireland in 1948 formally severed that relationship and ended any remaining role for the British monarchy in the Irish state.

ev

AN ACT TO REPEAL THE EXECUTIVE AUTHORITY (EXTERNAL RELATIONS) ACT, 1936, TO DECLARE THAT THE DESCRIPTION OF THE STATE SHALL BE THE REPUBLIC OF IRELAND, AND TO ENABLE THE PRESIDENT TO EXERCISE THE EXECUTIVE POWER OR ANY EXECUTIVE FUNCTION OF THE STATE IN OR IN CONNECTION WITH ITS EXTERNAL RELATIONS. [21st December, 1948.]

BE IT ENACTED BY THE OIREACHTAS AS FOLLOWS:—

1.—The Executive Authority (External Relations) Act, 1936 (No. 58 of 1936), is hereby repealed.

2.—It is hereby declared that the description of the State shall be the Republic of Ireland.

3.—The President, on the authority and on the advice of the Government, may exercise the executive power or any executive function of the State in or in connection with its external relations.

4.—This Act shall come into operation on such day as the Government may by order appoint.

5.—This Act may be cited as The Republic of Ireland Act, 1948.

---

5 "The Republic of Ireland Act, 1948," *Irish Statute Book,* http://www.irishstatutebook.ie.

DOCUMENT 63:

From the Ireland Act (1949)

> The Act was passed by the parliament of the United Kingdom in response to the Republic of Ireland Act of 1948. It formally recognized the new constitutional position of Ireland and addressed the issue of citizenship for residents of the Irish Republic, who up until 1948 had legally been British subjects.

ev

An Act to recognise and declare the constitutional position as to the part of Ireland heretofore known as Eire, and to make provision as to the name by which it may be known and the manner in which the law is to apply in relation to it; to declare and affirm the constitutional position and the territorial integrity of Northern Ireland and to amend, as respects the Parliament of the United Kingdom, the law relating to the qualifications of electors in constituencies in Northern Ireland; and for purposes connected with the matters aforesaid.

[2nd June 1949]

Be it enacted by the King's most Excellent Majesty, by and with the advice and consent of the Lords Spiritual and Temporal, and Commons, in this present Parliament assembled, and by the authority of the same, as follows:—

1 Constitutional provisions.

(1) It is hereby recognized and declared that the part of Ireland heretofore known as Eire ceased, as from the eighteenth day of April, nineteen hundred and forty-nine, to be part of His Majesty's dominions.

(2) It is hereby declared that Northern Ireland remains part of His Majesty's dominions and of the United Kingdom and it is hereby affirmed that in no event will Northern Ireland or any part thereof cease to be part of His Majesty's dominions and of the United Kingdom without the consent of the Parliament of Northern Ireland.

(3) The part of Ireland referred to in subsection (1) of this section is hereafter in this Act referred to, and may in any Act, enactment or instrument passed or made after the passing of this Act be referred to, by the name attributed thereto by the law thereof, that is to say, as the Republic of Ireland.

2 Republic of Ireland not a foreign country.

(1) It is hereby declared that, notwithstanding that the Republic of Ireland is not part of His Majesty's dominions, the Republic of Ireland is not a foreign country for the purposes of any law in force in any part of the United Kingdom or in any colony, protectorate or United Kingdom trust territory, whether by virtue of a rule of law or of an Act of Parliament or any other enactment or instrument whatsoever, whether passed or made before or after the passing of this Act, and references in any Act of Parliament, other enactment or instrument whatsoever, whether passed or made before or after the passing of this Act, to foreigners, aliens, foreign countries, and foreign or foreign-built ships or aircraft shall be construed accordingly.

(2) The person who, in the United Kingdom, is the chief representative of the Republic of Ireland or of the Government thereof shall, whatever the style of his office, have the same privileges and exemptions as to taxation and otherwise as fall to be accorded under the law for the time being in force to High Commissioners and Agents General within the meaning of section nineteen of the [13 & 14 Geo. 5. c. 14.] Finance Act, 1923, and his staff shall have the same privileges and exemptions as to taxation and "otherwise as fall to be accorded under the law for the time being in force to their staffs....

5 Provisions as to operation of British Nationality Act, 1948.

(1) A person who—

(a) was born before the sixth day of December, nineteen hundred and twenty-two, in the part of Ireland which now forms the Republic of Ireland; and

(b) was a British subject immediately before the date of the commencement of the British Nationality Act, 1948, shall not be deemed to have ceased to be a British subject on the coming into force of that Act unless either—

(i) he was, on the said sixth day of December, domiciled in the part of Ireland which now forms the Republic of Ireland; or

(ii) he was, on or after the tenth day of April nineteen hundred and thirty-five, and before the date of the commencement of that Act, permanently resident in that part of Ireland; or

(iii) he had, before the date of the commencement of that Act, been registered as a citizen of Eire under the laws of that part of Ireland relating to citizenship.

(2) In relation to persons born before the said sixth day of December in the part of Ireland which now forms the Republic of Ireland, being persons who do not satisfy any of the conditions specified in paragraphs (i), (ii) and (iii) of subsection (1) of this section, sections twelve and thirteen of the said Act (which relate to citizenship of the United Kingdom and Colonies and to British subjects without citizenship) shall have effect and be deemed always to have had effect as if, in paragraph (a) of subsection (4) of the said section twelve, the words "or a citizen of Eire" and in subsection (1) of the said section thirteen, the words "or of Eire" were omitted.

(3) So much of the said Act as has the effect of providing that a person is, in specified circumstances, to be treated for the purposes of that Act as having been a British subject immediately before the commencement thereof shall apply also for the purposes of this section.

(4) Nothing in this section affects the position of any person who, on the coming into force of the British Nationality Act, 1948, became a citizen of the United Kingdom and Colonies or a British subject without citizenship apart from the provisions of this section.

DOCUMENT 64:

From *A Catholic Handbook for Irish Men & Women Going to England* (1953)

Ireland had high rates emigration beginning with the Great Irish Famine and continuing through most of the twentieth century. The Ireland Act of 1949 (Document 63) meant that Irish people could easily emigrate to England for work. This guidebook handed out to emigrants on boarding boats bound for England sought to help young Irish people adjust to life in England and to preserve their Catholic faith, a significant concern for Church leaders.

❧

For many years now, economic difficulties—especially the scarcity of work in counties like Mayo, Kerry and Galway—have caused boys and girls to leave their homes in Ireland to seek a living in the land across the water. Away from their homes and families, often with few or no friends, they have tried to settle down to a new kind of life. They have found it hard to get suitable lodgings, to discover the whereabouts of the Catholic church, to get used to the ways of the English people in general, and English Catholics in particular. It is no wonder that many have fallen away from their religion, that others have grown weak and careless in their service of God, that only those who have a strong faith and a sound knowledge of what their religion means have remained good, practising Catholics.

When we think of the tragedy which the loss of even one soul means to God, we begin to realise how awful it is that so many of the emigrants drift away from serving Him. It is in order to help you to be loyal to Our Lord while in England that this "Handbook" has been drawn up....

The Average Englishman

English people may seem cold and aloof at first but they will become friendly as they get used to you. They rarely lose their temper and look on peace and quiet as the great aim in life. While this is good in many ways, it means that the average Englishman does not live by fixed principles or beliefs. He finds it difficult to understand them in others. Yet he has a real respect for people who stick to their principles even if it is difficult to do so. He often tries to conceal the respect he has for a good Catholic by ridiculing the Catholic religion. His knowledge of God is very sketchy because for many years now the children in English State schools have been taught very little about serving God. It is no use merely arguing about these things with him. You, being Irish, will probably lose your temper; he, being English, will keep calm.

Nor is it any use trying to answer all the questions he will ask you. But, if you can answer some of his questions, his respect for you and your religion will grow; if he is really interested, he will listen while you explain things about the Church. Something you say may start him thinking—and you will have started some one on the way to becoming a Catholic. After all, every year in England and Wales alone, some 12,000 people become Catholics.

DOCUMENT 65:

From Oliver Reilly, *A Worker in Birmingham* (1958)[6]

Birmingham was a significant industrial city in England. Following World War II it suffered a labor shortage and so the city was a popular destination for Irish immigrants. Oliver Reilly was an organizer for Muintir na Tire, a voluntary organization focused on community development. He traveled to Birmingham for three weeks to observe the Irish community there for the *Furrow*, an Irish Catholic magazine.

℘

In June of last year, with the permission of the National Executive of Muintir na Tire, I set sail for Birmingham, England, to find out for myself the truth about the lot of our people over there. I decided I would go as the thousands of others go, with just a few pounds, accepting their ways of living, working conditions, living conditions, etc., especially the conditions applying to the unskilled workers, who form the greater pecking order the many who go....

I share a room with a grand lad from Mayo. He drives the buses. He introduces me to his girl friend, also from the West of Ireland. They are engaged and are saving up to get married. She is a lovely girl of twenty-two, and he a fine lad of twenty-four. He earns £15 per week with overtime, and she about £7 or £8. She sleeps next room, and they share food and she washes his shirts. "When will you be married?" I ask, and am told "some-time." "But it is not exactly right living together like this," said I. She says: "you are old-fashioned, Oliver, we are here for the past couple of years, and can take care of ourselves. We do not want to get married for a while as we can not have children in houses; landlords will not allow you to stay." Poor couple, I liked them very much. They send home some money to help their parents each week. They are very bitter against Irish clergy, but speak kindly of priests over here. "The priests in Ireland don't care a hang what happens us, they are snobs."...

I met Father Murphy of the Irish Centre, and was shown over this eight-roomed establishment, where a cup of tea, a list of land ladies, and a few hours rest is given to any Irish emigrant who is on the rocks. The place is doing a great job under trying conditions; money is badly needed, and voluntary workers have a heavy task in meeting trains as early as 5 a.m. There is no doubt but that the clergy are doing everything humanly possible to save the people. Went into a café where the waitress told me she was a native of Thurles, and that the girl on the lift was from Cork. Both are

---

6   Oliver Reilly, "A Worker in Birmingham," *The Furrow*, vol. 9, no. 4, April 1958.

married and have no children. "We have to work and children would be a hindrance," they told me. They talked of Irish governments and bemoaned the fact of no work at home. Bitterness at the neglect of clergy at home, who do not use their power to help. All the emigrants I have met and they were many seemed to have the notion that Church and State combined against them at home, and that the opposite prevails in England. The only ones they held dear and with any power to influence those exiles are their old folk at home. "The old man" or "the old woman" are words spoken with the deepest feeling of love and affection: "The only ones I care about," "I must send a few bob." "I wouldn't like them to know." Stand in any group of Irish, let them be ever so tough, and I guarantee you will hear some of the foregoing words within five minutes....

Now my time is nearly over and my boat sails tomorrow. What did I find?

No. 1. I found out that the Irish leave home for economic reasons and I mean the huge number of unskilled or semi-skilled workers which form the greater portion of the emigrants.

No. 2. That work and conditions of work (overtime, breaks, wages) are excellent, and leave little to be desired.

No. 3. That living conditions for people unable to purchase their own house are very bad; often workers are forced to live four and five to a room with great danger to health and morals; accommodation is scarce and very expensive.

No. 4. That landladies will not allow children in houses let. Hence birth control is practised freely.

No. 5. That since women work and can get plenty of it there is no home life, and of course no family.

No. 6. That the Irish lose the faith is without doubt, or to say the most for them, the girls drift and hold on a little but men drift completely. I will put it this way, a boy and girl of twenty-one may hold on to the faith, but their children have little hope at all.

No. 7. That Irish care only for their parents, and that if any thing is to be done to save our boys and girls it must have the whole hearted support of the parents.

No. 8. That of the hundreds of professionals who emigrate each year it can truly be said that they are a credit to themselves and Ireland, and it is true to say that they are doing wonderful work in many spheres to help the less fortunate along. I met many who in their spare time went from house to house (being insulted at times) contacting Irish men and girls.

No. 9. That where Muintir na Tire comes in is by way of education. I really believe that a wonderful amount of good can be done by preparing people for what lies ahead. I believe, too, that Muintir na Tire could use its influence with parents to make an all-out effort to have their boys and girls home at least once a year, and in this way keep constant contact with people away from home. This will also let them see that somebody cares and is interested in their welfare.

No. 10. That every exile I spoke to would gladly come back to Ireland and accept half what he is getting in England if they could be sure of constant employment.

No. 11. I recommend that a small grant be given towards the new Irish Centre and that literature and photos be sent for display in windows. While there I saw many photographs of football matches, horse-racing, sports, dances, etc. from various parts of Ireland. We at home should show our goodwill in every concrete way.

DOCUMENT 66:

From Sean Lemass, Statement to the European Economic Community (18 January 1962)[7]

Sean Lemass (1899–1971) was an Irish politician and member of the Fianna Fáil political party. He served as Taoiseach from 1959 to 1966. He spent much of his time in office focusing on economic expansion. The major foreign policy goal of his administration was to obtain membership in the European Economic Community (the European Union). This statement is from Ireland's unsuccessful application for membership in 1962. Ireland's application was turned down because the United Kingdom's was also rejected and it was felt that Ireland was too dependent on trade with the United Kingdom.

Mr. Chairman:

I would like, at the outset, on behalf of the Government of Ireland, to thank you for your kindness in arranging this meeting. We appreciate very much the opportunity you have thus provided for an exchange of views on Ireland's application for membership of the European Economic Community with the representatives of the Governments of the member States. I hope that what I shall say will be of help to you in considering our application. I am also pleased that the Commission is represented at this meeting.

Ireland belongs to Europe by history, tradition and sentiment no less than by geography. Our destiny is bound up with that of Europe and our outlook and our way of life have for fifteen centuries been moulded by the Christian ideals and the intellectual and cultural values on which European civilisation rests. Our people have always tended to look to Europe for inspiration, guidance and encouragement.

It is thus natural that we in Ireland should regard with keen and sympathetic interest every genuine effort to bring the peoples of Europe closer together, so as to strengthen the foundations of our common civilisation. We were happy at the development in the years following the last war of a strong movement towards closer European union; and we have participated actively from the outset in the two organisations established to promote cooperation between European States, the Organisation for European Economic Cooperation and the Council of Europe. While Ireland did not accede to the North Atlantic Treaty, we have always agreed with the

7 "Statement by Sean Lemass (Brussels, 18 January 1962)," available at www.cvce.eu.

general aim of that Treaty. The fact that we did not accede to it was due to special circumstances and does not qualify in any way our acceptance of the ideal of European unity and of the conception, embodied in the Treaty of Rome and the Bonn Declaration of 18 July last, of the duties, obligations and responsibilities which European unity would impose.

The Treaty of Rome, as an expression of the ideal of European unity, brought into being a more closely integrated organisation than either the Council of Europe or the Organisation for European Economic Cooperation. Political considerations, we know, played a considerable part in the motivation and the successful outcome of the negotiations for the Treaty and the aims of the European Economic Community go much beyond purely economic matters. The Contracting Parties in the preamble to the Treaty affirmed their determination to lay the foundations of an ever closer union between European peoples and their resolve to strengthen, by combining their resources, the safeguards of peace and freedom. Their call to other peoples of Europe to join in their effort was addressed to those "who share their ideal." In the Bonn Declaration, they reaffirmed their resolve to develop their political cooperation with a view to the union of their peoples and set in motion procedures designed to give statutory form to this union....

Our principal concern in the agricultural sphere relates to the manner in which British agricultural and food import policy will be harmonised with that of the Community. As you know, a high proportion of our agricultural exports goes to the United Kingdom, and we have long-standing trade agreements which reflect our economic relations with that country. We realise that, when a common agricultural policy is in full operation in an enlarged Community including—as we hope it will—the United Kingdom and Ireland, our economic arrangements with the United Kingdom would become merged in a greater whole, but we expect that in the normal course of things the United Kingdom market will continue to provide an outlet for a considerable proportion of our agricultural exports. The nature of the arrangements which have yet to be settled in relation to the agricultural and food import policy of the United Kingdom in the context of her membership of the Common Market will be of vital concern to us....

External trade, particularly trade with Western Europe, is of great importance to Ireland's economy. Exports represent almost one-quarter of gross national product, while imports exceed one-third. In relation to gross national product, Ireland's external trade is the second highest in Europe. Four-fifths of our exports go to, and almost two-thirds of our imports come from, the United Kingdom and the present member States of the Community. As far as industrial exports are concerned, we have enjoyed for many years in the British market conditions of free entry similar to those which the Rome Treaty will have established between the member States when the Common

Market is finally in being. These advantages we shall henceforth be sharing progressively with many Continental countries. We are, therefore, disposed to look to Continental Europe for new scope and opportunity for the expansion of industrial exports. As yet, our export trade in industrial products to the Continent is small. Indeed, there is at present a significant lack of balance in our general trade relations with the Community; we import from the existing members over three times as much as we export to them....

Because of the close inter-relationship of the economy of Ireland and that of the United Kingdom, and the vital interest of Ireland in agricultural trade, the Irish Government would hope that the discussions for the admission of Ireland to the Community might be brought to completion at the same time as those for the United Kingdom. We would greatly appreciate being granted the opportunity of following closely the course of the discussions with the United Kingdom and other countries on matters of concern to Ireland and of having our views taken into consideration before conclusions are reached.

DOCUMENT 67:

From Terence O'Neill, *Ulster Stands at the Crossroads* (1968)[8]

Terence O'Neill (1914–90) was the prime minister of Northern Ireland
from 1963 until 1969 and leader of the Ulster Unionist Party. Following the
Anglo-Irish Treaty of 1921, Northern Ireland became a separate country with
its own internal government dominated by a Protestant elite. In the 1960s a
growing movement for Catholic civil rights was frequently met with violence
by the police. As the nation became increasingly unstable O'Neill, a moderate
unionist, gave this televised speech in 1968.

Ulster stands at the crossroads.

I believe you know me well enough to appreciate that I am not a man given
to extravagant language. But I must say to you this evening that our conduct
over the coming days and weeks will decide our future. And as we face this
situation, I would be failing in my duty, to you as your prime minister, if I
did not put the issues calmly and clearly before you all. These issues are far
too serious to be determined behind closed doors, or left to noisy minorities. The time has come for the people as a whole to speak in a clear voice.

For more than six years now I have tried to heal some of the deep divisions in our communities. I did so because I could not see how an Ulster
divided against itself could not hope to stand. I made it clear that a Northern
Ireland based on the interests of any one section, rather than on the interests
of all, could have no long term future.

Throughout the community many people have responded warmly to my
words. But if Ulster is to become the happy and united place it could be there
must be the will throughout our Province, and particularly in Parliament,
to translate these words into deeds....

But these considerations, important though they are, are not my main
concern. What I seek—and I ask for help and understanding of you all—is
a swift end to the growing civil disorder throughout Ulster. For as matters
stand today we are on the brink of chaos where neighbour could be set
against neighbour.... We must tackle root causes if this agitation is to be
contained. We must be able to say to the moderates of both sides: Come
with us into a new era of co-operation and leave the extremists to the
law. But this I also say to all Protestants or Roman Catholic, **Unionist** or
Nationalist:—Disorder must now cease....

Unionist: Someone in
Northern Ireland who wants
to remain part of the United
Kingdom.

Nationalist: Someone
in Northern Ireland who
wants independence from
the United Kingdom and a
united Ireland.

---

8   Terence O'Neill, "Ulster at the Cross Roads," available at https://cain.ulster.ac.uk.

And now I saw to say a word directly to those who have been demonstrating for **Civil Rights**. The changes which we have announced are genuine and far-reaching changes and the Government is totally committed to them. I would not continue to preside over an administration which would water them down or make them meaningless…. I believe that most of you want change, not revolution. Your voice has been heard and clearly heard. Your duty now is to play your part in taking the heat out of the situation before blood is shed….

But I have a word too for all those others who see in change a threat to our position in the United Kingdom. I say to them unionism armed with justice will be a stronger cause than unionism armed merely with strength. The bully-boy tactics we saw in **Armagh** are no answer to these grave problems: but they incur for us the contempt of Britain and the world—and such contempt is the greatest threat to Ulster. Let the Government govern and the police take care of law and order….

And now a further word to you all. What kind of Ulster do you want? A happy and respected province, in good standing with the rest of the United Kingdom? Or a place continually torn apart by riots and demonstrations, regarded by the rest of Britain as a political outcast? As always in a democracy, the choice is yours. I will accept whatever your verdict may be. If it is your decision to live up to the words "Ulster is British," which is part of our creed, then my services will be at your disposal to do what I can. But if you should want a separate, inward-looking, selfish and divided Ulster, then you must seek for others to lead you along that road. For I cannot and will not do it. Please weigh well all that is at stake and make your voice heard in whatever way you think best, so that we may know the views not of the few, but of the many.

Civil Rights: The Northern Ireland Civil Rights Association was committed to non-violent protest; it sought to end gerrymandering and discrimination against Catholics in employment and public housing.

Armagh: A peaceful civil rights march was attacked by Unionist counter-protestors; this became very common.

DOCUMENT 68:

From Bernadette Devlin, Maiden Speech in the House of Commons (1969)[9]

Bernadette Devlin (b. 1947) is an Irish civil rights leader who was elected to parliament in 1969 and served until 1974. Devlin came from a Catholic family with Irish Republican politics. Traditionally, Irish Republicans from Northern Ireland do not take their seats in parliament as a matter of political principle. Devlin ran on a platform that she would take her seat and ensure representation for the people of her district. At 21 she was the youngest member of the House of Commons and the youngest woman ever elected to parliament.

_ev_

I understand that in making my maiden speech on the day of my arrival in Parliament and in making it on a controversial issue I flaunt the unwritten traditions of the House, but I think that the situation of my people merits the flaunting of such traditions.

I remind the honourable Member for Londonderry (**Mr. Chichester-Clark**) that I too was in the Bogside area on the night that he was there. As the honourable gentleman rightly said, there never was born an Englishman who understands the Irish people. Thus a man who is alien to the ordinary working Irish people cannot understand them, and I therefore respectfully suggest that the honourable gentleman has no understanding of my people, because Catholics and Protestants are the ordinary people, the oppressed people from whom I come and whom I represent. I stand here as the youngest woman in Parliament, in the same tradition as the first woman ever to be elected to this Parliament, **Constance Markievicz**, who was elected on behalf of the Irish people....

We came to the situation in Derry when the people had had enough. Since October 5th, it has been the unashamed and deliberate policy of the Unionist Government to try to force an image of the civil rights movement that it was nothing more than a Catholic uprising. The people in the movement have struggled desperately to overcome that image—but it is impossible when the ruling minority are the government, and control not only political matters but the so-called impartial forces of law and order. It is impossible then for us to state quite fairly where we stand.

How can we say that we are a non-sectarian movement and are for the rights of both Catholics and Protestants when, clearly, we are beaten into

Mr. Chichester-Clark: James Chichester-Clark (1923–2002) was a Unionist politician in Northern Ireland; he succeeded Terence O'Neill as leader of the Ulster Unionist Party and prime minister of Northern Ireland.

Constance Markievicz: Markievicz (1868–1927) was an Irish revolutionary who fought in the Easter Rising; she was the first woman elected to the House of Commons in 1918 although as an Irish Republican she did not take her seat and instead served in the breakaway First Dáil.

9   HC Deb 22 April 1969 vol. 782 cc262–324, available at https://api.parliament.uk.

the Catholic areas? Never have we been beaten into the Protestant areas. When the students marched from Belfast to Derry, there was a predominant number of Protestants. The number of non-Catholics was greater than the number of Catholics. Nevertheless we were still beaten into the Catholic area because it was in the interests of the minority and the Unionist Party to establish that we were nothing more than a Catholic uprising—just as it is in the interest of the honourable Member for Londonderry to come up with all this tripe about the IRA....

The Unionist policy has always been to divide the people who are dependent upon them. The question of voting is tied up mainly with the question of housing, and this is something which the House has failed to understand. The people of Northern Ireland want votes not for the sake of voting but for the sake of being able to exercise democratic rights over the controlling powers of their own areas. The present system operates in such a way that Unionist-controlled councils and even Nationalist-controlled councils discriminate against those in their areas who are in the minority. The policy of segregated housing is to be clearly seen in the smallest villages of Ulster. The people of Ulster want the right to vote and for each vote to be of equal value so that, when it comes to the question of building more houses, we do not have the situation which we already have in Derry and in Dungannon....

Tory: A British term meaning Conservative.

There is no denying that the problem and the reason for this situation in Northern Ireland is social and economic, because the people of Northern Ireland are being oppressed not only by a **Tory** Government, a misruling Tory Government and an absolutely corrupt, bigoted and self interested Tory Government, but by a Tory Government of whom even the Tories in this House ought to be ashamed and from which they should dissociate themselves....

I should like in conclusion to take a brief look at the future. This is where the question of British troops arises. The question before this House—in view of the apathy, neglect and lack of understanding which this House has shown to these people in Ulster—is how in the shortest space it can make up for 50 years of neglect, apathy and lack of understanding. Short of producing miracles, such as factories overnight in Derry and homes overnight in practically every area, what can we do?

If British troops are sent in I should not like to be either the mother or sister of an unfortunate soldier stationed there. The honourable member ... may talk 'till Domesday about "our boys in khaki," but it has to be recognised that the one point in common among Ulstermen is that they are not very fond of Englishmen who tell them what to do.

Possibly the most extreme solution, since there can be no justice while there is a Unionist Party, because while there is a Unionist Party they will by their gerrymandering control Northern Ireland and be the Government of Northern Ireland, is to consider the possibility of abolishing **Stormont** and ruling from Westminster. Then we should have the ironical situation in which the people who once shouted **"Home rule is Rome rule"** were screaming their heads off for home rule, so dare anyone take Stormont away? They would have to ship every Government Member out of the country for his own safety—because only the "rank" defends, such as the Prime Minister and the Minister of Agriculture.

Another solution which the Government may decide to adopt is to do nothing but serve notice on the Unionist Government that they will impose economic sanctions on them if true reforms are not carried out. The interesting point is that the Unionist Government cannot carry out reforms. If they introduce the human rights Bill and outlaw sectarianism and discrimination, what will the party which is based on, and survives on, discrimination do? By introducing the human rights Bill, it signs its own death warrant. Therefore, the Government can impose economic sanctions but the Unionist Party will not yield. I assure you, Mr. Speaker, that one cannot impose economic sanctions on the dead.

Stormont: The building where Northern Ireland's independent parliament sits.

Home rule is Rome rule: A popular unionist slogan dating from the nineteenth century.

DOCUMENT 69:

From William Whitelaw, *The Future of Northern Ireland* (1972)[10]

William Whitelaw (1918–99) was a British Conservative politician. He served as secretary of state for Northern Ireland from 1972 to 1973, during which time this report was produced. As secretary of state for Northern Ireland Whitelaw introduced Special Category Status for paramilitary prisoners and attempted to negotiate with the Provisional Irish Republican Army, although this produced no lasting peace.

℮

The British Government have a clear objective in Northern Ireland. It is to deliver its people from the violence and fear in which they live today and to set them free to realise their great potential to the full.

We want to help them to draw together; to find a system of government which will enjoy the support and the respect of the overwhelming majority. If it is to do so, such a system must emerge in large measure from the ideas and the convictions of the Northern Ireland people themselves. This is why there has to be a lengthy process of consultation, which I started on arrival, have been continuing ever since, most recently at the Darlington conference for Northern Ireland parties, and which I shall now seek to bring to fruition over the coming weeks.

But the stage has now been reached at which we must take a step forward in shaping the future. This is the purpose of this Paper for Discussion. It does not set out any single cut and dried scheme for the future but sets out some fundamental conditions (including the clear pledges of successive British Governments) which any settlement must meet. It places the Northern Ireland situation in the wider context of certain unalterable facts of life—political, economic and military—which must fundamentally influence any settlement.

This Paper is intended to provide a comprehensive basis for further discussions which I now propose immediately to put in hand. These must go ahead with the utmost urgency. What is at issue is the future of Northern Ireland, and I have set out in the first paragraph of this Foreword what the Government aim to achieve for its people. But the future of any community depends upon the will of its own people to live, to work and to make progress together; in the last resort responsibility for bringing about a peaceful future lies with them. This Paper seeks to provide, as its title and sub-title indicate, a basis for discussion as to how that may best be achieved....

---

10 William Whitelaw, *The Future of Northern Ireland: A Paper for Discussion*, available at cain.ulster.ac.uk/hmso/nio1972.htm.

Of particular importance was that wide area of public policy which may be described as "law and order and security." On the one hand the Northern Ireland Parliament's general grant of powers charged it with responsibility for peace and order, as well as for good government; on the other, the United Kingdom Parliament reserved to itself responsibility for the defence of the realm and for the raising of any kind of military force. In practice, however, this division of power was not easy to observe in the face of developments in Northern Ireland itself. Although the Act of 1920 by no means envisaged the Irish border as an international frontier, it steadily assumed that character as Southern Ireland became first the Irish Free State and ultimately the Irish Republic. The partition of Ireland was deeply resented, and the new institutions of Northern Ireland were opposed; militant elements of the republican tradition launched violent attacks upon the Province and its institutions both from within Northern Ireland and across the border....

The most striking feature of the executive government of Northern Ireland throughout this period of more than half a century was its virtually complete concentration in the hands of a single political party, the Ulster Unionist Party. At every General Election from 1921 to 1969 this Party secured an absolute majority of the seats in the Northern Ireland Parliament. Thus, following the general convention governing such matters in the United Kingdom, successive leaders of that Party were invited by the Governor to form an Administration, and did so almost entirely from fellow members of the Party in one or other House of the Northern Ireland Parliament, (two of the three notable exceptions being appointed in 1971—Mr. Bleakley, and Dr. Newe, a Roman Catholic)....

The alternation of governing Parties which has for so long been a characteristic of the British political system, and which has undoubtedly contributed in a marked degree to the stability of Parliamentary Government in Great Britain, accordingly did not exist in Northern Ireland. It is true that there are other democracies, whether sovereign States or self-governing areas within them, of which this can also be said. The special feature of the Northern Ireland situation was that the great divide in political life was not between different viewpoints on such matters as the allocation of resources and the determination of priorities, but between two whole communities. The "floating vote" for which rival parties would normally compete was almost non-existent. Thus the relationship between the parties was not fluctuating and uncertain, but virtually fixed from one Election to another. Such a situation was unlikely to foster either sensitivity on the part of the permanent majority, or a sense of responsibility on the part of the permanent minority....

There were, however, persistent protests on behalf of the Roman Catholic minority that they were being excluded by deliberate policy from their fair share of the benefits of increasing prosperity, and from that legitimate political influence which would permit their claims to be more effectively advanced. While some of these complaints were undoubtedly justified, in some cases opportunities to participate were not taken up, and in others the minority, detecting an unfavourable position resulting from other circumstances, genuinely believed that there had been bias or malice where none existed. Thus a higher rate of unemployment in a comparatively remote area which had a predominantly Roman Catholic population could be attributed by that population to governmental bias against it; but could also result from the real practical problems of promoting new economic development in a remote area. What is incontestable is that the continuous and complete control of central government by representatives of the majority alone was virtually bound to give rise to such suspicions....

By 1968 there had emerged an active and articulate movement demanding changes in the area of civil rights, such as the acceptance of universal adult suffrage as the basis for all elections, the redrawing of electoral boundaries, and the ending of discrimination in employment and housing. From the start this movement was largely (though not exclusively) Roman Catholic, and although it undoubtedly attracted support from militant republicanism, its declared aim was to achieve the objectives by non-violent means. On 5 October 1968, however, a violent confrontation with the police occurred when a Civil Rights march took place in Londonderry in defiance of an Order made by the Minister of Home Affairs for Northern Ireland....

When the process of consultation has been completed, the United Kingdom Government have the responsibility of putting forward proposals, and of recommending them to Parliament. They will do this in the knowledge that there is no definite answer to questions as difficult and long-standing as these; no panacea which can transform strife into harmony. Whatever the constitutional arrangements may be, many difficult practical problems will remain. There is not least the great need to rid Northern Ireland of the presence and threat of violence. Both political theory and practical experience show that no scheme of government, however carefully drawn, can do more than present an opportunity for progress. It is in the hearts and minds of the people of Northern Ireland, and not just in the aims of Government or the words of Acts of Parliament, that the capacity for working and living together must flourish. For the ultimate truth is that the people of Northern Ireland need each other, and that to squander their great talents in bitter conflict is to diminish the prospects of them all. It is the profound wish and hope of the United Kingdom Government that this fundamental truth will be recognised, and will be the basis on which all concerned will take part in the further consultations for which this Paper is intended to provide a basis.

From Jack Lynch, Speech at the Dáil Éireann (21 March 1972)[11]

Jack Lynch (1917–99) was an Irish Fianna Fáil politician and Taoiseach of
Ireland from 1966 to 1973 and 1977 to 1979. The high point of his first term,
and perhaps the most significant accomplishment of his career, was securing
Ireland's entry into the European Economic Community (now the European
Union). Ireland was officially admitted along with the United Kingdom and
Denmark on 1 January 1973. In this speech given to the Dáil he announces a
national referendum which was held on the issue of Ireland's joining the EEC.

❧

The purpose of the debate is to give the Dáil the opportunity to discuss in
advance of the referendum the terms negotiated for this country's accession to the Communities and the Government's assessment of accession
on these terms as set out in the White Paper and the supplement. If the
people approve in the referendum the amendment proposed in the **Third
Amendment of the Constitution Bill**, 1971, and I am confident that they
will, a motion will be introduced by the Government in Dáil Éireann in
accordance with the requirements of **Article 29** of the Constitution seeking
approval of the **Treaty of Accession**, the text of which has already been
circulated to Deputies....

The Government entered into the negotiations because they were
convinced after the fullest examination that, given satisfactory terms for
accession, our national interests would best be served by membership. The
negotiations were essentially concerned with transitional arrangements
necessary to enable the applicant countries to adapt to the obligations of
membership. It was obvious that the views of the applicant countries and
the Community itself would differ as to the kind of transitional arrangements which would best serve their interests. Ideally, we would have liked a
longer period for the removal of industrial protection and a shorter period
for participation in the benefits of the common agricultural policy. Britain
would have preferred to have it the other way round, while Denmark's best
interest would be in a short transitional period in both sectors....

The achievement of these aims represents a formidable task. The question we must ask ourselves is whether we are more likely to succeed in this
task within the Community than outside it. The conditions of membership
are clearly set out in the White Paper. The Government are convinced that

Third Amendment of the Constitution Bill: An amendment to the Irish Constitution which permitted Ireland to join the EEC; it was approved by national referendum in 1972.

Article 29: This article of the Irish Constitution of 1937 (Document 59) focuses on international relations.

Treaty of Accession: The international agreement, approved by referendum in Ireland in 1972, which permitted Ireland to join the EEC. The same treaty was approved by referendums in the United Kingdom and in Denmark.

---

11   Jack Lynch, "Speech by Jack Lynch at the Irish Parliament (21 March 1972)," available at
https://www.cvce.eu.

these conditions, together with the transitional arrangements obtained in the negotiations, afford the best and perhaps the only opportunity we are likely to have of achieving those national economic aims. I am not seeking to play down the difficulties which will have to be overcome in some sectors. The Government have never pretended that the structure of industry would remain unaffected by the transition from a highly-protected market to free trading conditions. Over the years, they have spared no effort to facilitate this transition both by encouraging existing industry to adapt to a changing environment and by attracting new export-based industries on a large scale. Notwithstanding all that has been done there are likely to be some losses. These losses will be more than offset by the gains that can flow from membership of the Community, gains which will enable us to pursue our national economic aims with far greater prospect of success than would otherwise be possible....

This is not all. If we are to remain outside the enlarged Community which will include Britain, the Community barriers which would be erected against our exports to the British market, which at present accounts for 80 percent of our total agricultural exports, would have disastrous effects on Irish agriculture and the repercussions would damage the entire economy. Then, there is the matter of access to the Community's funds. The Agricultural Guidance and Guarantee Fund in addition to providing market support for agricultural production has the function of assisting the structural improvement of agriculture in the Community. The European Social Fund provides funds for the training of workers and is assuming an increasingly important role in this area. The European Investment Bank is a major source of funds for development projects. Additional means of Community assistance are also being devised with the special object of dealing with the problem of regional and structural disparities within the Community. We could not expect that access to these various sources of Community assistance which would be of great benefit to our economic and regional development would be open to us if we were not a full member of the Community....

The same sort of confused thinking is evident also in the argument put out by the anti-Common Market lobby that joining the Community would perpetuate the division of our country and this, despite the disappearance of economic frontiers within the EEC and the commitment of the Community to an ever closer union of its peoples. It passes comprehension how anybody could support that view. Surely it is self-evident that if we were to remain outside the Community we would be conferring on the Border the status of a frontier, both economic and political, between ourselves and the rest of Europe. Moreover, since Britain would continue to be the major market for agricultural products any agreement which we would make with the EEC as a non-member country would depend largely on the goodwill and favour of the British. Not alone, therefore, would we be copper-fastening Partition but by remaining outside the EEC we would be also increasing our dependence on Britain. Can any Irishman seriously want this?

The logical conclusion is that the political, economic and other interests of our country and our people are best served by membership of the Community. In saying this, it is not my intention to hold out membership of the Community as a universal panacea to cure all our ills. The Community has its defects as have all manmade institutions. Its most noteworthy feature however is the extraordinary progress it has achieved over the short period of its existence, a mere 13 years. In so far as the Community has defects, it would be for us as a member to work with our fellow members in order to remedy these defects.

From Radio Interview with British Prime Minister Margaret Thatcher (8 December 1980)[12]

Margaret Thatcher (1925–2013) was prime minister of the United Kingdom from 1979 until 1990. In this radio interview given in advance of the Anglo-Irish summit of 1980 she addresses the then ongoing first hunger strike by Irish republican prisoners in the Maze prison. That strike was called off after 53 days on 18 December 1980. A new hunger strike began on 1 March 1981 that lasted until 3 October; it resulted in the deaths of 10 men.

e

Peter Murphy: (1923–2011) an Irish radio and television presenter on RTE, the national broadcaster of the Republic of Ireland.

Peter Murphy: If I can ask you first of all Prime Minister, did the Irish Government seek any changes in your attitude to the hunger strikers?

Margaret Thatcher: No. Because our attitude to the hunger strikers [is] very well known. First, there can be no question of political status, murder is murder and those who wish to take explosives to risk other people's lives are criminals. There is no question of political status. Secondly, before the hunger strike began we had already been considering whether prisoners in Northern Ireland should be allowed to wear civilian clothing, issued by the governor of the prison. And we had agreed before the hunger strike began that they should—it is available to all prisoners. And thirdly, we issued a statement last Thursday setting out all the rights and privileges which are available to prisoners in Northern Ireland, provided they are not on the **blanket** or the **dirty protest**, and that is a very impressive list on humanitarian grounds. I think people who saw it for the first time were amazed at how humane and how extensive the list is. And it so happens that a number of things that people have been asking for are already available. So now it is a question of trying to get the message over to those on hunger strike. But all Parties in Northern Ireland have condemned the hunger strike, many parties in Southern Ireland the Church has condemned it. There is no point in carrying on.

Blanket: Reference to the blanket protest by republican prisoners in Northern Ireland in which prisoners refused to wear prison uniforms and wore blankets instead to protest not being classified as political prisoners.

Dirty protest: Protest by republican prisoners in Northern Ireland over not being classified as political prisoners in which they refused to empty their chamber pots and instead smeared excrement on the walls of their cells.

Murphy: Were there any suggestions though put forward by the Irish Government for …

---

12 Radio Interview for IRN (Anglo-Irish Summit), https://www.margaretthatcher.org/document/104458.

Thatcher: … no new suggestions, no new suggestions. Indeed I think it would be very, very difficult to find any new suggestions bearing in mind that we cannot possibly have political status.

Murphy: While the strike continues, though, there is a potentially explosive situation in Northern Ireland. Do you have much hope that it might be cooled off before somebody dies?

Thatcher: Well, of course, because it is such a waste of lives particularly when a number of things they are demanding are already available to ordinary prisoners in Northern Ireland.

Murphy: Turning to other matters, you spoke in your joint statement about possible new institutional structures. What exactly did you mean by that?

Thatcher: Nothing more than that. We curiously enough until recently we had closer relationships between the United Kingdom and France, the United Kingdom and Germany and the United Kingdom and Ireland [sic: Italy?] than we had between the United Kingdom and Ireland. In a way you could say that we already have an institutional structure because we now have regular talks with the Republic of Ireland and they come here. But what we are really saying is that there are a number of things we might consider. We already have very good security co-operation. We could consider much greater economic co-operation and energy co-operation and whether because there is a unique relationship between the Republic and the United Kingdom in that we have a land border and there are special citizenship rights and provisions between the United Kingdom and the Republic of Ireland. And I understand that **Mr. Haughey** is considering reciprocal voting rights. Whether it is possible or not to give any institutional expression to that unique relationship, and we shall just have to see whether it is possible or not.

Mr. Haughey: Charles Haughey (1925–2006) was Taoiseach of Ireland at the time.

Murphy: It has been suggested from Dublin that one of the areas to be examined is a possible confederation between Great Britain and Northern Ireland.

Thatcher: There is no possibility of a Confederation.

Murphy: That is a complete red herring.

Thatcher: There is no possibility.

Murphy: The problem of dealing with Northern Ireland and talks with the Southern Irish Government is there always seems to be some misunderstandings afterwards and the Unionists in particular seem worried.

Thatcher: With respect, I don't think there is any misunderstanding between those who took part in our bilateral talks. What happens is that people try to seek meanings to words which aren't there. When you talk about, as we did in this communique, joint studies included possible new institutional structures, citizens rights, security matters, economic co-operation, measures to encourage mutual understanding, don't we want greater mutual understanding, don't we want greater economic co-operation? We are trying to bring an end to violence, we are trying to replace violence with understanding and co-operation. Surely that is the right way to go about it?

Murphy: Finally, the last proposals for changes in Northern Ireland came to nothing in fact. Have you got any new plans for **devolved Government?**

Thatcher: No not at the moment. It is not possible to go forward to legislation on the basis of the White Paper in Northern Ireland which the Humphrey Atkins Secretary of State for Northern Ireland proposed. We have just tried to find new ways of securing greater co-operation and greater understanding between the communities in Northern Ireland.

Murphy: Thank you very much.

Devolved Government:
Northern Ireland at the time was being directly governed from England. A devolved government would mean the Northern Irish assembly was meeting and governing locally.

DOCUMENT 72:

From *An Camchéacta/The Starry Plough*, "Why it is murder ..." (June 1981)[13]

The Starry Plough or *An Camchéacta* was the official newspaper of the Irish Republican Socialist Party. The name is a reference to the starry plough flag of the Irish Citizen Army, a socialist republican organization that participated in the Easter Rising of 1916. In this article they address the still ongoing Hunger Strike of 1981 which had begun in March and had already resulted in the death of four men by June. The republican prisoners in the Maze were protesting the loss of Special Category Status, a distinction they held prior to 1976 in which they were treated as prisoners of war rather than as criminals.

ev

Bobby Sands, Francie Hughes, Ray McCreesh and Patsy O'Hara were murdered. They were murdered by the refusal of Thatcher to negotiate with the prisoners.

All the official statements say that they took their own lives. But nothing could be further from the truth.

They were murdered because they refused to conform to Britain's rules—to wear convicts' uniforms, to call prison warders "sir," to call themselves "criminals" and to call their struggle a criminal struggle.

Since they were teenagers Bobby, Francie, Ray and Patsy experienced what it was like to be a second-class citizen in their own country. That because they were Catholics, they were the last in line for any jobs going—and the last in line for housing. And they knew that if they opened their mouths in protest they would be kicked back into place by the **RUC** and **B Specials**.

They knew that their future under the present set-up in the six counties was more of the same—that there would be no change in the daily struggle to tear some dignity out of their lives.

ANGER

All four took-up arms to end all of this. Bobby, Francie and Ray in the Provisional IRA, Patsy in the Irish National Liberation Army.

> **Bobby Sands:** Sands (1954–81) was a member of the Provisional Irish Republican Army; he was the leader of the 1981 hunger strikers; he was elected to parliament in the midst of his hunger strike. He died of starvation on 5 May 1981.

> **RUC:** The Royal Ulster Constabulary, the police force in Northern Ireland.

> **B Specials:** Also known as the Ulster Special Constabulary, a quasi-military reserve force in the RUC.

13 http://www.hungerstrikes.org/documents/why_it_is_murder.html.

They had seen the peaceful protests, pickets, marches, demonstrations and rent strikes. All of them had failed. For the struggle for civil rights was answered by military might. The first 6 people who died in the Six Counties troubles were Catholics killed by the RUC and B Specials. And when more people joined the protests Britain responded by murdering 14 civil rights marchers on **Bloody Sunday.**

The republican people knew that there was going to be reform, but not while the **Stormont** set-up lasted. And they knew that Stormont would last as long as Britain backed it—and murdered all who opposed it.

And that's why the people turned to the armed struggle. Because there was no other way to overthrow the injustice and oppression foisted on them by Britain.

DEATHS

And there was nothing criminal about that decision. Which is the point at issue in the **H-Blocks** and **Armagh.**

Thatcher maintains that all who oppose British mis-rule in Ireland are criminals. Irish people know differently. We know that the prisoners are motivated by political reasons and are engaged in that struggle not from evil but against evil.

And that despite Thatcher's murders they will triumph.

From The Good Friday Agreement (1998)[14]

The Good Friday Agreement or the Belfast Agreement is a pair of agreements that ended most of the conflict in Northern Ireland known as the Troubles. The agreement was the result of multi-party negotiations between the British and Irish government as well as eight political parties or groups in Northern Ireland. Representatives of both the Unionist and Republican/Nationalist communities took part in the negotiations. It was signed on Good Friday, 10 April 1998. The Agreement was later approved by voters in both Northern Ireland and the Republic of Ireland.

DECLARATION OF SUPPORT

1. We, the participants in the multi-party negotiations, believe that the agreement we have negotiated offers a truly historic opportunity for a new beginning.

2. The tragedies of the past have left a deep and profoundly regrettable legacy of suffering. We must never forget those who have died or been injured, and their families. But we can best honour them through a fresh start, in which we firmly dedicate ourselves to the achievement of reconciliation, tolerance, and mutual trust, and to the protection and vindication of the human rights of all.

3. We are committed to partnership, equality and mutual respect as the basis of relationships within Northern Ireland, between North and South, and between these islands.

4. We reaffirm our total and absolute commitment to exclusively democratic and peaceful means of resolving differences on political issues, and our opposition to any use or threat of force by others for any political purpose, whether in regard to this agreement or otherwise.

5. We acknowledge the substantial differences between our continuing, and equally legitimate, political aspirations. However, we will endeavour to strive in every practical way towards reconciliation and rapprochement within the framework of democratic and agreed arrangements. We pledge

---

14 "The Agreement," available at https://cain.ulster.ac.uk.

that we will, in good faith, work to ensure the success of each and every one of the arrangements to be established under this agreement. It is accepted that all of the institutional and constitutional arrangements—an Assembly in Northern Ireland, a North/South Ministerial Council, implementation bodies, a British-Irish Council and a British-Irish Intergovernmental Conference and any amendments to British Acts of Parliament and the Constitution of Ireland—are interlocking and interdependent and that in particular the functioning of the Assembly and the North/South Council are so closely inter-related that the success of each depends on that of the other.

6. Accordingly, in a spirit of concord, we strongly commend this agreement to the people, North and South, for their approval.

ANNEX A

DRAFT CLAUSES/SCHEDULES FOR INCORPORATION IN BRITISH LEGISLATION

1. (1) It is hereby declared that Northern Ireland in its entirety remains part of the United Kingdom and shall not cease to be so without the consent of a majority of the people of Northern Ireland voting in a poll held for the purposes of this section in accordance with Schedule 1.

(2) But if the wish expressed by a majority in such a poll is that Northern Ireland should cease to be part of the United Kingdom and form part of a united Ireland, the Secretary of State shall lay before Parliament such proposals to give effect to that wish as may be agreed between Her Majesty's Government in the United Kingdom and the Government of Ireland.

2. The Government of Ireland Act 1920 is repealed; and this Act shall have effect notwithstanding any other previous enactment....

AGREEMENT BETWEEN THE GOVERNMENT OF THE UNITED KINGDOM OF GREAT BRITAIN AND NORTHERN IRELAND AND THE GOVERNMENT OF IRELAND

The British and Irish Governments:

Welcoming the strong commitment to the Agreement reached on 10th April 1998 by themselves and other participants in the multi-party talks and set out in Annex 1 to this Agreement (hereinafter "the Multi-Party Agreement");

Considering that the Multi-Party Agreement offers an opportunity for a new beginning in relationships within Northern Ireland, within the island of Ireland and between the peoples of these islands;

Wishing to develop still further the unique relationship between their peoples and the close co-operation between their countries as friendly neighbours and as partners in the European Union;

Reaffirming their total commitment to the principles of democracy and non-violence which have been fundamental to the multi-party talks;

Reaffirming their commitment to the principles of partnership, equality and mutual respect and to the protection of civil, political, social, economic and cultural rights in their respective jurisdictions;

Have agreed as follows:

ARTICLE 1

The two Governments:

(i) recognise the legitimacy of whatever choice is freely exercised by a majority of the people of Northern Ireland with regard to its status, whether they prefer to continue to support the Union with Great Britain or a sovereign united Ireland;

(ii) recognise that it is for the people of the island of Ireland alone, by agreement between the two parts respectively and without external impediment, to exercise their right of self-determination on the basis of consent, freely and concurrently given, North and South, to bring about a united Ireland, if that is their wish, accepting that this right must be achieved and exercised with and subject to the agreement and consent of a majority of the people of Northern Ireland;

(iii) acknowledge that while a substantial section of the people in Northern Ireland share the legitimate wish of a majority of the people of the island of Ireland for a united Ireland, the present wish of a majority of the people of Northern Ireland, freely exercised and legitimate, is to maintain the Union and accordingly, that Northern Ireland's status as part of the United Kingdom reflects and relies upon that wish; and that it would be wrong to make any change in the status of Northern Ireland save with the consent of a majority of its people;

(iv) affirm that, if in the future, the people of the island of Ireland exercise their right of self-determination on the basis set out in sections (i) and (ii) above to bring about a united Ireland, it will be a binding obligation on both Governments to introduce and support in their respective Parliaments legislation to give effect to that wish;

(v) affirm that whatever choice is freely exercised by a majority of the people of Northern Ireland, the power of the sovereign government with jurisdiction there shall be exercised with rigorous impartiality on behalf of all the people in the diversity of their identities and traditions and shall be founded on the principles of full respect for, and equality of, civil, political, social and cultural rights, of freedom from discrimination for all citizens, and of parity of esteem and of just and equal treatment for the identity, ethos and aspirations of both communities;

(vi) recognise the birthright of all the people of Northern Ireland to identify themselves and be accepted as Irish or British, or both, as they may so choose, and accordingly confirm that their right to hold both British and Irish citizenship is accepted by both Governments and would not be affected by any future change in the status of Northern Ireland.

ARTICLE 2

The two Governments affirm their solemn commitment to support, and where appropriate implement, the provisions of the Multi-Party Agreement. In particular there shall be established in accordance with the provisions of the Multi-Party Agreement immediately on the entry into force of this Agreement, the following institutions:

(i) a North/South Ministerial Council;

(ii) the implementation bodies referred to in paragraph 9 (ii) of the section entitled "Strand Two" of the Multi-Party Agreement;

(iii) a British-Irish Council;

(iv) a British-Irish Intergovernmental Conference.

ARTICLE 3

(1) This Agreement shall replace the Agreement between the British and Irish Governments done at Hillsborough on 15th November 1985 which shall cease to have effect on entry into force of this Agreement.

(2) The Intergovernmental Conference established by Article 2 of the aforementioned Agreement done on 15th November 1985 shall cease to exist on entry into force of this Agreement.

ARTICLE 4

(1) It shall be a requirement for entry into force of this Agreement that:

(a) British legislation shall have been enacted for the purpose of implementing the provisions of Annex A to the section entitled "Constitutional Issues" of the Multi-Party Agreement;

(b) the amendments to the Constitution of Ireland set out in Annex B to the section entitled "Constitutional Issues" of the Multi-Party Agreement shall have been approved by Referendum;

(c) such legislation shall have been enacted as may be required to establish the institutions referred to in Article 2 of this Agreement.

(2) Each Government shall notify the other in writing of the completion, so far as it is concerned, of the requirements for entry into force of this Agreement. This Agreement shall enter into force on the date of the receipt of the later of the two notifications.

(3) Immediately on entry into force of this Agreement, the Irish Government shall ensure that the amendments to the Constitution of Ireland set out in Annex B to the section entitled "Constitutional Issues" of the Multi-Party Agreement take effect.

In witness thereof the undersigned, being duly authorised thereto by the respective Governments, have signed this Agreement.

DOCUMENT 74:

From Tony Blair, Address to the Dáil Éireann (26 November 1998)[15]

Tony Blair (b. 1953) is a British Labour politician and was prime minister of the United Kingdom from 1997 to 2007. In that capacity he assisted in negotiating the Good Friday Agreement (Document 73). In November of 1998 he became the first British prime minister to ever address the Dáil Éireann.

ر

Dáil: The lower house of the Irish legislature.

Seanad: The upper house of the Irish legislature.

Oireachtas: The combined houses of the Irish legislature.

Go raibh mile maith agaibh: "Thank you all very much" in Irish.

Members of the **Dáil** and **Seanad**, after all the long and torn history of our two peoples, standing here as the first British prime minister ever to address the joint Houses of the **Oireachtas**, I feel profoundly both the history in this event, and I feel profoundly the enormity of the honour that you are bestowing upon me. From the bottom of my heart, **go raibh mile maith agaibh**.

Ireland, as you may know, is in my blood. My mother was born in the flat above her grandmother's hardware shop on the main street of Ballyshannon in Donegal. She lived there as a child, started school there and only moved when her father died; her mother remarried and they crossed the water to Glasgow.

We spent virtually every childhood summer holiday up to when the troubles really took hold in Ireland, usually at Rossnowlagh, the Sands House Hotel, I think it was. And we would travel in the beautiful countryside of Donegal. It was there in the seas off the Irish coast that I learned to swim, there that my father took me to my first pub, a remote little house in the country, for a Guinness, a taste I've never forgotten and which it is always a pleasure to repeat.

Even now, in my constituency of Sedgefield, which at one time had 30 pits or more, all now gone, virtually every community remembers that its roots lie in Irish migration to the mines of Britain.

So like it or not, we, the British and the Irish, are irredeemably linked.

We experienced and absorbed the same waves of invasions: Celts, Vikings, Normans—all left their distinctive mark on our countries. Over a thousand years ago, the monastic traditions formed the basis for both our cultures. Sadly, the power games of medieval monarchs and feudal chiefs sowed the seeds of later trouble.

Yet it has always been simplistic to portray our differences as simply Irish versus English—or British. There were, after all, many in Britain too

---

15   Tony Blair, "Address to Irish Parliament," http://www.historyplace.com/speeches/blair.htm.

who suffered greatly at the hands of powerful absentee landlords, who were persecuted for their religion, or who were for centuries disenfranchised. And each generation in Britain has benefited, as ours does, from the contribution of Irishmen and women.

Today the links between our parliaments are continued by the British-Irish Parliamentary Body, and last month 60 of our MPs set up a new all-party "Irish in Britain Parliamentary Group."

Irish parliamentarians have made a major contribution to our shared parliamentary history. Let me single out just two:

Daniel O'Connell, who fought against injustice to extend a franchise restricted by religious prejudice; Charles Stewart Parnell, whose statue stands today in the House of Commons and whose political skills and commitment to social justice made such an impact in that House.

So much shared history, so much shared pain.

And now the shared hope of a new beginning.

The peace process is at a difficult juncture. Progress is being made, but slowly. There is an impasse over the establishment of the executive; there is an impasse over decommissioning. But I have been optimistic the whole way through. And I am optimistic now. Let us not underestimate how far we have come; and let us agree that we have come too far to go back now....

No one should ignore the injustices of the past, or the lessons of history. But too often between us, one person's history has been another person's myth.

We need not be prisoners of our history. My generation in Britain sees Ireland differently today and probably the same generation here feels differently about Britain.

We can understand the emotions generated by Northern Ireland's troubles, but we cannot really believe, as we approach the 21st century, there is not a better way forward to the future than murder, terrorism and sectarian hatred.

We see a changed Republic of Ireland today: a modern, open economy; after the long years of emigration, people beginning to come back for the quality of life you now offer; a country part of Europe's mainstream, having made the most of European structural funds but no longer reliant on them; some of the best business brains in the business world; leaders in popular culture, U2, the Corrs, Boyzone, B-Witched; a country that had the courage to elect its first woman president and liked it so much, you did it again; and the politics of Northern Ireland would be better for a few more women in prominent positions too.

And you see, I hope, a Britain emerging from its post-Empire malaise, modernizing, becoming as confident of its future as it once was of its past.

The programme of the new Labour government: driving up standards in education; welfare reform; monetary and fiscal stability as the foundation of a modern economy; massive investment in our public services tied to the challenge of modernization; a huge programme of constitutional change; a new positive attitude to Europe—it is a program of national renewal as ambitious as any undertaken in any western democracy in recent times.

It is precisely the dramatic changes in both countries that allow us to see the possibilities of change in our relationship with each other....

But I want our co-operation to be wider and more fundamental still—above all in Europe.

It is 25 years since we both joined what was then the EEC. We have had different approaches to agriculture, to monetary union, to defence. But increasingly we share a common agenda and common objectives: completion of the Single Market and structural economic reform; better conditions for growth and jobs in Europe; successful enlargement; a united and coherent foreign policy voice for Europe; a more effective fight against crime, drugs, illegal immigration and environmental damage; flexible, open and accountable European institutions.

We must work to make the single currency a success. Unlike Ireland, we are not joining in the first wave. But we have made clear that we are prepared to join later if the economic benefits are clear and unambiguous. For my government, there is no political or constitutional barrier to joining. There is no resistance to full-hearted European co-operation wherever this brings added value to us all.

Enlargement will increasingly test our political and economic imaginations, as we struggle with policy reform and future financing. The international financial system must be reformed. We must learn to apply real political will and harness our skills and resources far more effectively to solve regional problems—notably in the Balkans and the Middle East. Above all, Europe must restate its vision for today's world, so that our people understand why it is so important. This means defining the priorities where common European action makes obvious sense and can make a real difference, like economic co-ordination, foreign and security policy, the environment, crime and drugs. It also means distinguishing them from areas where countries or regions can best continue to make policy themselves, to suit local circumstances, while still learning from each other—for example, tax, education, health, welfare.

That is why I want to forge new bonds with Dublin. Together we can have a stronger voice in Europe and work to shape its future in a way which suits all our people. It is said there was a time when Irish diplomats in Europe spoke French in meetings to ensure they were clearly distinguished from us. I hope those days are long behind us. We can accomplish much more when our voices speak in harmony.

Our ministers and officials are increasingly consulting and coordinating systematically. We can do more. I believe we can transform our links if both sides are indeed ready to make the effort. For our part, we are.

This must also involve a dramatic new effort in bilateral relations, above all to bring our young generations together. We need new youth and school exchanges, contact through the new University for Industry, better cultural programs in both directions. We need to work much more closely to fight organized crime and drugs. We can do much more to enrich each other's experience in areas like health care and welfare.

None of this threatens our separate identities. Co-operation does not mean losing distinctiveness....

That is my ambition. I know it is shared by the **Taoiseach**. I believe it is an ambition shared by both our nations. The 21st century awaits us. Let us confront its challenge with confidence, and together give our children the future they deserve.

Taoiseach: Bertie Ahern (b. 1957), Taoiseach from 1997 to 2008.

DOCUMENT 75:

Queen Elizabeth II, Speech at Dublin Castle (18 May 2011)[16]

Queen Elizabeth II (r. 1952–2022) and her husband Prince Philip (1921–2021) made a state visit to Ireland in May of 2011. This was the first time a reigning British monarch had visited the Republic of Ireland since its independence. A state dinner was held to honor the Queen at Dublin Castle, at which point the Queen gave this speech, which was widely praised in Ireland.

ev

A Uachtaráin agus a chairde :"President and friends" in Irish.

A Uachtaráin agus a chairde

Prince Philip and I are delighted to be here, and to experience at first hand Ireland's world-famous hospitality.

Together we have much to celebrate: the ties between our people, the shared values, and the economic, business and cultural links that make us so much more than just neighbours, that make us firm friends and equal partners.

Madam President: Mary McAleese (b. 1951), Uachtaran or president of Ireland from 1997 to 2011.

Madam President, speaking here in Dublin Castle it is impossible to ignore the weight of history, as it was yesterday when you and I laid wreaths at the Garden of Remembrance.

Indeed, so much of this visit reminds us of the complexity of our history, its many layers and traditions, but also the importance of forbearance and conciliation. Of being able to bow to the past, but not be bound by it.

Of course, the relationship has not always been straightforward; nor has the record over the centuries been entirely benign. It is a sad and regrettable reality that through history our islands have experienced more than their fair share of heartache, turbulence and loss.

These events have touched us all, many of us personally, and are a painful legacy. We can never forget those who have died or been injured, and their families. To all those who have suffered as a consequence of our troubled past I extend my sincere thoughts and deep sympathy. With the benefit of historical hindsight we can all see things which we would wish had been done differently or not at all. But it is also true that no-one who looked to the future over the past centuries could have imagined the strength of the bonds that are now in place between the governments and the people of our two nations, the spirit of partnership that we now enjoy, and the lasting rapport between us. No-one here this evening could doubt that heartfelt desire of our two nations.

---

16 "Full Text of speech by Queen Elizabeth II," *Irish Times*, 18 May 2011.

Madam President, you have done a great deal to promote this understanding and reconciliation. You set out to build bridges. And I have seen at first hand your success in bringing together different communities and traditions on this island. You have also shed new light on the sacrifice of those who served in the First World War. Even as we jointly opened the Messines Peace Park in 1998, it was difficult to look ahead to the time when you and I would be standing together at Islandbridge as we were today.

That transformation is also evident in the establishment of a successful power-sharing Executive in Northern Ireland. A knot of history that was painstakingly loosened by the British and Irish Governments together with the strength, vision and determination of the political parties in Northern Ireland.

What were once only hopes for the future have now come to pass; it is almost exactly 13 years since the overwhelming majority of people in Ireland and Northern Ireland voted in favour of the agreement signed on Good Friday 1998, paving the way for Northern Ireland to become the exciting and inspirational place that it is today. I applaud the work of all those involved in the peace process, and of all those who support and nurture peace, including members of the police, the Gardaí, and the other emergency services, and those who work in the communities, the churches and charitable bodies like Co-operation Ireland. Taken together, their work not only serves as a basis for reconciliation between our people and communities, but it gives hope to other peacemakers across the world that through sustained effort, peace can and will prevail.

For the world moves on quickly. The challenges of the past have been replaced by new economic challenges which will demand the same imagination and courage. The lessons from the peace process are clear; whatever life throws at us, our individual responses will be all the stronger for working together and sharing the load.

There are other stories written daily across these islands which do not find their voice in solemn pages of history books, or newspaper headlines, but which are at the heart of our shared narrative. Many British families have members who live in this country, as many Irish families have close relatives in the United Kingdom.

These families share the two islands; they have visited each other and have come home to each other over the years. They are the ordinary people who yearned for the peace and understanding we now have between our two nations and between the communities within those two nations; a living testament to how much in common we have.

These ties of family, friendship and affection are our most precious resource. They are the lifeblood of the partnership across these islands, a golden thread that runs through all our joint successes so far, and all we will go on to achieve. They are a reminder that we have much to do together to build a future for all our grandchildren: the kind of future our grandparents could only dream of.

So we celebrate together the widespread spirit of goodwill and deep mutual understanding that has served to make the relationship more harmonious, close as good neighbours should always be.

DOCUMENT 76:

Michael D. Higgins, Shadow and Shelter Speech (8 April 2014)[17]

Michael D. Higgins is an Irish politician as well as a poet and sociologist. In 2011 he was elected Uachtaran or president of Ireland; he was re-elected in 2018. In 2014 he visited the United Kingdom, the first official state visit to the United Kingdom by an Irish president. During a state banquet held at Windsor Castle he gave this speech reflecting on the nature of the relationship between England and Ireland.

❧

A Shoilse Banríon, A Mhargacht Ríoga:

Your Majesty, Your Royal Highness:

Thank you for your kind and generous welcome and for the warm hospitality you have extended to me, to Sabina and to our delegation.

That welcome is very deeply felt and appreciated by me, and by the people of Ireland, whom I represent. However long it may have taken, Your Majesty, I can assure you that this first State Visit of a President of Ireland to the United Kingdom is a very visible sign of the warmth and maturity of the relationship between our two countries. It is something to be truly welcomed and celebrated.

Your Majesty:

You famously used some words of Irish during **your State Visit to Ireland**. Today I would also like to draw from the oral tradition of our ancient language a seanfhocal, or wise saying, often applied to the mutuality of relationships. It observes simply:

Ar scáth a chéile a mhairimid.

Because scáth literally means shadow, this phrase is sometimes translated as we live in the shadow of each other. However, there is a more open and more accommodating meaning.

Scáth also means shelter. The word embodies the simple truth that physical proximity brings with it an inevitability of both mutual influence and interaction. But more importantly, I believe, it implies reciprocal hospitality and generosity; the kind of generosity reflected in your words this evening that encourages us to embrace the best version of each other.

your State Visit to Ireland:
See Document 75, p. 252.

---

17 Michael D. Higgins, "Full text of President Higgins address to State Banquet," *Irish Times*, 8 April 2014.

Ireland and Britain live in both the shadow and in the shelter of one another, and so it has been since the dawn of history. Through conquest and resistance, we have cast shadows on each other, but we have also gained strength from one another as neighbours and, most especially, from the contribution of those who have travelled between our islands in recent decades.

The contribution of Irish men and Irish women to life in Britain, which Your Majesty has acknowledged with such grace, is indeed extensive and lends itself to no simple description. It runs from building canals, roads and bridges in previous decades, to running major companies in the present, all the while pouring Irish personality and imagination into the English language and its literature.

Like so many of our compatriots, Sabina and I feel very much at home when visiting Britain, which should be the case with our nearest neighbour and our close friend.

Tonight we celebrate the deeply personal, close neighbourly connection which is embodied in the hundreds of thousands of Irish and British people who have found shelter on each other's shores.

Your Majesty:

History evolves, if we are fortunate, into greater mutual understanding between peoples. The welcome that is so naturally afforded to British visitors in Ireland today was, I think, wholeheartedly expressed on the occasion of your State Visit in 2011. Your gracious and genuine curiosity, your evident delight in that visit, including its equine dimension, made it very easy for us to express to you and, through you to the British people, the warmth of neighbourly feelings. It laid the basis for an authentic and ethical hospitality between our two countries.

Admirably, you chose not to shy away from the shadows of the past, recognising that they cannot be ignored when we consider the relationship between our islands. We valued your apt and considered words when you addressed some of the painful moments of our mutual history, and we were moved by your gestures of respect at sites of national historical significance in Ireland.

These memorable moments and these moving words merit our appreciation and, even more, our reciprocity. While the past must be respectfully recognised, it must not imperil the potential of the present or the possibilities of the future ar fidireachta gan teorainn our endless possibilities working together.

This present occasion, which completes a circle begun by your historic visit three years ago, marks the welcome transformation in relations between our countries over recent years, a transformation that has been considerably progressed by the advancement of peace in Northern Ireland.

We owe a great debt to all of those who had the courage to work towards, and make manifest, that peace. I wish to acknowledge here the remarkable contributions of my predecessors **Mary Robinson** and Mary McAleese. I am especially pleased that former President McAleese, and her husband Martin, are here with us this evening.

Mary Robinson: Uactharan from 1990 to 1997.

We must, however, never forget those who died, were bereaved, or injured, during a tragic conflict. As the French philosopher Paul Ricoeur wrote, to be forgotten is to die twice. We owe a duty to all those who lost their lives, the duty to build together in peace; it is the only restitution, the only enduring justice we can offer them.

We share, also, the imperative to be unwavering in our support of the people of Northern Ireland as we journey together towards the shelter and security of true reconciliation. We celebrate what has been achieved but we must also constantly renew our commitment to a process that requires vigilance and care.

Your Majesty:

We have moved on from a past where our relations were often troubled, to a present where as you have indicated—Ireland and the United Kingdom meet each other in mutual respect, close partnership and sincere friendship. That friendship is informed by the many matters of mutual interest in which we work together and support one another.

In recent times we have seen our two Governments working ever more closely together in the European Union and in the United Nations. We have seen deepening partnership in the area of trade, as well as in development aid where we both share a common commitment to tackling hunger and upscaling nutrition.

The future we each desire, and seek to work towards is one where Ireland and the United Kingdom stand together to seek common opportunities and to face common global challenges as partners and friends.

Your Majesty:

Ar scáth a chile a mhairimd. The shadow of the past has become the shelter of the present. While we grieve together for lost lives, we will not let any painful aspect of our shared history deflect us from crafting a future that offers hope and opportunity for the British and Irish people.

We again thank you for the hospitality that allows us, on this most joyous occasion, to celebrate the bonds of mutual understanding between our two peoples, and the warm, enduring friendship on which we have so happily embarked.

I therefore invite you, distinguished guests, to stand and join me in a toast:

To the health and happiness of Her Majesty and His Royal Highness, and the people of the United Kingdom;

To a creative cooperation and a sustainable partnership between our countries and our peoples; and
To valued neighbours whose friendship we truly cherish.
Go raibh maith agaibh go léir.

Go raibh maith agaibh go léir: "Thank you all very much" in Irish.

GLOSSARY OF KEY FIGURES AND TERMS

Acts of Union: Acts passed in the parliament of Great Britain and the parliament of Ireland in 1800 which created the United Kingdom and dissolved Ireland's independent parliament.

Church of Ireland: The Anglican (Church of England) in Ireland. Established in 1534, it was the legally established state church in Ireland until 1869.

Dominion: A term used to refer to a self-governing nation within the British Empire; the Irish Free State gained dominion status in 1922.

European Union: A political and economic union of European states, first established as a free trade community in 1951.

Great Britain: An island in the North Atlantic that consists of England, Scotland, and Wales—most of the United Kingdom.

Northern Ireland: A region that is part of the United Kingdom, it consists of the six north-eastern counties of the island of Ireland. It was partitioned from the rest of Ireland in 1921.

Parliament: A legislative body governing the United Kingdom and based in Westminster, London. Ireland had an independent parliament based in Dublin from 1297 until 1800.

Plantation System: A sixteenth- and seventeenth-century English policy in Ireland whereby large amounts of land were confiscated from Irish owners and colonized with settlers from Great Britain. The Plantation of Ulster was the largest of these projects.

Repeal Movement: A nineteenth-century political movement in Ireland to repeal the Act of Union and restore an independent parliament to Ireland.

Republic of Ireland: Éire in Irish. A country consisting of the 26 southern and western counties of the island of Ireland.

Strongbow: Richard de Clare, 2nd Earl of Pembroke (1130–76), an Anglo-Norman nobleman who led the Anglo-Norman invasion of Ireland.

United Kingdom: A nation-state currently consisting of England, Scotland, Wales, and Northern Ireland. It contained all of the island of Ireland until 1922.

SELECT BIBLIOGRAPHY

Black, Jeremy. *A History of the British Isles.* 4th ed. London: Palgrave Macmillan, 2017.

Canning, Ruth. *The Old English in Early Modern Ireland: The Palesman and the Nine Years' War, 1594–1603.* Woodbridge: Boydell Press, 2019.

Canny, Nicholas. *Making Ireland British, 1580–1650.* Oxford: Oxford UP, 2001.

Connolly, S.J. *Religion, Law and Power: The Making of Protestant Ireland 1660–1760.* Oxford: Oxford UP, 1995.

Conway, Stephen. *Britain, Ireland, and Continental Europe in the Eighteenth Century: Similarities, Connections, and Identities.* Oxford: Oxford UP, 2011.

Cope, Joseph. *England and the 1641 Irish Rebellion.* Woodbridge: Boydell Press, 2009.

Ellis, Steven G. *Ireland in the Age of the Tudors 1447–1603: English Expansion and the End of Gaelic Rule.* New York: Longman, 1998.

Fanning, Ronan. *Fatal Path: British Government and Irish Revolution 1910–1922.* London: Faber & Faber, 2013.

Foster, R.F. *Paddy and Mr Punch: Connections in Irish and English History.* London: Faber & Faber, 2011.

Frame, Robin. *Ireland and Britain 1170–1450.* London: Bloomsbury, 1998.

Graham-Campbell, James, and Michael Ryan, eds. *Anglo-Saxon/Irish Relations before the Vikings.* Oxford: Oxford UP, 2009.

Hayton, David. *Ruling Ireland, 1685–1742: Politics, Politicians and Parties.* Woodbridge: Boydell Press, 2004.

Heal, Felicity. *Reformation in Britain and Ireland.* Oxford: Oxford UP, 2003.

Kenny, Gillian. *Anglo-Irish and Gaelic Women in Ireland, c. 1170–1540.* Portland: Four Courts Press, 2007.

Kenny, Kevin, ed. *Ireland and the British Empire.* Oxford: Oxford UP, 2006.

Kidd, Colin. *British Identities before Nationalism: Ethnicity and Nationhood in the Atlantic World, 1600–1800.* Cambridge: Cambridge UP, 1999.

Matthew, Kevin. *Fatal Influence: The Impact of Ireland on British Politics, 1920–1925.* Dublin: U College Dublin P, 2004.

O'Duffy, Brendan. *British-Irish Relations and Northern Ireland: From Violent Politics to Conflict Regulation.* Dublin: Irish Academic Press, 2007.

Ohlymeyer, Jane. *Making Ireland English: The Irish Aristocracy in the Seventeenth Century.* New Haven: Yale UP, 2012.

Williams, William. *Tourism, Landscape, and the Irish Character: British Travel Writers in Pre-Famine Ireland.* Madison: U of Wisconsin P, 2008.

Williamson, Daniel. *Anglo-Irish Relations in the Early Troubles 1969–1972.* London: Bloomsbury, 2016.

Wood, Ian. *Britain, Ireland, and the Second World War.* Edinburgh: Edinburgh UP, 2010.

PERMISSIONS ACKNOWLEDGEMENTS

Lynch, Jack. "Speech at the Irish Parliament," Parliamentary Debates Dáil Éireann, Volume 259, 21 March 1972. Copyright © Houses of the Oireachtas. Reproduced under the Oireachtas (Open Data) PSI Licence. https://www.oireachtas.ie/en/copyright-and-reuse/

O'Neill, Terence. "Ulster at Cross Roads," (1968) Press Notice, 9 December 1968, Government of Northern Ireland. Copyright © PRONI Public Records Office of Northern Ireland. Used under the Open Government Licence v3.0. https://www.nationalarchives.gov.uk/doc/open-government-licence/version/3/

Parliament of the United Kingdom. "Ireland Act," (1949). Copyright © UK Parliament. Used under the Open Parliament Licence v3.0. https://www.parliament.uk/site-information/copyright-parliament/open-parliament-licence/

Reilly, Oliver. "A Worker in Birmingham," (1958) *The Furrow*, 9.4 (April 1958): 217–24 [excerpted]. Copyright © 1958 The Furrow. Reprinted by permission of The Furrow, Maynooth, Co. Kildare, Ireland. https://www.jstor.org/stable/27657361

"The Republic of Ireland Act," (1948). *Irish Statute Book*. Copyright © Government of Ireland. Reproduced under the Oireachtas (Open Data) PSI Licence. https://www.oireachtas.ie/en/copyright-and-reuse/

Thatcher, Margaret. Radio "Interview with British Prime Minister Margaret Thatcher for IRN (Anglo-Irish Summit)," 8 December 1980. Crown © Copyright. Used under the Open Government Licence v3.0. https://www.parliament.uk/site-information/copyright-parliament/open-parliament-licence/

Valera, Éamon de. "Response to Churchill," (1945) reproduced as "Taoiseach's Broadcast to the Nation on the conclusion of the War in Europe," *The Irish Press*, 17 May 1945.

Whitelaw, William. "The Future of Northern Ireland: A Paper for Discussion," (1972) Northern Ireland Office, published in London by Her Majesty's Stationery Office, 1972. Crown © copyright. Used under the Open Government Licence v3.0. https://www.nationalarchives.gov.uk/doc/open-government-licence/version/3/

"Why it is murder...," *An Camchéacta/The Starry Plough*, June 1981. Used by permission of the Irish Republican Socialist Party.

From the Publisher

A name never says it all, but the word "Broadview" expresses a good deal
of the philosophy behind our company. We are open to a broad range of
academic approaches and political viewpoints. We pay attention to the
broad impact book publishing and book printing has in the wider world;
for some years now we have used 100% recycled paper for most titles.
Our publishing program is internationally oriented and broad-ranging.
Our individual titles often appeal to a broad readership too; many are
of interest as much to general readers as to academics and students.

Founded in 1985, Broadview remains a fully independent
company owned by its shareholders—not an imprint
or subsidiary of a larger multinational.

To order our books or obtain up-to-date information,
please visit broadviewpress.com.

broadview press

www.broadviewpress.com

This book is made of paper from well-managed FSC® - certified
forests, recycled materials, and other controlled sources.